FINANCIAL
ACCOUNTING

FINANCIAL ACCOUNTING

A Canadian
Casebook with
Multiple-Subject
Cases

L.S. Rosen
York University

Prentice-Hall Canada Inc.
Scarborough, Ontario

Canadian Cataloguing in Publication Data

Rosen, L.S. (Lawrence Sydney), 1935-
    Financial accounting: a Canadian casebook with multiple-
subject cases.

ISBN 0-13-315911-6

1. Accounting – Canada – Case studies. 2. Accounting – Canada –
Problems, exercises, etc. I. Title.

HF5635.R666   657′.0971   C82-094093-3

©1982 by Prentice-Hall Canada Inc.
Scarborough, Ontario

Prentice-Hall Inc., Englewood Cliffs, New Jersey
Prentice-Hall International, Inc., London
Prentice-Hall of Australia, Pty., Ltd., Sydney
Prentice-Hall of India, Pvt., Ltd., New Delhi
Prentice-Hall of Southeast Asia (PTE) Ltd., Singapore

ISBN 0-13-315911-6

Production Editor: C.G. Leatherdale
Designer: Gail Ferreira

Printed and bound in Canada by John Deyell Company
Composition by York Typographers, Inc.
7 8 9 10 JD 92 91 90 89

CONTENTS

Preface

For several years the author has deeply felt that traditional accounting education in Canada has inadequately prepared students to cope with change. Inadequate attention was given to preparing students for a shift away from stewardship accounting, and for the many other changes that had occurred as diverse objectives and user needs grew in prominence. Accounting courses often stressed memorization of authoritative pronouncements, even though they were quickly growing obsolete. Students were somehow led to believe that accounting had "correct" or "true" answers, and that its principles were firmly set, and not subject to change. Mythical merchandising and manufacturing companies were used as textbook illustrations.

Confirmation of the deficiencies of accounting education in Canada appeared only too glaringly when changes were made in some professional accounting examinations. Many students were not able to explain "why" they were recommending particular procedures. Responses to questions asking students to choose accounting principles for a new company brought forth incredible and embarrassing comments, or even blank paper in some answer books. Accounting students were stunned by questions asking what a user's reaction would likely be to a specific type of disclosure.

What had gone wrong? A combination of factors could be pointed to. Some of these were: (1) rapid changes in financial accounting; (2) heavy demand for accounting courses at university, with resulting large classes and hiring of unqualified instructors; (3) preference for easy-to-mark examinations; (4) an absence of modern Canadian textbook material; (5) a shortage of senior accounting faculty to help train other instructors; and (6) inadequate liaison among accounting academics, practitioners, standard-setters and various user groups. Unfortunately, several of these factors still exist today.

In order to be properly prepared, students must approach accounting as a practical, professional subject. They must learn to assess facts and to apply their knowledge, realizing that there are no simple solutions for complex problems.

Most of the cases in this book are less directive abstracts of real life problems, thanks to Clarkson Gordon, Price Waterhouse, Touche Ross & Co., and Arthur Andersen & Co. The problems and orientation have been varied to make the material suitable for both potential users and for accounting majors. The cases are based on, or inspired by, information relating to practice situations provided to me by the four firms. However, the information has sometimes been modified, disassembled and combined in a somewhat artificial way to disguise the actual situation and yet not change the accounting issues that required attention. Some of the cases are simple; others are complex. These cases are neither easy, nor inordinately difficult. If students and instructors are to combat the glaring deficiencies in accounting preparer and user education in this country, they will want to become accustomed to using material such as that provided in this book.

The challenge and the necessity face us. Let us respond positively. Comments from readers are welcome.

L.S. Rosen
Toronto, Canada.

Acknowledgments

Many people have helped the author try to enrich the students' study of accounting through providing real-life material that can be used to teach the students to analyze, diagnose, apply, integrate and, in general, to become better users or preparers of financial statements and accounting information. Prime appreciation has to be expressed to the following partners of Clarkson Gordon: Chuck Austin, Ken Carr, Alex Milburn, John Richardson, Ron Scott and Ross Skinner. Ken, Alex and Ross have allowed my colleagues and me to class-test disguised case situations over the past nine years, so that we might find better ways of helping the students cope with a subject and an educational process that is in transition.

In recent years I have been assisted in this project by several practitioners, in particular J. Bruce Dunlop of Price Waterhouse, Naju B. Shroff of Arthur Andersen & Co., and Don R. Fenwick and Dan B. Rubenstein of Touche Ross & Co. Each provided me with disguised mini case material to use in class and on examinations. I am grateful to each of them.

Gordon D. Richardson, former secretary to the Board of Examiners who administer the Uniform Final Chartered Accountancy examinations, read most of the material and provided responses to many of the mini cases. His suggestions and encouragement are much appreciated.

Thanks must be expressed to J. M. Donovan of Falconbridge Nickel Mines Limited and D. H. Ford of Noranda Mines Limited for allowing me to reproduce portions of the 1980 annual reports of each company. Joe W. Bolla, Tom H. Beechy, John Friedlan, Bill King, John Switzer and Henry McCandless gave me suggestions on how to improve several mini cases. Many other instructors gave helpful advice.

Nancy Johnstone and her staff, Teresa Colavecchia and Joan Howard, ably typed several versions of the manuscript and worked hard to produce the material on time. Their devotion to the task made my job easier.

L.S. Rosen

List of Mini Cases

Introductory-Intermediate

An Inheritance
Beedle Developers Ltd.
Benoit Limited
Blaine Manufacturing Limited
Burke Limited
Butterworth Products Ltd.
Canadiana Products Ltd.
Canadian Candy Inc.
College Books Limited
Credit Services Corporation
Direct Imports Limited
Eckel Sales Limited
Feature Furniture
Finney Limited
Funnel Hotels Limited
Galvin Disposal Company
Gibbins Insurance Limited
Goodale Corporation
Haileybury Manufacturing Limited
Jewelry Products Limited
Johns Construction Limited
Jones, Jones & Jones
Kennedy Corporation
Laimon Limited
Lead Barrier Mines Limited

Leisure Distributing Limited
Leisureproducts Limited
Lemke Limited
Marchant Automobiles Limited
McDonald Forest Products Limited
Mercantile Printing Limited
Miller Metals Limited
Mitchell Canada Limited
Murphy Properties Limited
Newlife Limited
Northern Grocers Limited
Precious Metals Inc.
Prentice Oil Limited
Queen City Drugstores
Reel Estates Limited
Scrumptious Bread
Seaside Resorts Limited
Stollar Furniture Stores
Sweeney Limited
Thomas Toys
Toronto Builder Inc.
Weintrop Insurance Brokers Limited
Williams Estates (A Partnership)
Williams Estates Limited

List of Mini Cases

Intermediate-Advanced

Adanac Transportation Corporation
Arctic Equipment Limited
Baxter Resources Limited
Betty Boutiques Limited
Brennan Airlines Limited
California Corporation
Carter Corporation
Chalcopyrite Limited
Commercial Helicopters Limited
Davis Oil and Gas Limited
Denham Limited
Donamar Corporation
Enchanted Forest Products Limited
Grammas Foods
Graul Explorations Limited
Hanna Corporation Limited
Herauf Limited
Island Manufacturing Limited
Joplin Distributors Limited
Kaiser and Son
Laughlin Pipeline Limited
Lease-A-Car Limited
Lemon Corporation
Lightening Electronics Limited
Marble Installations Limited
National Communications Limited
Natural Steel Limited

Northern Explorations Limited
Olympic Brothers
Osmosis Pipeline Limited
Park Estates Limited
Parkinson Limited (A)
Parkinson Limited (B)
Peaceful Gardens Corporation
Philips Investments Limited
Planet Limited
Pleasant Mines Limited
Portage Limited
Portion Mining Limited
Radio GAAP Limited
Revamp Limited
Saltspray Mines Limited
Schandl Limited
Seymour Manufacturing Limited
Shaw Brothers Builders' Supply
Smooth Limited
Southern Mines Limited
St. Denis Softdrinks Limited
Switch Limited
Taylor Pipeline Limited
Thornton Transportation Limited
Tiessen Coffee Corporation
Waterhouse Protection Systems
Western Steel Supply Limited

Whelan Farms Limited
Wholesum Grain Terminal

Zipair Limited

Multiple-Subject

Adams Corporation
An Acquisition
Antiques Limited
Bell Enterprises Limited
Mann Oil Limited
Modern Metalworks Limited

Mount Royal Manufacturing Limited
Urban Magazine Limited
Xavier Softdrinks Limited
Yarmouth Steel Corporation Limited
Yarrow Corporation
Zeballos Fishing Company Limited

FINANCIAL ACCOUNTING

Section 1:

Introduction and Analytical Techniques

CHAPTER 1

Less Directive Questions

```
┌─────────── LEARNING OBJECTIVE ───────────┐
│                                           │
│    Why cases or less directive questions  │
│        are an essential part of your      │
│      accounting and business education.   │
│                                           │
└───────────────────────────────────────────┘
```

Educational Rationale

Why is it essential that mini cases or less directive problem material be used in accounting courses? Although many responses can be provided to this question, one simple reply tends to stand out and be more convincing than others: *Clear-cut answers do not exist to a large percentage of activities and transactions that have to be accounted for in real life.* Frequently, we are not able to refer to a book of rules and find a "right answer." Instead, as preparers of financial information we must reason from "similar" situations, making sure that we have fully recognized any differences in facts, purposes of accounting and legal restrictions between the various situations. Or, if we are readers or users of financial statements, we must recognize the degree of judgment that has been exercised in the preparation of financial figures and explanations. As users we must understand the limitations, as well as the strengths, of financial reports.

Most students are accustomed to what might be called a "knowledge recall" approach to education. Under such an approach directive material tends to be used. ("Directive" simply means that students tend to be held by the hand, and directed or pointed towards an answer.) Questions tend to oblige students to recall and write out their accounting knowledge. Memorization plays an important role in this educational approach.

Sometimes, under directive learning, students are given practice in applying their new knowledge. That is, a problem situation could be provided that allows them to apply exactly the new knowledge that they have just acquired. The problem situation does not ask for any more or any less than what the students know. Such problems might be called "knowledge recall with highly directive applications."

When we are training bookkeepers, "knowledge recall with highly directive applications" makes sense because it is cost effective. That is, the method "works" and does not cost as much money as an alternative approach to training. However, we must remember that the bookkeeper who has been trained in a highly directive manner has to be closely supervised so that he or she avoids applying the limited knowledge to the wrong situation. An incorrect application can be costly and may mislead readers and invite a lawsuit against us.

Suppose, for example, that you have just taught a younger brother and sister how to change a tire on your Chevrolet. They have watched you change the tire from the time you got out the tools until you delivered the flat tire to a repair garage. You have given them an oral quiz wherein they repeated the steps in the process. They passed your oral test with high grades.

Are they now ready to change flat tires on all makes of automobiles? How can you find out? If you give them an examination that asks them to change a tire on the same Chevrolet (in other words, a directive examination problem), you are not going to find out how ready they are to change all types of tires. Why? There are many reasons, but one simple one is that they may not know how to raise the frame of every type of automobile. Jacks vary in where they are placed and how they operate. If you cannot lift the automobile, your knowledge about changing tires is useless.

Your course involving one automobile was therefore inadequate if you wanted your brother and sister to be capable of changing all types of tires. What could you have done to better prepare them? Maybe all you needed was an additional explanation of the different types of lifting devices and where they are to be placed on different types of automobiles. Maybe they require practice in changing tires on sample types of automobiles. Yet, it still may be necessary to give them an update course every time a new type of lifting device appears on the market. Or, they may be capable of reasoning from their broad knowledge and experience to any new situation. Your course of action should be decided after you think about the complexity of the task (changing tires) and the abilities of your brother and sister.

Accounting is somewhat more complex than changing flat tires. Nevertheless, the general approach to educating and training has to consider the issues just raised. How complex is accounting? What type of students should we attract to educational programs? How much can users understand? What should be taught first? Might we attract the "wrong" people to accountancy or financial analysis if we do not portray the subject as it exists in real life? Accounting is not simply a collection of rules. It is a subject that is constantly evolving and therefore needs people who can adapt to change.

In summary, less directive problem material has to be used in accountancy courses because few accounting rules exist and the subject is changing rapidly in response to economic and environmental changes. Regardless of whether students are preparers or users of accounting information, they have to be prepared for the world of tomorrow. They cannot be subjected to a hand-holding education and nothing more.

In its worst form, the "knowledge recall" and directive type of accounting course tends to stress rules that may be obsolete by the time the students graduate. These courses may stress memorization beyond what makes sense in a subject that is in a state of continual change. Directive courses do not provide students with the full range of skills needed to understand the subject.

Accepting Responsibility

It takes at least two parties (instructors and students) to bring about the existence of highly directive, knowledge recall courses. Such courses are easy for both the instructor and the students. The instructor can avoid many real-life complexities by teaching what students come unwisely to regard as a general purpose model or answer. Examinations are simple to set and mark. Indeed, marking may be delegated to junior people once a "correct answer" has been provided. Thinking and creativity are played down, and worship of authority is encouraged. Unfortunately, in accounting, the views of authorities change quickly. Memorizing what the authorities say in today's environment has serious drawbacks because their opinion could very well be different tomorrow.

Some students respond to the high structure or directive style of pure knowledge recall courses. They like the certainty; they like to know exactly what will be covered in examinations. When they finish an examination they know what their mark will be. In short, they have been granted the joys of a make-believe world.

What do students receive from highly directive courses? Do they, for example, believe that their course reflects what happens in the real world? Do they believe that there are universal accounting "truths?" Do they lock in to an attitude about the subject that is not easily changed in later life? Do they understand the important role that judgment plays in the preparation and interpretation of financial statements? Do they understand that a different accounting technique could have resulted in a much different net income, or balance-sheet figure?

These questions are not easily answered. Much depends on the attitude and capability of each student. One serious danger of highly directive accounting courses is that they mislead some students into thinking that accounting is precise. Hence, people who like precision and certainty may be attracted to accountancy, instead of those people who are better able to cope with a career that involves diagnosing problems, assessing the importance of the problems, evaluating evidence, making judgments and so forth.

Students have to decide what type of education they desire. If they agree that diagnostic and judgmental skills are needed for their career, then they have to accept the less secure atmosphere that goes with less directive problem material and mini cases. Students have to focus on the approach and process more than on the final answer. They have to learn to accept lower grades on cases (but not necessarily lower final grades in the course) when they miss the main points. If students force markers to give high grades for poor quality mini case responses, they are defeating themselves. They will inadvertently persuade themselves to write down anything in response to a case, because the range of grades given by the instructor will be narrow.

In summary, instructors who choose to assign mini cases require support from students. Students have to avoid taking out on the instructor the frustration that accompanies mini case learning. Students should consider the alternatives to less directive mini cases: Are the alternatives worth the effort? Do they prepare one adequately for a career in interpreting or preparing financial statements?

Striking a Balance

A balance has to be struck between providing directive course material and less directive material. On the one hand, students need some knowledge before they can apply it. In accounting this knowledge of techniques often can be provided in a cost effective manner by directive teaching methods. On the other hand, students should not be allowed to proceed too far into a course without being required to comprehend the strengths, weaknesses and sensible applications of this knowledge. If students proceed too far into directive material many of them somehow develop the unfounded belief that their knowledge has universal use or application.

Junior instructors often are dismayed by student answers to their first case. If the case is assigned after their textbook chapter on, say, receivables has just been completed, the student answers tend to pick out receivables problems in virtually every paragraph in the case. However, if the *same* case is assigned after completion of the chapter on inventories, students think that there are endless inventory valuation problems. In other words, students have a tendency to apply the last thing they have learned, whether it fits the facts and circumstances or not.

Consequently, it becomes necessary for instructors to rearrange cases so that they might test knowledge acquired earlier, or even call for knowledge that students have not yet fully acquired. The latter is a particularly useful approach to help students evaluate new knowledge. (Is the new knowledge that was just taught similar to what students anticipated in a case considered the previous week? If not, what are the differences? Why do they exist?)

There is a vast range of Canadian business activity. Instructors ought to be confident that what they are teaching can apply to the full range, not just to a small group of enterprises. But if a narrow approach is taken in courses, students ought, as a minimum, to be taught where they can sensibly apply what they have learned. It is vital that they be taught where their new knowledge does *not* apply. The cases in this book attempt to help students assess the knowledge that they are learning in textbooks. Accordingly, for best results the cases can, and should, be used from week to week throughout courses taught at introductory, intermediate and advanced levels.

Needed Skills

Both users of financial statements (such as financial analysts employed by underwriters, brokers and trust companies, bankers or current and potential shareholders) and preparers (such as controllers or, perhaps, auditors) need the following "cognitive skills"*: knowledge, comprehension, application, analysis, synthesis and evaluation. These skills are similar to those needed by most professionals.

Consider the skills required of a doctor. He or she must learn to ask patients many questions about the symptoms that they are experiencing, how serious the symptoms are, how frequently they occur, and so on. The doctor must tentatively diagnose the problem, and decide what further tests (X-ray, blood) are needed to confirm the diagnosis. It would be rare that a patient would arrive at a doctor's office knowing precisely what the problem was, and what treatment was needed.

Preparers and users of financial statements are in a similar situation. The problem often is not clear, and considerable investigation is needed to uncover the main problem, as opposed to symptoms of the problem. This is unlike the questions and problems at the end of the chapters in most accounting textbooks. Textbook questions tend to tell you what the main issue is, and direct you to the technique that ought to be chosen to solve the problem. As a result you often are not taught to be a

---

* Benjamin S. Bloom, ed. *Taxonomy of Educational Objectives, Handbook I: Cognitive Domain* (Longmans, Green & Co., 1956).

manager. Instead, you are being taught to be a junior who has to be supervised, perhaps closely.

In general, this book is trying to encourage students to develop an analytical technique that can be used in solving accounting and business problems. At the end of their formal training, students have to be ready to solve problems they have not seen before. If they are not ready, their education has been a failure to an important degree.

One analytical technique is shown in Exhibit 1-1.

EXHIBIT 1-1

An Analytical Framework

1. Ascertain the *objectives* or purposes of the financial statements, or accounting system.

2. Identify the problems in the situation, and rate their *importance* (serious, minor, in between) in light of the objectives in 1.

3. Identify any legal or professional *constraints* (such as corporate or securities legislation, or professional accounting pronouncements) that confine your possible answer or limit your choice of solutions.

4. Gather necessary *facts* (or make assumptions when crucial facts are missing) that help you assess the nature of the problem and help to point towards possible solutions.

5. List the *possible* feasible *solutions* to the main problems, and list the pros and cons of each in light of the objectives in 1.

6. Choose the best solution and *explain* why it is the best of those available. The solution may not be ideal, but it should be better than the alternatives. It should help attain the objectives in 1, and be compatible with facts and constraints in 3 and 4.

7. If required, implement your solution.

As the course progresses you ought to be developing an analytical framework that you feel comfortable with. It should be comprehensive and credible. After all, you are trying to convince others (especially an instructor) that you know how to diagnose, apply, assess, evaluate and so forth.

Summary

Less directive questions can be frustrating for students because there is no one "right answer." Various diagnostic, judgmental and integrative skills have to be honed, and this takes time. Sometimes progress is slow, and you may wonder whether the end result is worth the effort.

At times when your morale is low, consider alternative educational patterns. One pattern involves giving highly directive questions that leave you with the impression that your education can apply anywhere. On graduation you will not be ready for a position of much responsibility; you will have to be closely supervised. Worst of all, you will have to *unlearn*. You will have to assess your education and note that it has limited application. And then you will have to start learning how to solve problems that you have never encountered before.

CHAPTER 2

Financial Accounting Overview

┌─────────── **LEARNING OBJECTIVES** ───────────┐

1. Understanding that financial accounting and reporting tend to be tailored to fit: (a) the purposes or *objectives* of accounting, (b) the *facts* of the situation and (c) any legal or professional *constraints*. That is, students must avoid seeking the all-purpose method of accounting for each transaction.

2. Recognizing that few accounting principles apply to all of the vast range of business enterprises in Canada, and that educational emphasis therefore has to be placed on learning what fits where—that is, what principle applies in which situations. This means that it is necessary for students to develop a learning attitude that not only involves grasping how the principle or accounting technique works, but comprehending where it can and where it cannot be applied.

3. Comprehending that the material in this chapter cannot be fully grasped until students have read it several times and completed many accounting cases.

└──┘

Objectives of Financial Accounting

Professional groups and authors tend to have different listings of the objectives, or purposes, or reasons for the existence of financial accounting. Over time the relative importance of each objective will change because users' wants or needs will change. Naturally, it is useful for us to know what the prime objectives of accounting are at any one point in time; but such knowledge is far less important to students than having them grasp the fundamental reality that *more than one* objective exists. Do students understand what the learning implications are in situations where multiple objectives exist? Memorization, for example, becomes less important than learning how to *apply* knowledge that may have been obtained by memorization, or other means.

Preparers and users of financial statements ought to be communicating with each other. This communication will not occur if the preparer has compiled a financial statement in accordance with one objective of accounting whereas the reader/user believes that the financial statement is useful for another objective—or worse, for every objective.

The message for students of accounting, regardless of whether they will be users or preparers, should be clear. Your study of the subject should be approached from the viewpoint of trying to learn *where each* accounting principle, procedure, or technique mentioned in your principal textbooks *applies*, and *where* it does *not*. If, instead, you try to approach your learning by seeking an all-purpose answer, at least two dangerous effects probably will occur:

1. You will tend to apply your "all-purpose answer" in an improper setting and arrive at senseless results that could confuse many people. The confusion could lead to a misallocation of funds and resources.
2. You might delude yourself into giving greater permanency in your mind to "*the* answer" when "the answer" may be a temporary one only, that fits only a limited circumstance. What is worse, accounting authorities may change "the answer" shortly after you have learned it. Your knowledge could become obsolete quickly.

Consider, again, the environment and task of the doctor. It would be ridiculous for a doctor to order head X-rays for everybody who came to her office. It would be equally ridiculous to have medical training and education consist solely of memorizing the symptoms and progression of individual ailments. Real-life practice is required. Recognition of situations where multiple ailments and conflicting symptoms exist is essential. Without such understanding, incorrect diagnoses will occur.

Analogies between doctors and accountants are incomplete and can be misleading. For example, doctors spend a year or more in hospitals in a training position. During this time they see a wide range of medical problems. Graduates of business schools, whether they are potential users or preparers of financial information, rarely receive the equivalent type of broad exposure shortly after graduation that doctors receive. Indeed, accounting majors may see only the most mundane parts of business for two or three years after graduation. Thus, greater pressure exists on universities to give a broader view of the subject so that graduates are more than specialized technicians. Graduates must be able to fit their day-to-day practical experience into an all-inclusive picture of accounting and business.

The first step in painting ourselves an all-inclusive picture of accounting involves looking at the more common objectives of financial accounting. The objectives can be fitted into three categories:

A. *General purpose* reports. (Only *one* general purpose report may be issued per financial period by an organization; and the report might be employed by a variety of users having different needs.) There tend to be four main subcategories of general purpose reports:

1. stewardship-type report (or financial statement);
2. report for income tax purposes (or income tax postponement);
3. report to aid those who are attempting to estimate or predict cash flows (cash receipts less cash disbursements) that will be generated in future years (hereinafter called "cash flow predictions"); and
4. report to aid those who want to evaluate corporate management's efforts during the most recent financial period (hereinafter called "management evaluation").

B. *Specific* or *special purpose* reports. (Many different specific purpose reports could be issued by an organization in a period to supplement or augment the organization's general purpose report. Special or specific purpose reports tend to be issued to those who have legal or other power to require the organization to disclose more, or a different type of, information than is in its general purpose report. An example may be a banker who wants a projected cash flow report to show that the bank loan can be repaid within a specified number of years.)

C. *Internal control* systems. (Some organizations, such as certain charities, do not have to issue a financial statement; but they still would like the benefit of good control systems to safeguard their assets. Hence, accounting textbooks often contain descriptions of bank reconciliations or perpetual inventory systems that are primarily record-keeping in purpose, and have little to do with financial reporting. Even double entry bookkeeping is a form of internal control check.)

An organization might have one or more of the above financial accounting objectives. A charity that does not issue income tax receipts for donations may have internal control as a sole objective. A small proprietorship may have two objectives: internal control and income tax postponement. Whenever there is more than one objective it may become necessary to ascertain which is more important than the other(s). For example, in a case where the objectives are contradictory, it becomes necessary to know which objective is of the greatest importance because that is the one that will be catered to first. Large publicly-owned companies could have several reporting objectives.

Accounting policies, techniques, principles, procedures and practices are chosen for the longer term, and are not altered every year in order to pursue a different objective of accounting. Consistency plays an important role in financial reporting. Therefore, all organizations have to think out their longer-term needs and select accounting policies that fit their objectives, as well as any constraints and environmental facts. A closer look at the objectives previously listed is essential.

General Purpose Reports

A(1) *Stewardship*. The term "stewardship" means different things to different people. It might, for example, include all of the four objectives listed under "general purpose reports." However, a narrow definition has been selected for this book, and the term will mean "complying with the law." The "law" will be explained later in this chapter under the heading 'Constraints'.

Owners of limited liability companies are granted privileges and must assume responsibilities. One privilege is that they are entitled to annual financial statements from the managers, or stewards, of their company. This privilege is set out in the corporate legislation under which the company has been incorporated. Some legislation in Canada specifies in detail what the financial statements shall contain. Other legislation allows quite brief financial reporting. When companies are publicly owned, securities legislation may specify additional financial reporting requirements.

A company that has stewardship as its sole objective of financial accounting will merely comply with the law, and not show additional information in its financial statements. This approach might be taken to save money (or minimize accounting and auditing costs), or because no great need to communicate with the owners-/shareholders is felt. A mining company that no longer needs funds for expansion of its one mine is an example of a situation where stewardship could be the most important objective. The mining company wishes to comply with the law at the lowest possible cost. It does not wish to incur costs of reporting if it is not likely to receive benefits greater than the costs.

Stewardship accounting might be the only objective or reason for financial reporting in many other situations. Two more examples might aid understanding. Some Canadian corporate legislation specifies a size test for privately-held companies. For instance, one Corporate Act states that if sales exceed $10 million or assets exceed $5 million, the financial statements have to be audited. But the financial accounting statements may not be wanted by the owners. The owners may have their own sources of information, such as management accounting reports, and use these internal reports to judge corporate performance and to make predictions. If so, they will want only low cost, minimum disclosure stewardship financial statements in order to comply with the law.

Sometimes the company's banker wants a general purpose report, audited or not, to send to the bank's head office along with, perhaps, a special purpose financial report. If most of the information needed to support a request for a bank loan is in the special purpose report (which usually is not audited), then the general purpose report can be skimpy, possibly in a stewardship vein.

A(2) *Income tax requirements.* The Department of National Revenue (or Revenue Canada—Taxation) requests that financial information accompany the business taxpayer's income tax return. For many small businesses this requirement may be the only reason they are interested in financial accounting. For others there may be two objectives: a stewardship-type report for their banker, and an income tax report for Revenue Canada. If appropriate financial accounting policies are chosen, one general purpose report could serve both needs.

Roughly speaking, income tax law as it affects accounting can be divided into two categories. First, there are several situations specified in the tax law where the policy for computing taxable income (or income subject to taxation) must be handled Revenue Canada's way. An example of this is depreciation (called capital cost allowance). The tax law requires taxpayers to use a specified method and capital cost allowance/depreciation rate. *But* a *different* method of depreciation and rate can be used in general purpose reports where the objective is stewardship or cash flow prediction or management evaluation. In a limited sense, there are "two sets of books": one for tax purposes and one for other general purpose objectives.

Second, the vast majority of situations and transactions encountered in practice are not regulated by specific income tax laws. Companies are not entirely free to choose their own accounting principles, but they have considerable freedom in choosing one method from a group of "generally accepted accounting principles." Income tax assessors are willing to accept most common sense methods provided that they are applied consistently over a certain minimum of years.

It is this second category that causes us to pay particular attention to a company that has implicitly adopted income tax as a prime objective of financial accounting. (Companies do not specify their objectives in an overt way in their financial statements. However, their choice of accounting policies and methods provide clues.)

A company that regards income tax as its prime objective of accounting will be attempting, in general terms, to keep taxable income to a minimum. Tax legislation, with a few exceptions, does not specify which of several methods of recognizing revenue a company must use. Hence, whenever facts are unclear, a company with an income tax objective of accounting would attempt to delay revenue recognition as long as possible. Similarly, few policies for recognizing expenses are restricted by, or specified in, income tax legislation. Thus, where facts are not clear, attempts will be made to recognize expenses as soon as possible.

When income tax minimization is a prime objective of accounting, a company would select long-term revenue and expense recognition policies that minimize taxable income, and as a consequence, income tax. Having selected such policies, the company must use them in its one general purpose report for the financial period.

What are the implications for readers/users? Suppose that you are a banker reading a general purpose financial statement of a customer who has requested a loan. Suppose also that the net income of the company for the current year is barely above zero. What does this low amount signify? If you know that the customer's prime objective of financial accounting is income tax minimization, then three possibilities exist: (1) the company has been successful in minimizing income tax; (2) the company is not overly profitable; or (3) the low figure is a combination of (1) and (2). With some astute questioning of the customer you can soon determine which of the three represents reality.

However, if you are not aware of the importance of objectives of accounting you may (perhaps foolishly) conclude that the company is not profitable and does not merit a loan from you. In fact, the company could be well managed. The managers could be saving interest expense by postponing income tax payments for a year or more. That is, if the company recognized revenue in an earlier financial year it would have increased its taxable income and income tax. In order to pay the income tax it may have needed a bank loan, or it may have been forced to sell some interest-yielding marketable securities. Either way, earlier revenue recognition is more costly (results in an increase in interest expense or a decrease in interest revenue) than later recognition.

It is important to observe that the company cannot change its revenue and expense recognition policies every year in order to minimize taxable income. Tax assessors would not allow such a practice. Auditors would object to frequent changes because the credibility of financial statements would be destroyed. Thus, the future has to be anticipated and a company's accounting policies must be set to acknowledge longer-term objectives of financial accounting.

A(3) *Cash flow prediction*. Although financial accounting reports are based on the past, they reflect limited anticipation of the future as it is perceived by preparers. For example, the statements might indirectly show anticipated returns of goods, expected warranty costs, bad debts or expected lives of depreciable assets. Thus, the financial statements might give some clues about the net cash inflow (receipts less disbursements) that could appear in the future. Note that we are not primarily referring to cash flow arising from acquiring fixed assets or by selling bonds or shares. "Cash flow prediction" usually connotes the net inflows from regular company operations. For a merchandising company regular operations would consist of buying and selling goods, paying salaries, interest expense, income taxes and so forth. This net cash flow represents a return on investment, or repayment for capital investment.

A general purpose report that is designed to meet a cash flow prediction objective would contain much more information than a stewardship report. Rather than merely having indirect references to the future through such financial statement items as liabilities for estimated warranty expense, the information about the future would be in notes to financial statements, or in accompanying schedules. In those cases where it is not prohibited by legal constraints, information could be captured in direct valuations (such as present value or replacement cost) in the financial statements.

Note that we must draw a distinction between forecast financial statements and a cash flow prediction type of statement. Financial forecasts, such as what next year's net income will be, are generally prohibited by securities legislation. This prohibition exists to prevent manipulation of investors' funds. That is, a company could falsely say that net income will triple, in the hope that the price of its common shares would rise.

A cash flow prediction type of statement is based on the past (the financial period(s) just ended), but includes much more information about possible future activities than does a stewardship financial statement. A forecast financial statement, in contrast, focuses on balance sheets and income statements for future years.

Why would a company issue a cash flow prediction type of financial statement? There could be several reasons, but one of the most common is a desire to attract new bondholders and shareholders. Funds may be needed for expansion, and funds might be available at a cheaper rate if the company is less secretive about its future prospects. Another reason might involve management's desire to increase the future price of its common shares, because management holds incentive share option certificates.

Before we proceed, a brief comparison between stewardship and cash flow prediction statements is in order. It is not unusual to encounter the following situations in practice:

1. Net income, or balance sheet, figures are needed to assist in distributing income to partners, or those entitled to periodic profit bonuses, and so on.
2. Purchase and sale prices of an entire company might (perhaps foolishly) be tied in part to income statement, funds flow, or balance sheet figures.

The concern in these situations is with the past, and therefore stewardship statements are desired. Of *no* concern, or virtually none, are additional disclosures pertaining to the future. Measurement of the past is the only focus when bonuses or selling prices are tied to income, and/or balance sheet figures.* Disclosure by way of footnotes is not relevant to the users of the statements.

In contrast to the two situations just described is a scenario where an investor or potential investor is trying to decide whether to buy, hold or sell common shares in a company. A wise investor will try to obtain information about future prospects for the company from many sources. One such source is financial statements *if* they contain more information than that typically shown on stewardship or income tax postponement/minimization type reports.

---

* Some authors might mention the subject of "agency theory" while discussing distributions such as profit bonuses. Agency theory and the definition of stewardship chosen in this book have similarities.

For example, the statements might show the following types of items:

1. profitability of main products or geographical regions as well as the total profitability;
2. cash flows needed to meet lease obligations/liabilities for each of the next several years;
3. cash flows expected for pension obligations;
4. cash flows required when depreciation exceeds capital cost allowance and cash payments are higher than that shown as income tax expense;
5. unfilled sales orders as of the end of the year.

Some people believe that such information helps them predict future cash flow (or earnings per share). They can thereby establish the worth of the company because, in theory at least, current worth of a company is the present value of future cash flows.

What sort of information would be included in a set of financial statements designed to attain a cash flow objective of accounting? In general terms the statement ought to include details to help readers establish the *amount, timing* and *uncertainty* of future cash flows. That is, we have to know how much cash flow, when it will appear, and the likelihood that the cash amount could be higher or lower because of various risks. If we have all of this information, and we know what interest/discount rate is appropriate, then we can compute a theoretical present worth.

For several reasons not all of the information needed to perform a present value or worth calculation is available in financial statements. Some reasons are: (1) who can predict the future?; (2) preparers of financial statements are subject to legal liability for furnishing unsubstantiated information (i.e., preparers can be sued for misleading user/readers); (3) information costs money to prepare and have audited where necessary; and (4) some information may be helpful to competitors.

Given cost and liability considerations, and the fact that large amounts of detail may confuse unsophisticated users, some accountants argue against pursuing cash flow type objectives. However, if sophisticated users can understand the information and *if* such information helps to reduce a company's borrowing cost, then benefits to the company could exceed costs. For instance, by providing such detail about the future, a company might be able to reduce the interest rate by 1 percent on a new $10 million, 20-year bond payable. The lenders would be willing to reduce the interest rate because less uncertainty about the amount and timing of cash flows appeared to exist now that they knew more about the company's operations.

In the past few years the cash flow prediction type objective has received considerable attention, especially in the United States. Larger public corporations have been asked to furnish additional statements and schedules giving such data as inflation and current cost effects, profitability by segments of the company and, on a trial basis for some resource companies, the estimated worth of oil and gas reserves in the ground.

A(4) *Management evaluation.* This objective is the least understood of the four that we have included under the general purpose category. But there clearly are accounting methods and techniques in practice that are seemingly designed to help users evaluate the abilities of current management. For example, some accountants prepare financial statements based on current cost. One reason for a current cost system is to ascertain the change in current cost during a year, or period of time. (The opening balance presumably attaches to the efforts of a previous management or the current management's previous actions.) Some users believe that future success of a company is more assured if the company has good management.

Attempts to have outsiders evaluate senior management by examining financial statements are plagued by two accountability problems. First, under Canadian corporate law, *management* prepares the reports that it sends to shareholders. Although the reports are usually audited, the auditor's role is merely to attest that the statements are "fair in accordance with generally accepted accounting principles (GAAP)." The word "fair" is qualified by the reference to GAAP, and GAAP can include a wide range of choices. In a sense, thus, management is preparing its own report cards and assigning its own performance grades.

Second, how is it possible to separate good luck from good management? If current costs of assets rise, is this the result of good management? If they drop, is this bad luck or bad management?

In practice, there are other implications of the management evaluation objective. For example, one must look out for obvious attempts to blame a prior management. A new management might attempt to write off large amounts of assets (inventory, or long-lived) so that it cannot help but look good in a future period. That is, it could sell the assets for well in excess of written-down cost, or it would not have to incur much future depreciation expense.

The management evaluation objective has other drawbacks, such as the time period. Management actions of today often may not result in noticeable improvements for two or more years. The opening of a major new assembly plant may not add to profits until many years later. Measuring the benefit from cost expenditures is not easy. Sometimes the cost-benefit comparison may have to occur over a period much longer than one year.

If a company chooses to have management evaluation as a prime objective of accounting, what would it do in its financial statements? Generally, it would provide more information than what is in a stewardship report. The information could take the form of notes indicating such matters as the market value of securities, or inventory (if selling price is well in excess of cost) or of other assets. These figures may or may not be audited, depending on the legal constraints. The information may also be supplementary in nature, and consist of current cost financial statements. Sometimes realized gross profit might be separated between holding gains (difference between original cost, and current cost at the date of sale) and trading gains (selling price less current cost at the date of sale). Such a split helps to separate this year's results from those of a previous year, thereby providing some information on management's current actions.

Sometimes it is not easy to identify the particular financial accounting objectives that are being followed by a company in its general purpose report. Students have to avoid frustrating themselves with an obsession to pin down each of the four objectives briefly explained above. Emphasis should be placed instead on recognizing that multiple objectives exist, and that accounting techniques are designed for different purposes.

If you expect to be a user of financial statements, focus on techniques that might apply to particular types of companies. If you then obtain employment with an organization that can demand more information from a company (e.g., a potential lender of money) you will know what to ask for, and why.

Special Purpose Reports

The subject of specific or special purpose reports tends to be given little attention in textbooks. One reason for the lack of exposure is that such reports run counter to some authors' attempts to teach students one particular model or approach to accounting. Too frequently the stress on one model causes students to unwisely believe that, in reality, only one method of accounting exists.

Special purpose financial accounting reports can be used for a variety of reasons. At one extreme would be those financial reports that are close to general purpose reports in design and coverage. These might include the financial statements in a prospectus° or in a private placement circular. The latter is like a prospectus but offers securities to a limited number of buyers, perhaps one insurance company. Usually the financial statements at this one extreme are audited, and GAAP would apply as a minimum standard.

At the other extreme the financial reports would not be audited and would be based on whatever principles met the needs of users and preparers. The financial reports could bear little relationship to GAAP. For instance, the reports could be for a specialized "industry" such as hospitals, insurance companies, school boards, a provincial or the federal government, or charitable institutions. Ideally, the reports should contain a description of the accounting principles that were followed in compiling the report. Sometimes the principles would be spelled out in whole, or in part, by an association or government body that is the main recipient of the report.

Special purpose reports are usually prepared for those who have the power or influence to demand more than a general purpose report. From the viewpoint of education, it is important for students to learn to ask the following questions:

1. Would a special purpose report instead of a general purpose report better serve the information needs of the user?

° Often the most recent two years' balance sheets and five years' income, retained earnings and statement of changes in financial position, and notes, are included in the financial statement package.

2. Would the cost of preparing the special purpose report be less than anticipated benefits received by the preparer and the user?
3. Would the special purpose report have to be audited in order to be credible? (Would the added cost affect the response to question 2?)
4. Could the number of users of the special purpose report be restricted so that the preparer does not become exposed to extra liability (in potential lawsuits) as a result of the accounting principles that were applied and misunderstandings that might result?

Users generally want all of the information about a company that they can get. Why should they act otherwise? Generally they receive the information at no cost to them. Hence, when the preparer views the cost-benefit equation, the benefits have to be assessed more in terms of benefit to the preparer than to the user.

Since there are many types of special purpose reports, it is not possible to illustrate all or most of them. (Indeed, one of the reasons why the book is stressing the use of mini cases is to establish general analytical thinking that students must acquire *because* it is not possible to illustrate everything that they will later encounter.) One common special purpose report for small businesses would be a financial projection for the company's banker to show that, if certain assumptions turn out correctly, the loan will be repaid in, say, four years. The report likely would consist of cash receipts and cash disbursements, on perhaps a quarterly basis, for the next four years.

In some government agencies reports may have to be filed with another senior government body to show how actual expenditures compared with projected expenditures. The report might also request a particular level of financing or funding for next year. In a sense the agency is trying to show that value was received for the funds allocated by the senior government (value-for-money accountability).

Sometimes the special purpose reports take on characteristics of both financial and managerial accounting. An example would be a charity that is appealing for donations and wants to show what previous donations were used for, and what plans exist for future donations.

Overall, the same educational theme as has been stressed before applies to special purpose reports. As a user, learn to recognize where a special purpose report might serve your needs better than a general purpose report. If you have the necessary power over the preparer (e.g., you are a lender of funds) and need the special purpose report, then you should request it. As a preparer, consider whether a special purpose report might better serve a user's needs. You might be able to cater better to conflicting user needs if you issue one general purpose report, and one or more special purpose reports for restricted distribution.

Internal Control Objective

Although there have been some discussions in the United States about issuing external reports that explain the state of a firm's internal control system, most accounting textbooks tend to ignore the reporting aspects of internal control. Internal control is shown as an objective of accounting in this book because accounting includes more than reporting. As users and preparers we have to recognize that some organizations (e.g., some charities) want nothing more than internal control out of their accounting system. Other companies may choose a procedure (e.g., perpetual inventory methods) because of its internal control benefits rather than for any other reason.

Hence, when we state that a particular organization's accounting is a function of its objectives, facts and constraints we include the internal control objective in order to be complete in our observation. We do not want users of financial statements seeking complex reasons for a particular procedure when the choice may have been motivated by a simple internal control objective.

Constraints

We have stated that many organizations are not completely free as to the accounting principles and reporting procedures that they may adopt in their financial statements. For instance, a company may believe that its prime objective is furnishing information to those who wish to conduct cash flow predictions, and thereby establish a present worth for the company. Yet the company may be constrained by the following:

1. the legislation under which it is incorporated (for example, the Canada Business Corporations Act);
2. securities legislation in each province in which it sold bonds, or preferred or common shares that are presently outstanding;
3. U.S. securities legislation, if it previously sold securities that are still in the hands of U.S. investors; or
4. generally accepted accounting principles (GAAP), if:
   a. such are prescribed by 1 or 2;
   b. a chartered accountant is performing an audit and is required to follow GAAP;
   c. a user who has the power to demand particular information requests GAAP; or
   d. an auditor who is not a chartered accountant chooses to follow GAAP.

The existence of the constraints may prohibit the company from totally furnishing the type of general purpose report that is being sought. Yet some information that is not required by GAAP, and is also not prohibited by GAAP, may still be supplied. Often this additional information will take the form of more extensive note disclosure or perhaps supplementary schedules, possibly on a current cost or other basis.

In many cases the constraints noted above are not as confining as students may expect. For instance, Securities Acts and Regulations may state that GAAP as prescribed in the *CICA Handbook* should be followed. Yet a search of the *CICA Handbook* and other sources of Canadian GAAP will reveal nothing pertaining to the particular problem that we are trying to resolve. (Generally, because we are trying with this book to encourage students to learn analytical techniques, solutions to the case problems are not readily obtainable by examining the *CICA Handbook*.) The only real constraint may therefore turn out to be, from the preparer's point of view, whatever he *cannot* persuade the firm's auditor to accept. Well-documented reasoning by the preparer may be the key factor in persuading an auditor to accept a method or reporting procedure that is very close to the one that the auditor could not accept moments before.

In practical situations accountants often determine the constraints that they face before they consider objectives or purposes of accounting, and various facts. When the constraints are minor, accounting and reporting become a function of facts and longer-term objectives of accounting. When constraints are many and complex, they dictate the accounting and reporting that must be followed. Objectives and facts therefore assume much less or no importance.

Students have to be on guard and not fall into a trap where they believe that more knowledge of the constraints, gleaned from sources such as the *CICA Handbook*, will make the case problems easier to solve. More knowledge is always helpful, but the key to understanding the subject of accounting is learning to reason from fundamental notions such as the purposes of accounting. Learning to apply one's knowledge is essential in a practical subject such as accounting.

Facts

In a three-tiered framework, such as objectives-facts-constraints, one of the three will tend to serve as the catch-all for ideas that do not conveniently fit under the two tiers. We are not advocating strict adherence to the three tiers in any analysis, and therefore do not want students to waste time deciding whether something is a constraint or a fact. However, for purposes of explanation in this book the term "constraints" has been given a legal connotation (e.g., *CICA Handbook*, GAAP, or companies legislation). Constraints arising from other factors, such as user ignorance, have been called "facts."

A fact, for purposes of our analysis, is something of importance that may cause us to seriously consider, or even choose, one particular accounting or reporting procedure instead of another. Thus, in determining which revenue recognition method may be appropriate, besides objectives of accounting and constraints, we would look at such facts as:

1. the credit worthiness of the customer (Will receivables be paid promptly?);
2. the quality of the product that we are selling (Will customers return some of our products? How many? When?);

3. the terms of sale (Will we allow a large portion of the items to be returned? Are we providing a warranty? How much might this cost?); and
4. the interest rate that we are charging on receivables (Are we subsidizing the sale price by foregoing interest revenue in future periods?).

Obviously, many more facts could enter into our deliberations.

Facts are important to us for various reasons, but mainly they help to support the credibility of our conclusions. We can say to listeners: "As a result of these facts...we have concluded...." If listeners dispute the facts then we have to provide evidence.

When the facts clearly favor one particular accounting procedure over another, we ought to follow what the facts tell us, or we will lose our credibility in financial reporting. For example, if we sold the goods to the federal government on the basis that no returns are permitted and no warranty is provided, and payment is due in 30 days, it would not make sense to delay revenue recognition beyond the delivery of the goods. It would also not make sense to provide a bad debt allowance against the federal government's account receivable.

Thus, despite our objectives of accounting, when the facts strongly point in one direction we have to follow it. However, if the facts point in different directions, objectives can take precedence over facts. For instance, if the sale is to a reliable buyer, but returns are permitted and large warranty costs may be incurred, it is not obvious that one revenue recognition basis is more sensible than another. Hence, if the company's prime objective is to postpone income tax payments, then revenue recognition would tend to be delayed as long as would be credible to an income tax assessor. In contrast, if cash flow prediction were more important, early revenue recognition would make sense.

What would we do if both cash flow prediction and income tax postponement were of equal (50 percent each) importance? (The total of 100 percent shows that no other objectives exist.) We would have to delay revenue recognition in the accounts, to cater to the income tax objective; otherwise, we would be taxed on the income that resulted. We might also be able to give effective note disclosure as opposed to direct measurement on the income statement, disclosure that could help those wishing to predict. We say "might" because much depends on the abilities of the readers, and what information we disclose in the notes.

At this point we must stress again that accounting principles, policies, procedures and methods are selected for the *longer term*, not for every separate transaction. Thus, we would choose a limited number of revenue recognition policies in the company, one for each type of transaction. (We might have one policy for sales of new merchandise, and another for the sale of repossessed goods that have to be resold over longer terms with no down payment.) These policies would be reviewed and possibly changed if facts, objectives or constraints changed. When reporting, we would have to explain what changes we made from the policies that we employed in our last report.

The notes that we design for those who want to predict cash flows may tell our readers that we have used a particular revenue recognition measurement basis, and hint that we did this for income tax purposes. The notes might go on to say how much has already been sold on terms that would generate revenue in the next period (when we would have to pay income tax). The exact disclosure would depend on constraints that we faced.

User Knowledge

Preparers have to address the point of user sophistication whenever they are considering other than basic stewardship or income tax postponement objectives. Stewardship accounting often implicitly assumes that readers are naive and that everything dealt with must be objective, conservative and so forth in accordance with stewardship definitions.

In contrast, when we consider management evaluation or cash flow prediction we have to think about the "efficient market hypotheses." In particular, we have to look at the *semi-strong* form, which has these characteristics or implications.*

1. Information that is *publicly* made available is assessed for relevance by investors and is incorporated into share prices in an unbiased fashion within hours of its release.
2. Information that is not publicly available is guessed at, and guesses or anticipated results will tend to be captured in share prices; the guesses are revised as better information becomes available.
3. Knowledgeable people with moderate or large amounts of money will tend to make share trading of a particular company efficient in the semi-strong form because they will follow and assess all public releases of information, and through buying or selling adjust share prices accordingly.
4. Avoidance of guesswork about accounting figures can only occur when accountants explain the dollar effect of choosing different accounting policies or principles instead of the one that was used to measure income and assets. (Suppose that a company is using FIFO accounting for inventories and cost of goods sold. During periods of inflation analyst readers will want to know what cost of goods sold would be if LIFO or replacement cost values were in use. Accountants typically do not provide the alternative valuations for LIFO and replacement cost in their general purpose report. Hence, readers will have to guess. Accountants may, however, provide supplementary schedules showing replacement cost. This helps to prevent guesswork.)
5. Share prices, under a semi-strong form, will not necessarily reflect a so-called "true value" because guesswork is necessary when information is not available, and uncertainty exists about the future.

For our purposes the preparer/user implications boil down to whether or not the company in the case under consideration has sophisticated readers of its financial statements in a semi-strong sense of "market efficiency." If they do, we do not have to be concerned about the *location* of disclosure (i.e., whether incorporated into measurements on the income statement or mentioned in the notes to the financial

---

*For a thorough explanation see G. Foster, *Financial Statement Analysis*, (Englewood Cliffs: Prentice-Hall, 1978), especially pages 212 and 357.

statements). But we still have to be concerned about guesswork. We should not expect the semi-strong market to guess perfectly when we have not provided the information. Readers may guess at replacement cost of goods sold; but they may or may not be close.

In addressing the cases in this book that seem to involve cash flow prediction, management evaluation and perhaps stewardship, students must look for evidence of market efficiency in the semi-strong form. The same procedure applies in the real world. A company with many shareholders and with several types of shares listed on stock exchanges would be a likely candidate for a student's assumption of efficiency in the semi-strong form. This would be because a number of investors would likely be closely following the company's activities. In contrast, when the financial statements are to be read by one person, say the company's banker, the "efficiency" presumption would make less sense.

In summary, we should check the facts of the case and look for possible hints about "market efficiency." We should not automatically assume that all readers of financial statements are naive. We should also not assume that sophisticated investors will guess correctly when information is not available.

In keeping with our desire to learn how to diagnose problems, we should, as part of our studies, compile checklists of questions that must be asked so we can ascertain the facts. In simulated environments such as a classroom, one effective way of encouraging learning of diagnostic skills is to require yourself to make *and state* assumptions whenever facts are missing. An assumption, when stated on an answer paper, tells the instructor whether you know the fruitful questions to ask. The tendency of a student to proceed to an answer or recommendation without learning the facts should make an instructor suspicious. One suspicion that instructors will entertain is whether the student thinks there is one correct answer regardless of objectives, facts and constraints.

Other Facts

To obtain the greatest benefit from using mini cases such as those in this book, a student should attempt to compile a list of relevant questions as he proceeds from chapter to chapter in the main textbook. Besides asking himself where a procedure or technique can be sensibly applied, a student might consider the following types of questions while studying or analyzing a textbook chapter or case:

1. Does the procedure apply only in arm's-length situations, or under any conditions?
2. What would happen if economic conditions changed?
3. What would occur if risks increased? Who would be upset?
4. Did this situation occur before? How did we handle it then?
5. What will be the effect on minority shareholders, if any?
6. Are any restrictions imposed by debt or preferred share agreements (called "restrictive covenants")?

Naturally, many other questions have to be asked to learn all of the important facts.

Basic Concepts

Since many of the cases in this book, most of which are adaptations of real situations, are not easily responded to by looking at a source such as the *CICA Handbook*, where does one go for help? A variety of publications or sources may have to be consulted in practice. The more common ones would be surveys of what other companies are doing, files of similar problems, accounting theory books, publications of the Financial Accounting Standards Board (FASB) in the United States in its *Statement of Financial Accounting Concepts* series, research studies, magazine articles and industry accounting guidelines.

Students should probably rely on their textbooks, accounting theory books such as R.M. Skinner *Accounting Principles: A Canadian Viewpoint* (CICA), and the FASB *Concepts* series. If students are facing a stewardship objective, they will have to reason from such stewardship concepts of matching, objectivity, consistency, revenue recognition, conservatism and so on. If students are interested in management evaluation and prediction, concepts such as representational faithfulness, that are listed in the FASB series, should prove helpful.

Financial accounting is undergoing rapid change. Students must accept this state of change, and not hide from it by studying obsolete knowledge. The sooner students become accustomed to using the facilities of a modern library the better educated they will become.

Summary

This chapter has attempted to provide a framework that may be used to view financial accounting as it exists in Canada and as it pertains to mini case analysis. If possible, students should attempt to devise their own analytical framework.

We have stressed the objectives-facts-constraints framework as an analytical guide only; or in a sense, as a partially directive device, until students develop a way of looking at a problem from all sides. The three-tiered framework is designed to combat memorization approaches that lead students to believe that only one tier, such as constraints, exists in accounting.

We have mentioned the importance of learning diagnosis, application, synthesis and similar skills weekly, as we proceed from chapter to chapter in our main textbook. Accounting has to be tailored to suit objectives-facts-constraints. In order to learn how to do this tailoring, extensive practice with cases is required. Tailoring does not signify that dishonesty is being advocated. We are not trying to deceive readers. On the contrary, we are merely accepting the fact that the world is complex and is evolving, and that accounting and accounting education must evolve with it.

CHAPTER 3

Elementary Case Analysis

```
┌─────────────── LEARNING OBJECTIVES ───────────────┐
│                                                    │
│  1. Observing differences in objectives, facts and │
│     constraints.                                   │
│  2. Obtaining practice in solving less directive   │
│     mini cases and in assessing and applying       │
│     knowledge.                                     │
│                                                    │
└────────────────────────────────────────────────────┘
```

Introduction

This chapter is the first of three that provide an opportunity for those who wish to tackle a mini case and compare their responses to ones suggested by other analysts. The examples here are kept simple so that students enrolled in an introductory accounting course ought to be able to obtain some useful practice. The earlier students start with learning how to assess the strengths and limitations of their knowledge, and where to apply it, the easier applications will become, and the easier it will be to grasp the full nature of financial accounting as an evolving discipline.

Similar, but Different

Two short cases are provided to highlight the significance of an objectives-facts-constraints framework. Each case should first be responded to on its own. Then, to gain maximum benefit, students should compare objectives, facts and constraints in the two situations. Where are they the same? Where do they differ? What effect does this have on accounting and financial reporting?

Treat each mini case as an open book examination. Refer to Chapters 1 and 2 in this book, and to your principal textbook, for help. Remember to consult Exhibit 1-1 to ensure that you set out your reasoning process fully.

GERRARD CONVENIENCE SHOPPE

Gerrard Convenience Shoppe (GCS) is owned by Mr and Mrs Ruthjohn. They received $50,000 as a wedding present from relatives on condition that they open GCS.

GCS consists of one retail store of about 500 square feet located on the ground floor of a large, new, residential building. The space has been leased for two years for $600 per month, with an option to renew for a further two years at an increase in rent. The lease was signed on May 10, 19x2 for occupancy commencing June 1, 19x2. However, the owners of GCS were able to make the necessary renovations in May 19x2 and opened for business on June 3, 19x2.

Mr and Mrs Ruthjohn live in a small one-bedroom apartment at the back of the store. The monthly rental is $500 and the lease is for the same period as for GCS. Some parts of their apartment are used to store canned goods that are to be sold in GCS.

Most of the $50,000 was used to buy a cash register, refrigerators, shelving, and groceries for resale. Some of the long-lived assets (such as the cash register) were bought for cash, but others had to be financed. Most of the groceries are acquired on a "net 30 days" basis, but some have to be paid for in cash on delivery.

Leasehold improvements, such as permanent counters and limited storage space, cost GCS about $6,000 cash. Various permits and licences cost another $350. Burglar alarms cost $2,100 and have a life of 10 years at least, but are attached to the wall, windows and doors. Neon signs and advertising attached to the storefront cost $2,800 cash but are being paid for at $200 per month over 18 months, commencing June 30, 19x2.

It is hoped that the store can be staffed by Mr and Mrs Ruthjohn with occasional help from their relatives. The store is open seven days a week from about 07:00 until 24:00. All sales are for cash; no credit cards or personal cheques are accepted.

By rearranging the movable display counters, the owners hope to expand their line of goods beyond the usual groceries. They wish to include some bakery products and soft drinks that will be bought in small quantities by students at a community college across the street. The cost of this expansion is expected to be about $15,000 and the necessary funds probably will have to be borrowed by the Ruthjohns.

GCS has decided that its year-end will be January 31, with the first one being January 31, 19x3. It is now mid-January 19x3 and the owners have asked you to prepare financial statements for them for the period from commencement until January 31, 19x3. At the present time all of their records are on a cash basis, but they have a file of invoices available.

The owners would like you to select appropriate accounting and reporting principles for them, and to explain your choices. After they have discussed the choices with you, the financial statements may be prepared.

Required:

Choose appropriate accounting and external reporting principles for GCS and defend your selections.

OWL FOODS LIMITED

Owl Foods Limited (OFL) is a group of franchised convenience stores. One of the stores is "owned" by your client, Bo Lah, and is located in the Northgate Plaza. The store is separately incorporated under the name of Bo Lah Food Limited (BL).

The franchise agreement contains many clauses and restrictions. BL must buy all of its goods (excluding minor items such as newspapers) from OFL. All advertising is handled centrally and BL is charged its proportionate share of costs. In addition, a general management fee, based on sales, must be paid quarterly to OFL by all franchisees. Finally, a $50,000 franchise cost, which allows use of the Owl Foods name and provides research on merchandising techniques, must be paid at the rate of $10,000 per year for five years. The first payment of $10,000 was made on July 1, 19x2, the date BL opened for business. At the moment, Mr Bo Lah thinks that he may have to borrow in order to meet some of the further $10,000 payments.

Mr Bo Lah has started other small convenience stores and sold them when sales stabilized and someone with less business experience was able to take them over. He has found the practice very profitable. This is the first time he has acquired a franchise from OFL.

The Northgate Plaza Store is open 24 hours a day, seven days a week. Although most sales are for cash, Mr Bo Lah allows credit to some of the merchants in the mall and to a few steady customers. Payments for purchases must be made to OFL on the 10th and 25th day of each month.

The store space in Northgate Plaza is leased for five years with an option for another five years. The rent will increase annually. The cash register had to be bought from OFL because the machine is designed to record sales information by special categories. The freezers and shelving and accessories were acquired for $32,500 cash in June 19x2. Leasehold alterations and storage facilities cost $7,800 and were paid in June 19x2.

Mr Bo Lah works in the store about 60 to 70 hours a week. He has three employees, two of whom receive a small profit bonus based on quarterly gross profit, while the third is paid an hourly rate.

Under the terms of the franchise agreement, Mr Bo Lah must report sales information and inventory levels to OFL on a quarterly basis. He must also furnish an annual, audited financial statement. Mr Bo Lah has hired you to assist him with accounting and reporting matters. He wants you to recommend appropriate accounting principles and explain why they are needed.

Required:
Choose appropriate accounting and external reporting principles for BL and defend your selections.

Some Responses

Reflections

Most students will experience some discomfort after reading the two mini cases. One reaction may be that you need more knowledge before you can tackle each case. Another reaction may be that you have not been taught how to start at the beginning, when the company has not yet chosen its accounting principles. A third reaction may be that you now grasp what was mentioned in the first two chapters. That is, your education is not complete until you learn how to diagnose and then assess and apply your knowledge.

An analytical framework is often helpful in breaking the case down into "chewable bits," and in overcoming nervousness or other discomfort. Let us apply a combination of Exhibit 1-1 and general common sense in each case situation.

Similarities and Differences

Although both companies are in the same industry, so to speak, there are differences between the two. Let us try to pinpoint the similarities and differences.

	GCS	**BL**
1. Purposes or *objectives* of accounting and external reporting.	Very few readers of its financial statements; probably just needed for income tax purposes and maybe a lender such as a banker.	Probably more readers than for GCS; besides banker and income tax need, the employees having bonus incentives may be entitled to see the gross profit figures. Also, OFL requires information. Mr Bo Lah may want to show financial statements to a prospective owner.
2. *Constraints* of corporate law or accounting principles.	Not incorporated; no audit or review by a professional accountant seems required. Therefore no need to comply with *CICA Handbook* or GAAP.	Incorporated; audit required. Probably auditor will follow the *CICA Handbook* and GAAP.
3. *Facts* and assumptions.	All sales are for cash. Some accruals needed for long-lived assets; depreciation policy needed—what is the life of assets? Et cetera.	Some bad debts might have to be provided for. General accruals are needed. A conflict may exist because of differing objectives of accounting and external reporting. Et cetera.

Clearly, GCS's primary thrust will be towards external financial statements that help to minimize income taxes. Where possible and credible to income tax assessors, cash outlays will be expensed so as to lower taxable income of the owners. Perhaps special purpose reports on future cash flows will be needed by the company's banker. The basic financial statements of GCS that are furnished to Revenue Canada with the owners' income tax returns might have to be supplemented, orally or in writing, for negotiations with the company's banker. That is, policies of expensing might have to be explained so that the banker understands why income appears to be low.

Turning to specifics, GCS would probably do the following:

1. Recognize revenue when cash is received;
2. Charge a portion of the rent on the Ruthjohns' apartment to GCS to compensate for the space used to store canned goods;

3. Depreciate or amortize various expenditures on the basis of methods and rates that are permitted for income tax purposes;
4. Accrue expenses promptly.

The situation for BL is a little more complex. The objectives of accounting might conflict and force the owner to have to choose between principles that have a different effect on income and the balance sheet. For example, principles needed to lower taxable income and income tax (per BL's general purpose financial statements) may not make the company appealing to a prospective buyer who is naive about financial statements. Possibly OFL may want a form of reporting that permits it to make comparisons among its franchisees. A good response to the OFL/BL problem situation requires a discussion of trade-offs and pros and cons of selecting different principles of accounting and reporting. A massive application of everything in the *CICA Handbook* would be wasteful and pointless unless it is absolutely required by GAAP.

In terms of specifics, BL ought to:

1. Decide whether a prospective buyer of BL would believe special purpose report information. (The general purpose report has to be audited because of OFL's requirements, and likely would be in accordance with GAAP. If the prospective buyer would accept a special purpose report, BL could have a general purpose report in a stewardship vein and one that would help to postpone income tax payments. If the prospective buyer would want to give importance to a general purpose report, BL might have to prepare one constrained by GAAP but catering as much as possible to cash flow prediction. An income tax objective might have to be sacrificed.)
2. When (1) is decided, select suitable accounting principles, policies and disclosures. If cash flow prediction is given top priority, it will be necessary to spell out accounting policies in detail, rather than give a minimal description to comply with the *CICA Handbook* and GAAP. For instance, the period of amortization of leasehold improvements would be shown as either five or ten years. If the prospective buyer were to be on the naive side, revenue would be recognized as early as the facts allowed, and expenditures might be amortized over as long a period as would be credible.

Communication Strategy

The responses in the mini cases that are included in this chapter and the next two are in a teaching style rather than in the format noted in Exhibit 1-1. The reason for the teaching style is to permit us to show the effect of alternative objectives, facts and constraints on accounting and reporting. Many students believe that accounting has definite rules and do not see the need for mini case learning. Thus, it is necessary, chapter after chapter, to give examples of the consequences of alternatives.

Do not be misled by our style of response in these chapters. Most markers will give grades for *each* of the steps in Exhibit 1-1. Thus, it is not wise to bypass a step unless it does not apply.

In order to display your analytical ability, it is sensible to decide which objective or objectives apply in a case, and then systematically work through to recommendations as per Exhibit 1-1. Avoid wandering around, saying for example, "If this objective applied I would do that; however, if this other objective applied, I would do something else." The latter comes too close to memory regurgitation for comfort. It does not show what insight you possess about the particular situation. Let the marker know, *first*, that you can follow through to the consequences of a particular set of objectives-facts-constraints. Then, if time permits, go back in your analysis to where you have made an assumption that you are not convinced is clearly better than an alternative assumption. Explain the consequences of the alternative assumption if you can deduce them. But deal with alternatives *only after* you have worked right through the case with one set of objectives-facts-constraints.

Summary

This chapter is designed to show that two organizations, that appear on the surface to be similar, could have different accounting policies and different financial statements. The chapter also provides an opportunity to those who wish to test their diagnostic and application skills in a less directive setting. The next two chapters give two other approaches to different cases. The three chapters do not, of course, explain all of the types of cases that might exist.° At some point you will be on your own. We have to withdraw the "hand-holding" or we merely circumvent our own educational objectives.

° For additional assistance see L.S. Rosen and M. Granof, *Canadian Financial Accounting, Principles and Issues* (Prentice-Hall, 1980) and G. Richardson and L.S. Rosen, *Self Study Problems for Canadian Financial Accounting* (Prentice-Hall, 1980), especially Chapter 5 and others containing mini cases.

CHAPTER 4

Solved Case No. 1

```
┌─────────────── LEARNING OBJECTIVES ───────────────┐
│                                                     │
│  1. To obtain practice in resolving another mini case │
│     and checking your thought processes against      │
│     another analyst's response.                      │
│  2. Observing a slightly different analytical approach │
│     from that stated in Chapter 3.                   │
│                                                     │
└─────────────────────────────────────────────────────┘
```

Introduction

The mini case in this chapter is a disguised actual situation, as are most of the cases in this book. The case is not particularly complex, but it forces analysts to think out their response and defend their recommendations. Unless analysts can explain why their approach makes sense they will not be convincing to those who have requested the advice.

The vast majority of the cases in this book leave out a few pieces of information, some of which might be very important. A typical student reaction to missing information is: "In real life we would *know* the information. It would not be missing." This comment shows a serious misunderstanding of what happens in real life. *You would know only if you had asked the relevant questions* and assessed the completeness of the replies that you received. Very few people will ask your advice and tell you all the important facts. Most of the time you will encounter vague situations that force you to systematically ask a series of questions that uncover all of the facts and constraints and objectives. Students who believe that they would know all the facts probably have been exposed too long to directive, hand-holding learning environments.

Where possible the mini cases have been written up in the way that they were presented to the person who was asked for advice. Sometimes additional information has been provided when it was readily available. In summary, the analytical approach is to gather everything that seems relevant, and systematically work through the issues. Recommendations should be tied into objectives-facts-constraints or a similar framework.

SURFACE MINES LIMITED

The Mini Case Problem

Surface Mines Limited (SML) is incorporated under the laws of Canada and is listed on several Canadian stock exchanges. The company has operated an open pit copper mine in Western Canada for several years and this constitutes its principal source of revenue. Net income has recently been in the $10 million to $10.5 million range, but is naturally subject to worldwide copper price fluctuations.

A little over four years ago (19x3) the company leased a portion of the mining rights to lower grade ore to another company, Mosquito Mines Ltd. Mosquito pays SML a royalty based on tonnage mined, as follows:

First four years of contract: (19x3 to 19x6 inclusive)	$1.40 per ton on a minimum annual tonnage of 5,000,000 tons. (Minimum royalty is therefore $7 million.)
Remaining six years of contract: (19x7 to 19x12 inclusive)	$1.20 per ton on a minimum annual tonnage of 2,500,000 tons. (Minimum royalty is therefore $3 million.)
All 10 years of contract:	75¢ per ton on an annual tonnage mined in excess of above minimums set for royalty payments.

Mosquito has mined less than 2,500,000 tons in each of the four years which just ended on December 31, 19x6.

In about three months (it is presently late January 19x7) SML will have to switch a large proportion of its operations from open pit to underground mining. This will increase mining costs about 10 percent from last year's sum of $60 million. At present the company has a stockpile of about five months' unprocessed ore to be sold to a smelter under a long-term contract.

The accounts are being finalized for the year just completed, December 31, 19x6.

Required:

A. Assume the role of the chief financial officer of SML. What accounting treatment, if any, would you give to the above? Why?
B. Assume the role of SML's auditor. What posture would you take with regard to accounting and reporting in the 19x6 financial statements? Why?

A Possible Response

To obtain maximum benefit from this chapter you should not read beyond this sentence until you have tried your best to respond to the mini case. Most students desperately need an assessment of their analytical skills, and feedback on their response approach. Why not take advantage of an opportunity that is usually not readily available?

A quick overview of the problems can be obtained from the following schedule:

(Figures in millions)

	19x3	19x4	19x5	19x6	19x7	19x8	19x9	19x10	19x11	19x12
Sales to Mosquito Mines (19x7 to 19x12 sales are slightly overstated)	$7	$7	$7	$7	$3	$3	$3	$3	$3	$3
Mining costs				60	66					
				(53)	(63)					
Decline in net income =					10					
after income tax, at 40 percent =					(6)	?	?	?	?	?
Revenue from unprocessed ore				?	?					

It can be seen from the above figures that 19x7 net income will take a rather sharp drop, from $10 million in 19x6 to a figure as low as $4 million, depending on how much revenue the stockpile of ore will generate.

What should be done with respect to the 19x6 financial statements? Some students will quickly respond: "Do whatever the accounting rules say". This response, of course, misses the point because there are no set "rules" for the situation described. You cannot ask your boss what to do. She will ask you to "research the problem and make a recommendation."

The mini case asks you to assume two roles, the first being that of chief financial officer. In this role, the officer has to recognize that the financial statements must be audited. (The company is incorporated under the Canada Business Corporations Act and its revenues exceed $10 million. It also is a listed company and would likely have an auditor. Finally, although this is not in the body of the question, and therefore ought not to be considered as conclusive evidence, the "Required" mentions the role of auditor.) The officer therefore has to devise reasoning that will be accepted by the auditor. If the auditor will not accept the chief financial officer's solution to the problem, the auditor will qualify the 19x6 audit report. Students have to decide whether the chief financial officer wants to report only the bare essentials, to avoid an audit report qualification, or will give full disclosure.

The auditor will tend to push for as much disclosure as possible, but will settle for bare essentials or a minimum. By encouraging full disclosure the auditor becomes less subject to criticism and less vulnerable to lawsuits.

The case boils down to "What are the financial accounting objectives of SML?" If the company wants only minimum disclosure stewardship-type reporting, there is no need to report in the 19x6 financial statements that business conditions will change in 19x7. Transactions of 19x7 will be reported in 19x7. The 19x7 transactions are not "subsequent events" that need be reported in 19x6. Auditors would probably have to accept the absence of disclosure, but would not like to. The financial statements belong to the company. The auditor merely reports whether they are "fair in accordance with GAAP." If GAAP does not require the disclosure in 19x6, the auditor's bargaining power with SML is diminished.

If the company's objective is evaluation of management or cash flow prediction, the 19x6 financial statements would contain disclosure of what will happen in 19x7. The auditor and chief financial officer would have the same role, in effect, and no dispute would arise.

Those students who are studying accounting to learn how to become better users of financial statements should absorb an important message from the above. Do they know whether a financial statement that they are reading is based on stewardship minimum disclosure, or on some other objective(s)? Suppose that the 19x7 transactions or events were not reported in 19x6's financial statements. Would knowledge of the 19x7 transactions have affected their assessment of SML?

Another Analyst's Response

What follows are notes provided by another analyst of the SML case, who is following a more elaborate framework in order to try to be more convincing than the nutshell response given above.

This case presents interesting disclosure issues. The income measurement issues are less important.

OBJECTIVES OF ACCOUNTING INFORMATION:

1. Stewardship reporting to public shareholders. Income measurement issues are primarily related to this objective.
2. Prediction by public shareholders. Disclosure issues are primarily related to this objective. Do readers have a right to know about the fairly certain drop in net income in 19x7, under standards of "fair disclosure?" Securities commissions might monitor such disclosures. But is this part of the normal business operations? Or is there no obligation to disclose imminent, material income effects? Does the extent of disclosure depend on objectives of accounting?
3. Possibly, performance evaluation of management. The chief financial officer may not be too happy about disclosure in 19x6 of things about to happen in 19x7, especially if management participates in a stock or share option plan. Share prices would probably quickly adjust to the information content of any 19x6 note disclosures (efficient market assumption). Yet, is the purpose of the exercise one of furthering interests of the chief financial officer?

ACCOUNTING PROBLEMS:

1. Disclosure issues related to events about to happen in 19x7.
2. Measurement issues, such as revenue recognition for the royalty payments and the long-term contract.

ANALYSIS OF THE TWO PROBLEMS:

1. Readers probably (GAAP is not clear) have a right to know about important contracts such as the royalty contract. A note would be helpful, but, because of legal liability considerations of the preparer/auditor, the note may not say too little *or* too much. The auditor and management may have to engage in much debate over the wording of any such note. Perhaps consultation with lawyers may be needed. Students should discuss the content of such a note if it is required by fair disclosure standards. Such a note probably would contain *at least* the following:

   (a) minimum annual tonnage and minimum annual royalty payments, under the contract; and

   (b) revenue recognized to date, and the revenue recognition policy chosen.

   This information should help readers sort out cash flow implications. If the company intends to finance shortly by issuing a prospectus (cash flow prediction objective), prospective lenders should not be caught by surprise. Hence, a note may be more extensive.

   The increase in mining costs is another candidate for note disclosure. It is less obvious what standards of fair disclosure would require in this instance.

Management will probably resist disclosure, on the grounds that this is a normal business event. On the other hand, this is a material change in operations. Perhaps a communication with someone in authority from the securities commission, and with the company's solicitors, would be a good idea.

2. Not much information is given in the case about revenue recognition. This is a less important issue but worthy of some discussion. Revenue from royalties should probably be recognized as ore is extracted, on an accrual basis. Monthly statements of tonnage could be requested from Mosquito. Or, if cash collection is very uncertain, recognition could be delayed until cash payment.

Students should be given credit for identifying the problem of how to recognize revenue on the long-term contract. Not much information is given. If selling prices are not guaranteed, or the buyer is unreliable, recognition should probably wait until at least the point of shipment.

The above methods relate to stewardship income measurement. Complete accounting policies notes should help those who want to sort out and predict cash flow implications. A note outlining the long-term contract (quantities, terms, etc.) will help readers predict. This might be wise given the anticipated overall drop in net income in 19x7. Readers will want as much information now as possible, in order to predict.

RECOMMENDATIONS:

One approach is to assume that minimum stewardship reporting is the only important objective. Then little or no disclosure is required. The company could probably get away with saying very little about either the royalty contract or the upcoming change in operations. Management may want this approach, especially if they think the market will not learn about such events from other public sources (analysts, newspapers, etc.).

Another approach is to assume that prediction is an important objective, perhaps because a debt or share issue is imminent, and investors do not like surprises. The auditor is more likely to press for expanded disclosure of upcoming events, to help ensure fair disclosure. No doubt some compromise will be necessary to resolve conflict between auditor and management over how much to say in a footnote to the statements.

Summary

Two possible responses were provided to the SML case in this chapter. Neither gave the elaborate treatment suggested by Exhibit 1-1. This abbreviated approach was adopted in the interest of showing two approaches and yet saving space. Students should attempt to give a full response while they are learning how to handle less directive situations. Most markers will award grades for the full process from problem identification through to supported recommendations, and not just for "an answer." In real life you have to be convincing, and the more of your reasoning process you explain the better are your chances of persuading others. Alternative possible recommendations have to be examined, and reasons given why they are not as good as what you are suggesting.

CHAPTER 5

Solved Case No. 2

```
┌─────────────────── LEARNING OBJECTIVES ───────────────────┐
│                                                            │
│  1. For intermediate and advanced level students,          │
│     this chapter provides another opportunity to           │
│     respond to a case, and then compare their              │
│     approach to that provided by a more expe-              │
│     rienced analyst.                                       │
│  2. For professional accountancy level students it pro-    │
│     vides an opportunity to handle what might be           │
│     called a multiple-subject case question.               │
│                                                            │
└────────────────────────────────────────────────────────────┘
```

Introduction

Introductory level students will benefit from this chapter even though they may not have thought much about the case situation. After a careful reading or two they should better comprehend from the case and accompanying analysis why clear-cut accounting answers do not exist. Judgment and credibility play important roles in preparing financial statements. It is impossible for accounting standard-setting, or principle-setting, bodies to anticipate all possible situations and give universal remedies.

Students who are using this book to prepare for professional accountancy examinations should examine the case situation in great detail and look carefully for additional problems in the areas of auditing, management accounting, and income taxation. How would the auditor verify the figures if particular recommendations are suggested? What are the ethical and legal liability issues? What effect would particular recommendations for solving the problems have on income taxes, and on the firm's management accounting and internal reporting system? Would your overall response change when you looked at the problems in a broader perspective than just financial accounting?

Students registered in intermediate or advanced level financial accounting courses ought to take the mini case at face value and try to identify the important problems, and resolve them in light of probable objectives-facts-constraints. The response that follows the case views the situation as a financial accounting (rather than multiple-subject) mini case.

SI LIMITED

The Mini Case Problem

Si Limited (SL) is incorporated under Canadian federal corporate legislation and is publicly owned. Many of its business operations are in South America with its main subsidiary being 40 percent owned by the government of one of the South American countries.

SL produces a base metal under a patented refining process that uses petroleum as a heating fuel. All of SL's major world competitors have been using hydroelectricity as a heating fuel. A few years ago, SL had a major competitive advantage because petroleum was regarded as cheap relative to electricity. Now, competitive relationships are changing as petroleum prices increase.

SL invested $60 million in the plant and the foreign government contributed $20 million plus mining rights for 99 years. A switch-over to hydroelectricity is not practical because of the plant's location. The plant theoretically could operate for 50 to 100 years if annual maintenance was provided. Several scientists have predicted that petroleum supplies in the world will be exhausted in 40 or so years.

In the year just ended, 19x3, SL produced 100 million pounds of the metal and sold it on a contract basis to several buyers at an average price of $3.10 per pound. The selling price on December 31, 19x3, was $3.15 per pound. Average production cost, excluding depreciation, was $3.08 per pound in 19x3. Mainly because of petroleum price increases, costs have been rising much faster than revenue in the past four years.

SL anticipated a temporary selling price decline in 19x4, and in 19x3 sold 80 million pounds of metal at $3.11 per pound for delivery throughout 19x4. So far (late January 19x4) the price drop has not occurred. The selling price currently is $3.17 per pound.

Required:

Assume the role of auditor of SL. What accounting and reporting do you recommend for the years ended December 31, 19x3, and 19x4?

A Possible Response

OVERVIEW:

The prospects for the company (hereafter SL) do not look good. The subsidiary has a plant that is locked into petroleum use. Competitors have plants that use hydro-electricity. They can therefore charge a lower price for the base metal produced and still make competitive profits. On the assumption that competitive markets exist, SL is a price taker for both its basic input (petroleum) and its basic output (base metal). Picture the following:

Marginal Revenue;
Cost of Output
of Subsidiary Company

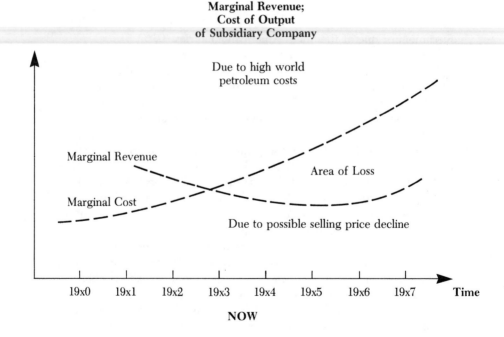

It is evident that the subsidiary could face a going concern problem, as marginal cost may exceed marginal revenue as early as fiscal 19x4. Will this endanger the future for SL as well?

This is mainly a problem recognition case. The above and other problems are not obvious ones in the direction provided by the case.

OBJECTIVES OF ACCOUNTING INFORMATION:

Some likely ones are:

1. Stewardship reporting subject to GAAP constraints to public shareholders. Security commissions in Canada could be watching for "fair" disclosure.
2. Prediction of future cash flows by public investors. See (1) above. This is especially important if SL will need new equity financing in the near future.
3. Performance appraisal of management by public investors. Are the events described in the Overview beyond management's control? What about the 19x3 contract obligation? Was this wise?
4. Income tax. Tax is likely not affected by long-term asset write-downs that are not yet realized, but might be affected by a loss accrual on the sales contract.

CONSTRAINTS:

Given the public nature of the company, the main constraints are GAAP and securities and companies legislation. The foreign country may impose some constraints on the subsidiary's financial reports, but not on consolidated financial statements of SL.

ACCOUNTING PROBLEMS:

1. Which accounting principles should be used for SL's subsidiary - that of the South American country? Canadian GAAP?
2. Loss recognition on the contract.
3. The going concern issue.
4. Any patents on the books of SL should possibly now be written down or off.
5. Foreign currency translation. Also, should the subsidiary be consolidated or shown at cost?
6. Inflation accounting.
7. Disclosure (stewardship versus prediction and management evaluation).
8. Should the subsidiary's plant be written down? By how much?
9. A possible revision of depreciation rates if the plant is not written down.

ANALYSIS:

Underlying all that follows is a need to assume *facts*. What is material? Is the subsidiary a going concern? Can world prices be predicted? Can the base metal price be predicted?

THE ACCOUNTING PROBLEMS ARE DISCUSSED IN THE ORDER NOTED ABOVE:

1. Canadian GAAP must be used for Canadian reporting purposes. Before translating the accounts of the subsidiary to Canadian dollars, the accounts must (possibly on a worksheet basis) be adjusted to Canadian GAAP.

2. See the *CICA Handbook* material (Section 3290) on contingencies. Is a future event *likely* to confirm the existence, in 19x3, of a loss due to the contract commitment? There is probably too much uncertainty regarding 19x4 base metal prices to justify loss accrual in 19x3. Note disclosure as a contingency would be required by Section 3290. See 7 below for a discussion of how *much* disclosure is required and which is optional. As always,the *CICA Handbook* spells out *minimum* disclosure requirements only.

3. See the Overview. Economic analysis reveals that the subsidiary may not be a viable economic concern. Is it premature to switch to a basis other than going concern for the subsidiary in 19x3? Facts are not yet clear. But heavy operating losses may commence as early as 19x4. Will the cash flow losses drag SL itself down? Will SL continue to be a going concern?

4. See 3. The decline in value of the patents is probably sufficiently evident, in 19x3, to support a write-off for consolidation purposes. This entry need not be made on the books of the subsidiary.

5. Students can discuss foreign currency translation issues, per the *CICA Handbook*. If and when the subsidiary's assets get written down to liquidation values (possibly as early as 19x4), they become amounts stated in current, not historic, dollars. A foreign currency translation gain or loss would be accrued in SL's consolidated income statements in accordance with the temporal or current rate methods.

6. This is worth bonus marks, although it is not a reporting issue. The cost of replacing the subsidiary's plant with one that could use some other energy source is no doubt a figure of interest to SL's Board of Directors. The accountant can be of some assistance in this regard.

7. Minimal stewardship disclosure with a GAAP constraint might require reporting of the existence of the sales contract, but not much more. See Section 3290 of the *CICA Handbook* regarding the constraints. Expanded disclosures might help the prediction and performance appraisal objectives if management believes that it will benefit from telling the whole story. It could be that the contract represents a wise hedge against future metal price declines.

8. See 3 and 4. The decline in value of the subsidiary's plant is perhaps now sufficiently evident to warrant a write-down. Is it likely that net book values of fixed assets will not be recovered? Other approaches are possible. Such an entry might have to be made on the consolidation worksheet and not in the accounts of the subsidiary. The minority government owner might refuse to make such an entry in the books of the subsidiary.

9. If the plant is not written down, then as a minimum fixed asset lives must be revised downwards. See the Overview. The subsidiary may not last three years, let alone 40 years.

RECOMMENDATIONS:

A critical fact is that the subsidiary cannot pass on higher purchase prices in the form of higher selling prices, since it is a price taker and competitors have a lower marginal cost curve. Students need only review their introductory economics to see this. This *fact* is strong enough to warrant a write-down of subsidiary patents and fixed assets in the consolidated accounts.

One approach is for SL to take the "big bath" in 19x3 and write off entirely its investment in the subsidiary. The logic is that this subsidiary is not a viable going concern and could not be sold. Alternatively, carrying values could be written down to current Canadian dollar equivalent liquidation values, if it is assumed the minority government partner will agree to liquidation. The auditor could probably live with this approach on the basis of conservatism.

Another approach is to wait and see, and merely revise depreciation rates in 19x3. This may cater to management's concern about the performance appraisal and perhaps bonus implications of such a write-down. Much will depend on when SL feels its income statement can best absorb the write-downs and write-offs. Are there restrictive bond covenants based on profit, and might they be violated by the lower resulting profits? Auditors must watch for an income-smoothing bias. Is one of the company's objectives fair and timely disclosure to readers? Much depends on assumed price trends and other facts.

The suggested amount of disclosure will depend on the assumed priority of the prediction and performance appraisal objectives. *If* the facts of the case are made available in 19x3 to Canadian markets, in some public form, then SL's share prices may quickly adjust if markets are efficient in the semi-strong form. Then the timing of write-downs may not matter so much. Much hinges on whether SL can control the timing and amount of information that reaches the public through available public information sources (newspapers, analysts, financial statements, and so on).

The auditor cannot easily take the posture that SL or its subsidiary is not a going concern. The very fact that the auditor assumes the absence of continuity (or going concern) may cause creditors to force bankruptcy upon the subsidiary, and perhaps upon SL. The auditor may be inviting lawsuits if he is the direct cause of subsequent bankruptcy.

Summary

Although the SL case is short, it is full of problems. Often one event can trigger a series of complications. Students have no alternative but to work towards comprehending that an answer that they receive to a question posed to obtain facts may open up a whole new world of issues that require resolution.

In an important sense this book challenges students to make the subject interesting, by drawing connections with other disciplines. Students are also challenged to overcome bad habits of regurgitating what they hope are all-purpose answers. Why miss an opportunity to enrich your education?

CHAPTER 6

Some Questions and Responses

┌─────────── LEARNING OBJECTIVES ───────────┐
│ Attempting to resolve some issues that arise │
│ when mini cases are used in the classroom.   │
└──┘

Clearing the Air

Every educational technique has advantages and disadvantages. Some students cannot handle less directive material and probably would be happiest in a setting where they would be closely supervised. Others can adjust to a variety of approaches. Still others may tend to resist change. This chapter is devoted to this last type of student, and to those who wish to convince possible resisters that there is much sense in mini case learning for accountants and those who have to use accounting reports.

1. *Question:* Is the mini case approach that is described in this book suggesting that preparers do everything that users want?

   Response: No. To be a good preparer you have to understand the needs of the users. To be a good user you have to understand the objectives of the preparer and the thinking that led to the financial statements that you are reading. We are suggesting an open learning environment. What actually happens in a specific situation varies with the factors described in Chapter 2 and elsewhere.

2. *Question:* Is it unethical to cater to an income tax postponement objective?

Response: No. You are entitled to do what the law allows. At one time in Canada educators tried to encourage students in the direction of one objective of accounting, namely, stewardship. However, in view of the diversity of businesses in Canada, such an approach does not make sense. Accounting is a practical subject; it has to evolve or it will become obsolete.

3. *Question:* Will my course grades be affected by having to learn case analysis?

Response: Not if your instructor uses cases on examinations, or gives homework projects that count in final grades, and maintains reasonable expectations. It would be unreasonable to expect students to give much attention to mini cases if examinations are highly directive.

4. *Question:* Is the tailoring approach advocating chaos in financial reporting, rather than uniformity?

Response: The tailoring to objectives-facts-constraints is simply recognizing the reality that accounting rules cannot cover all situations. Why pretend that ratio analysis of two companies in the same industry, for example, will provide informative results? The chances are great that the two companies have very different accounting policies.

5. *Question:* What are some typical errors that students make when they are learning to cope with mini case analysis?

Response: Many students will make recommendations that do not fit the objectives or constraints or facts that they have identified earlier in their analysis. Others will choose one objective of accounting, often income tax or stewardship, even when it does not seem to apply. Some students will not explain why their recommendations make more sense than other possible choices. (This last weakness comes from not having the technical knowledge that they thought they had acquired.)

6. *Question:* How do we know when we have the correct case answer?

Response: If you believe that there is one correct answer in practice or with cases, you have missed the point. Your task is to convince others that you have thought out the effects of possible alternatives, and have chosen the best of those available. You have to *anticipate* their questions and provide a credible response.

7. *Question:* Won't mini case analysis confuse students before they get their feet on the ground?

Response: This question could easily be the outcome of assuming that there is a particular concrete ground on which all accounting is built. The ground of accounting is evolving or shifting from one objective to another, virtually all the time. Providing a false ground can lead to serious problems of preparing or using dangerous information. Students ought to be taught the importance of disclosing the assumptions that they made to solve mini cases. This habit ideally could carry over to giving full disclosure of methods and assumptions used in preparing financial statements. Communication ought to improve with better user/preparer understanding of what assumptions underlie accountancy and accounting figures. Why pretend that a concrete ground exists when it does not?

8. *Question:* Mini case analysis is not being advocated as the sole method of teaching accounting, is it?

Response: Absolutely not. The theme of this book is that mini cases should be used alongside directive learning. One complements the other, and prevents students from jumping to false conclusions about the nature of accounting.

Section II:

Introductory and Intermediate Level

AN INHERITANCE

A student has just been informed that she is the recipient of an unusual inheritance. She is to be given a choice of being the sole owner of either Company A, Company B, or Company C (or receive nothing), and has been given 24 hours to decide which company to choose. The only information she has about the companies is noted below:

1. Each company commenced business at the beginning of this year with $1 million of cash. Each is in the steel warehousing business wherein they buy from steel mills and sell to many small users of steel.
2. Each company entered into identical transactions during the year— several purchases and one sale of steel.
3. The partial income statements of each company are:

	Company A	Company B	Company C
Revenue	$100,000	$100,000	$100,000
Cost of goods sold	70,000	80,000	90,000
Gross profit	$ 30,000	$ 20,000	$ 10,000

4. All three companies are located in Canada.
5. Each company is run by a skilled manager.
6. She is not allowed to interview any employees.

Required:
Which company would you advise her to choose? Why?

BEEDLE DEVELOPERS LTD.

Beedle Developers Ltd. (BDL) was incorporated under federal corporate legislation 15 months ago. The company is owned by a small group of investors. Most of the funds needed by BDL are borrowed from banks and from life insurance and trust companies that supply mortgages.

BDL's main operations involve building small apartments and residential properties, renting them, and then selling the rented properties to investors. A typical "contract" would consist of:

1. Acquiring land, usually including an old house, tearing down the old house and constructing a new house or apartment building (called a "property") on the land.
2. Obtaining a mortgage on the property at as high an amount as can be acquired at a reasonable interest rate.
3. Signing rental agreements with persons interested in living in the property.
4. Selling the completed, rented property and its mortgage at the current market price, plus an additional sum of 10 percent or more to cover a rental receipt guarantee. The guarantee by BDL ensures that the investor who buys the property will be paid a minimum rental per month regardless of whether BDL is able to find tenants (as mentioned in 3). Usually the guarantee is for three, four or five years.
5. Managing the property (handling maintenance, paying property taxes, arranging insurance, etc.). The management contract could be for three to 10 years. (The investor pays BDL a certain amount per month for management of the property.)

The sales of property to date have been for sums well in excess of the cost of acquiring the land and building the new house or apartment.

Most of the leases that have been signed with tenants are for a two-year period.

The owners of BDL have asked your advice on how they should account for their activities in the financial year that ended a few months ago. (An income tax return will have to be filed within six months of the year end of the company.)

Required:

Advise the owners of BDL.

BENOIT LIMITED

Benoit Limited (BL) is a small furniture manufacturer specializing in wooden tables, chairs, outdoor swings, picnic tables and similar items. Its one factory is located just outside Quebec City. The main markets for its products are Ontario and Quebec.

Lately the company has not been doing well: small profits and larger losses have been the pattern for the past four years. The company has been having difficulty repaying a $300,000 bank loan obtained four years ago and $235,000 remains unpaid at the end of 19x3.

You are the auditor of BL and have been called in by your client on behalf of the bank to prepare the financial statements for the year ended December 31, 19x3. During the course of your review you encounter the following data:

1. The financial statements currently show (before any needed adjustments) a net loss of $42,000.
2. The inventory of some wood used in furniture manufacturing is getting old because a large amount good for about eight years of production was bought four years ago in order to make some specialty items. The cost of the wood was $300,000; it is now one-half used and has a replacement cost of about $170,000 and a resale (net realizable value) price of $135,000.
3. Accounts receivable of about $40,000 are long overdue and payments of $4,000 per year are being made on this balance in accordance with a repayment scheme arranged between BL and the customer.

4. The company received a deposit of $5,000 from a customer who wants a special order. This $5,000 was used to buy some unusual wood. Neither of these sums is recorded on the company's books.

5. BL sells scrap wood to a local trucker who in turn sells it to nearby farmers. The company does not show this scrap on its books even though it has a value of $200 to $400 at any time. Revenue is recorded on receipt of cash from the trucker.

6. The company currently has orders for $120,000 of finished goods on hand and not yet started. 19x3's revenue from this source amounted to $700,000.

7. BL's buildings and machinery have a net book value of $300,000 but a net realizable value, if sold, of only $40,000.

Required:

Assume the role of auditor of BL. How would you handle each of the above in preparing financial statements of BL for 19x3?

BLAINE MANUFACTURING LIMITED

Blaine Manufacturing Limited (BML) is publicly owned and was incorporated under federal legislation 30 years ago. The company makes a line of cooking utensils and small appliances which until this year were marketed only in Eastern Canada.

In October 19x5 it signed an agreement with a distributor in Western Canada. The terms were as follows:

1. Specified quantities of the standard line of products are to be manufactured in November and December 19x5. These items will be physically separated in BML's warehouse and legal title will pass to the distributor on completion of manufacturing in early December 19x5.

2. The goods will be shipped to the distributor in February 19x6 after its year end of January 31, 19x6.

3. The distributor will pay 75 percent of the estimated purchase price of the items before December 20, 19x5. (BML received the distributor's cheque for $440,000 on December 19, 19x5.)

4. The distributor will be invoiced for the items before December 10, 19x5. The price can be adjusted downward, but not upward, if BML's selling prices drop in February 19x6, the delivery date.

5. The distributor can return up to 50 percent of the items before June 30, 19x6, if it is unable to sell them. BML will pay invoice price plus interest at 12 percent per annum on returned items.

BML is finalizing its financial statements for its year ended December 31, 19x5. It is now February 19x6 and the items have been shipped to the distributor; the price did not have to be adjusted downward. The controller is wondering how he should record the transactions with the distributor.

Required:
Advise the controller.

BURKE LIMITED

Burke Limited (BL) commenced business on January 12, 19x1, a few days after it was incorporated under federal corporate legislation. BL is owned by two young people who formerly worked for a large manufacturing organization. They pooled their financial resources, borrowed from various friends and the bank, and commenced the manufacture of plastic drinking cups.

The production process consists of feeding small resin chips into a machine which extrudes and forms a continuous plastic sheet. Various dies press against the sheet and stamp out a plastic cup. The cup is then separated from the remaining parts of the continuous sheet, and all unused sheet is fed back into the extruding and forming machine. The cups are either packed for storage in the company's warehouse, or packed and shipped directly to customers.

BL rents the building in which its manufacturing plant, warehouse and office is located for $4,000 per month. The lease is for five years. The extruding and forming machine and related equipment were leased for a monthly charge of $10,000. BL has an option to purchase them at the end of six years for $50,000.

BL produces most of its cups to meet customer specifications. As a service to customers BL will store specialized cups for periods of up to eight months. Customers are invoiced when the cups are shipped, and have 60 days in which to pay without interest being charged. Some cups are produced for general purposes such as sales to country fairs and various informal social events.

BL had to buy two company vehicles for sales and delivery purposes; both are financed with payments over a 20-month period. Packing boxes and resin are acquired in bulk every two or three months in order to obtain quantity discounts.

The owners of BL have come to you in January 19x2 and have asked for help in preparing the company's financial statements for the year ended December 31, 19x1. In particular they want to know what accounting principles they should select and which financial statements they should prepare and why. They already have noticed that inflation is causing costs to rise every few months.

Required:
Advise the owners of BL.

BUTTERWORTH PRODUCTS LTD.

Butterworth Products Ltd. (BPL) is incorporated under federal corporate legislation. The company has two physically separate divisions:
(1) manufacturing small appliances; and (2) manufacturing and distributing electronic components. BPL is owned by one family.

In recent years the appliance division has been profitable, but the electronics division has had a series of difficulties and losses in most of the years. In the year ended December 31, 19x6 the electronics division had a strike from mid-January to the end of August. Both the electronics manufacturing plant and its two distribution warehouses were closed during the period of the strike.

The following are some of the costs incurred in the electronics division during the strike or as a result of the strike:

1. Depreciation on the electronics manufacturing
   building $65,000
2. Depreciation on the electronics manufacturing machinery
   and equipment $54,500

3. Extra security guards hired for strike period $44,000
4. Interest on bank loan acquired to finance
   inventories $36,000
5. Inventory spoiled by workers in the few days preceding
   the strike $12,450
   (However, the net realizable value of the entire finished
   goods inventory is in excess of the cost including the $12,450.)
6. Salaries of sales and office staff $127,000

    BPL management is seriously considering debiting some or all of the above costs to a "Strike Cost" account and amortizing the amount over the 24 months commencing September 19x6. The period of 24 months is felt to be appropriate by management because this is the duration of the labor contract that was signed.

    You have been hired to advise management as to the appropriateness of its accounting and reporting.

Required:

Advise management.

CANADIANA PRODUCTS LTD.

Canadiana Products Ltd. (CPL) is incorporated under federal legislation and is privately owned. CPL has manufacturing facilities in several Canadian cities and began construction of a new facility in February 19x1 to produce a brand new product line. Although it had been very profitable in some years, CPL's history of earnings indicates that it has incurred losses in two of the 10 years prior to 19x1, with two other years being at approximately break even.

    Construction of the new plant was completed in December 19x1. Realizing it would probably have many start-up problems, management decided to defer all costs of the new plant during 19x2, offset by any revenue from the new product line. Because of the problems anticipated and some that were not, CPL had deferred net start-up costs of $12 million at December 31, 19x2. The net income from all other operations for the year then ended was $1 million.

Believing that most of the problems relative to the new facility had been resolved, it was announced to the shareholders that the deferring of costs would cease as of December 31, 19x2 and that the operating results of the new plant and product line would be included in CPL's income for 19x3.

CPL incurred a loss of $5 million before taxes for the year ended December 31, 19x3, consisting of a loss of $13 million on the new product line and profits of $8 million on all other operations. In order to minimize the loss, CPL's management set up a deferred tax benefit of approximately $2 million.

In the two succeeding years, results were as follows:

	Loss on New Line	Profit From Other Operations	Net Loss Before Taxes	Deferred Tax Benefit Recorded
19x4	$11 million	$5 million	$6 million	$3 million
19x5	$12 million	$4 million	$8 million	$4 million

Required:

You have been appointed auditor of CPL for 19x5. What disclosure and accounting treatment would you insist on for 19x5? Why?

CANADIAN CANDY INC.

Canadian Candy Inc. (CCI) is a medium-size manufacturing company producing various kinds of candies and chocolates. The company is incorporated under federal legislation and is privately owned. Due to the large influx of imported candies into the Canadian candies' market in recent years, CCI had been suffering declining sales and earnings.

The major raw material for CCI's products is sugar. Like cocoa, cotton and other commodities, the price and supply of sugar are very erratic. To hedge against the risk of fluctuating prices and ensure an adequate supply of the raw materials for production, CCI had been purchasing sugar futures contracts in the commodity market. Any unrealized gains and losses on the futures contracts has traditionally been deferred to the maturity dates of these contracts. On maturity CCI liquidates the contracts and obtains the raw materials needed for their candy operations.

In September 19x1, CCI hedged all estimated sugar purchase needs up to late 19x3 at approximately 17¢ per pound. Because of the world shortages of sugar caused by bad weather in most sugar producing countries in 19x1, there was heavy trading in sugar in the commodity market; the spot price of sugar eventually soared to 64¢ per pound.

Believing that the price of sugar had peaked and probably because the company could use additional earnings for 19x1, management decided to liquidate all contracts that mature in 19x2 and 19x3, reap the resultant 47¢ per pound profit and bring the gain into income in 19x1.

You are finalizing the audit of the financial statements of CCI for 19x1.

Required:

What is the minimum accounting and reporting treatment that you would insist on for 19x1? Why?

COLLEGE BOOKS LIMITED

College Books Limited (CBL) was owned by about 20 investors. It was incorporated under federal corporate legislation about 15 years ago prior to an expected increase in university and college age students. This year it was acquired by five new owners, who are friends of the original 20 investors.

CBL's operations involve:

1. Contracting with authors who write original manuscripts that CBL edits, publishes and distributes in Canada. Typesetting and printing are contracted to specialists in these fields.
2. Contracting with publishers in other countries to either: (a) import and distribute their books; or (b) prepare Canadian editions of foreign books.
3. Editing manuscripts, advertising new books, and storing the many books in a central warehouse in Toronto. CBL has about 12 salespersons who call on potential adopters, such as university and college teachers.

The teachers are issued free books so that they may review them and decide whether the students should read them. Teachers may use the book as a principal one, or a supplement. Salespersons are paid a salary plus commission, and try to convince teachers to adopt their book as a principal textbook for courses.

Inventory control is a problem for publishers like CBL. In order to be able to publish a book at an attractive price, editing, typesetting and office costs have to be spread over 5,000 to 10,000 or more copies. Printing must occur before the publisher knows how successful the book might be. A reprinting takes six to eight weeks if paper stock is available. Most of the sales occur in the June to August period in readiness for September classes. If the publisher runs out of stock, because teachers order the books too late in the year, or for other reasons, the reputation of the publisher can be affected. Teachers may not want to order their books in subsequent years.

Inventory problems are compounded by the fact that there are frequent paper shortages, and in order to protect themselves, CBL has to order a stock of paper well in advance of printing or reprinting dates. Inventory storage of paper or printed books can be costly being up to 30 percent per year of the cost of the inventory item. Sometimes costs are offset by inflation. Each year it costs more to produce and publish a book.

Publishers in Canada tend to allow bookstores to return any item that is still "in print." Some exceptions exist to the general policy. Returned books can vary in quantity and dollar volume from year to year. For example, a teacher may order 1,000 books, then change her mind about requiring students to buy the book. Or, some flaws may be discovered in the contents and re-ordering may not occur. Sometimes an active used book market will appear.

In addition to inventory, sales and office costs, royalties must be paid to authors. Royalties are based on the net price paid by a bookstore, which is usually 75 to 80 percent of the retail price of the book. Royalty rates tend to be between 5 to 15 percent of the net cash paid to CBL by bookstores. Authors are paid twice per year about 90 days after each six-month period.

Contract arrangements between CBL and foreign publishers vary widely. Generally CBL buys the "foreign" books at say one-half the retail price. Discounts of 20 to 25 percent are offered to bookstores.

CBL owns its office and warehouse in Toronto. Offices in other cities are leased, as are automobiles for sales staff.

Some of the books published by CBL are subsidized by grants from government and charitable organizations. Subsidies tend to be paid to

CBL on publication of the book, or 18 to 36 months after publication.

Most bookstores are given 60 to 90 days to pay their invoice amounts to CBL. Some bookstores go bankrupt.

Required:

You have been hired by the new owners of CBL to suggest appropriate accounting and reporting principles for the company. Advise the owners giving full explanations.

CREDIT SERVICES CORPORATION

Credit Services Corporation (CSC) is owned by several banks. CSC processes charges incurred by persons who hold credit cards issued by one of the banks. Processing involves buying credit card holders' purchase invoices from retailers for 96¢ on the dollar, tabulating and sorting them on a computer, sending monthly statements to credit card holders, collecting payments from the card holders, and conducting various credit worthiness checks. The banks lend money to CSC to finance unpaid balances of holders of their credit cards. Thus, the banks rather than the retail stores finance purchases made by credit card holders.

CSC was formed on the theory that it would make a small profit. That is, interest revenue received from charges to card holders (less interest expenses charged to CSC by the banks) plus the 4¢ discount charged to retailers should be in excess of administrative and operating costs of CSC. Whereas the 4 percent discount to retailers has been fixed by contract for several years, the interest revenue and interest expense can vary. Interest charged to card holders on unpaid balances is based on current market rates for the general public, and thus can fluctuate from year to year. The interest rate on money borrowed from the banks (needed by CSC to pay retail stores) is supposed to be, in theory, the "balancing" figure that allows CSC to make a small profit.

However, the rate has to be set several months in advance because it requires full agreement among the banks. This means that CSC has tended to operate at a loss in some years and at a profit in other years.

For instance, in 19x1 and 19x2 CSC had computer problems and was not able to balance the full value ($1.00, not the 96¢) of invoices acquired from retail stores with the total charges on monthly statements sent to credit card holders. In 19x1 the difference was about $500,000 and in 19x2 it was $260,000. Both were shortages or losses to CSC. In 19x3 and 19x4 the banks lowered their interest rate on loans to CSC, which then made a profit in excess of losses incurred in 19x1 and 19x2. In 19x5 CSC had a net loss of $10,000.

You were hired two weeks ago as the vice-president of finance of CSC. The former vice-president of finance resigned before you arrived, but before he left he had prepared the financial statements for the year just ended, October 31, 19x6.

On reviewing the 19x6 financial statements you discover that the reported net loss for the year is $880,000. The reported loss before income taxes is $1.6 million and a sum of $720,000 is shown as an "income tax recovery." The $720,000 also appears as a current asset "deferred income taxes."

Moments after your discovery you receive a telephone call from CSC's auditors, who were first appointed last year, and had signed the audit report included with the 19x5 financial statements. They inform you that the net loss for 19x6 is $1.6 million and that the $720,000 reduction is "not acceptable" to them. They ask you to provide them with revised financial statements.

Required:

Do you agree with the auditors? If so, explain. If not, give your reasoning.

DIRECT IMPORTS LIMITED

Direct Imports Limited (DIL) was incorporated under federal legislation three months ago, and commenced business on September 3, 19x2. DIL is owned by Mr and Mrs Brown, who obtained exclusive Canadian rights to distribute a line of German cutlery and a line of French food processors.

They have asked you to help them with financial and accounting matters. After some enquiries you learn the following:

1. The exclusive franchises are for five years, but can be renewed for additional five-year periods as long as specified conditions (such as buying a minimum quantity of goods from the manufacturer-franchiser) are met.

2. The following sales are expected in the three years ended August 31: 19x3, $360,000; 19x4, $480,000 and 19x5, $600,000. Roughly three-quarters of the sales will be on credit terms that will extend on the average for 45 days.

3. Inventory will have to be acquired in bulk from the foreign suppliers about four times per year in order to meet sales of the next quarter. Approximate delivery dates are early March, June, September and December. Payment is due 60 days after receipt of goods by DIL.

4. The Browns expect a gross profit of 40 percent on sales for the first three years.

5. Sales are expected to be seasonal with 50 percent occurring in October and November and the balance spread over the other 10 months.

6. DIL has rented its distribution warehouse and office on a 10-year lease requiring payments of $5,000 per month.

7. Selling and office expenses (excluding salary to Mr and Mrs Brown) in the year ended August 31, 19x3 are expected to be $90,000. They likely will be incurred evenly throughout the year. They are expected to rise by 15 percent per annum for the years after August 31, 19x3.

8. Incorporation costs and money needed to start up the business (to purchase long-lived assets) amounted to $160,000 in September and October 19x2.

9. The Browns invested $200,000 in common shares in September 19x2 in order to commence DIL.

10. The Browns opened a bank account in September 19x2.

Required:
Advise Mr and Mrs Brown about DIL.

ECKEL SALES LIMITED

Eckel Sales Limited (ESL) manufactures and sells special equipment used in a variety of manufacturing enterprises. Some of the equipment that ESL makes is in steady demand whereas other items are especially designed to meet the needs of a specific customer.

ESL is incorporated under federal legislation. Its voting shares are held by a small group of business people but its bonds are widely held by the general public.

Last year (19x7) competition appeared for one of its equipment products that had been in steady demand for five years. The competitor chose to compete by offering lower prices. Fortunately for ESL, its customers were suspicious about the service abilities of the competitor and continued to do business with ESL in 19x7.

Unfortunately, for ESL, this year (19x8) the competitor has strengthened its service department and further lowered the costs of its product. In order to meet competition ESL has elected to give to regular customers a rebate of 5 percent on all of their equipment purchases made since July 1, 19x7. ESL closed its accounts and issued its financial statements for the year ended December 31, 19x7 in March 19x8, three months ago.

Competition has also forced ESL to look to new markets in order to increase its sales volume. Management believes that it can find success in some different specialty sales markets. In order to compete successfully in these different specialty sales markets ESL will have to incur the following types of costs in addition to the usual ones applicable to all of its other products:

1. Engineering design costs related to the design of a special machine or product requested by the customer.
2. Manufacture of a prototype. This would involve the building of a sample machine to test operating performance. (Such would occur only when many machines are to be made under a prospective contract and a prototype is necessary to improve performance.)
3. Manufacture of special tools which are only useful for the specific contract.

Management is uncertain how to account for the rebates and the three types of costs.

Required:
Assume the role of auditor of ESL and advise management.

FEATURE FURNITURE

Feature Furniture (FF) acquires furniture from factories and sells it in two retail stores in a large Canadian city. FF was formed by the Feature brothers about 20 years ago and has been moderately successful during more than 10 of those years.

As a result of a serious illness suffered by one of the Feature brothers the company was recently (and somewhat quickly) sold for a price which was tied to the audited financial statements for the most recent year, ended December 31, 19x3. The terms of sale provide for an arbitrator in case of disputes between the buyer and seller over the accounting principles adopted by the Feature brothers and their auditor. The brothers were hoping to obtain about $4 million for FF.

You have been appointed auditor of FF for the year ended December 31, 19x3. The accounts were not audited in previous years. During your audit in April 19x4, you encounter the following matters that you must account for:

1. FF sold excess land and a building which it had used as a warehouse on October 1, 19x3, for $1.5 million of which $350,000 was paid in cash. Quarterly payments of $200,000 plus interest at 12 percent were arranged to pay the balance owing by the purchaser. The first payment was due December 30, 19x3. Unfortunately, the payment was not made on December 30, and as of April 19x4 FF has instituted foreclosure proceedings against the purchaser of the building. It is hoped that the building can be resold by November 19x4. At the present time the accounting records show a receivable of $1,184,500, which includes accrued interest to December 31, 19x3.

2. The balance sheet shows a sum of $100,000 for prepaid advertising. Investigation indicates that this is one-half of the cost of magazine advertising in October, November and December, 19x3.

3. The company sells most of its furniture on credit terms extending over six to 24 months. Interest is usually 18 percent per annum on outstanding sums. FF recognizes revenue on delivery of the furniture, and does not provide for bad debts even when goods are sold on a no down payment basis. Interest is accrued daily on the outstanding balance; goods are repossessed as required.

4. FF has traditionally expensed many expenditures on small assets and building improvements if less than $1,000 has been spent. It now wishes to capitalize these in the cost of its retail store assets.

Required:

A. Assume the role of auditor of FF. How would you record and report each of the above four matters? Why?

B. How would your answer in A. differ if you were:
   (i) acting on behalf of the purchaser;
   (ii) the arbitrator.

Be specific about each matter; explain your response.

FINNEY LIMITED

Finney Limited (FL) is a small, closely held retail store chain which sells shoes. Its five stores are located in shopping centres in a large Canadian city.

The company requires annual financial statements for the bank, and must file an annual income tax return; otherwise, it has no special need for accounting. Cash and inventory control are facilitated by a cash register which provides data for direct feeding to a computer that is owned by a financial institution. Reports of sales, purchases and inventory levels are provided monthly for each store by the computer owner. A public accountant prepares audited, annual financial statements and the company's income tax return.

The following conversation occurred recently between the president of FL and the company's public accountant:

President: "What do you mean that your fee will increase 30 percent this year? I can't increase shoe prices by 30 per cent. If I did I wouldn't have any customers! All I need the financial statements for is to keep the bank happy—and the banker doesn't even want an audit, just statements."

Public Accountant: "The banker wouldn't be very happy with unaudited statements. She wouldn't lend you as much money I'd guess—and you need a high loan in the autumn and spring when your inventory is high...Besides, you wouldn't save that much having only unaudited statements. By the time we prepare unaudited ones we've had to do a large amount of verification. The additional cost is minor."

President:	"Let's get back to the 30 percent increase."	
Public Accountant:	"Our costs are up. Your tax return is costlier to prepare because the regulations and legislation are more complex. In addition, we prepared a Statement of Changes in Financial Position for you this year."	
President:	"Why did you do that? Our financial position didn't change during the year."	
Public Accountant:	"The Statement of Changes in Financial Position is a relatively new type of statement. Public accountants across the country are introducing it to clients to improve financial reporting."	
President:	"I don't want something if it costs too much and doesn't tell me anything. What good does it do?"	

Financial Statements Prepared by Public Accountant:

FINNEY LIMITED
Balance Sheet
January 31, 19x2
(with comparative figures for 19x1)

	19x2	19x1
Assets		
Current:		
Cash	$ 22,750	$ 1,800
Accounts receivable	76,200	29,600
Inventory	361,600	420,600
Prepaid expenses	5,450	3,000
	466,000	455,000
Leasehold improvements and fixtures	162,000	160,000
Less accumulated amortization	128,000	124,000
	34,000	36,000
Deferred charges	19,000	22,000
	$ 519,000	$ 513,000

Liabilities and Equities

Current:

Bank loan	$ 160,000	$ 200,000
Accounts payable	114,700	86,900
Income tax payable	16,000	17,000
Other current	26,300	2,950
	317,000	306,850
Deferred income tax	5,000	4,000
Debt payable—12% due 19x2	—	120,000
Due to owners	23,850	20,000
Debt payable—14% due 19x9	100,000	—
Owner's equity:		
Common shares	40,000	40,000
Contributed surplus	10,000	10,000
Retained earnings	23,150	12,150
	73,150	62,150
	$ 519,000	$ 513,000

FINNEY LIMITED

Income Statement

Year ended January 31, 19x2

(with comparative figures for 19x1)

	19x2	19x1
Revenue	$1,200,000	$1,100,000
Cost of goods sold	800,000	714,800
Gross profit	400,000	385,200
Expenses		
Depreciation	4,000	4,000
Selling and administrative	265,000	246,000
	269,000	250,000
Income before income tax	131,000	135,200
Income tax (deferred: 19x2 and 19x1 $1,000)	60,000	50,000
Net income	$ 71,000	$ 85,200

FINNEY LIMITED
Statement of Retained Earnings
Year ended January 31, 19x2
(*with comparative figures for 19x1*)

	19x2	19x1
Beginning of year	$ 12,150	$ 6,950
Net income	71,000	85,200
	83,150	92,150
Dividends	60,000	80,000
End of year	$ 23,150	$$ 12,150

FINNEY LIMITED
Statement of Changes in Financial Position
Year ended January 31, 19x2

Sources:		
From operations:		
Net income		$ 71,000
Add: Leasehold amortization	$ 4,000	
Deferred charges	3,000	
Deferred income tax	1,000	
	8,000	8,000
Debt payable		100,000
From owners		3,850
		182,850
Uses:		
Leasehold improvements		2,000
Dividend		60,000
Repay debt		120,000
		182,000
Increase in working capital		$ 850

Required:

A. Analyze and comment upon the strengths and weaknesses of the Statement of Changes in Financial Position (SCFP) prepared by the public accountant for Finney Limited.

B. Revise the SCFP as best you can to make it more informative to the president of FL.

C. Explain the purpose or uses of the SCFP you prepared in B in language that the president of FL will likely understand.

FUNNEL HOTELS LIMITED

Funnel Hotels Limited (FHL) is incorporated under the laws of Canada. The voting shares are closely held, but the company's debt is owned by the general public throughout Canada and by institutional investors in foreign countries.

Funnel has just opened its fifth hotel, which is so large that it has almost doubled FHL's rental room capacity. As a result, management has decided to alter its policy of expensing opening costs in order to, in their words, "better match revenue to expired costs." Until now the company has capitalized expenditures prior to opening a hotel, and amortized them over five years from the opening of a hotel. Items included in this category are: interest on debt, advertising, salaries and a range of other daily costs. All amounts involved are material.

You have just taken over the audit of Funnel, and have been asked by management to agree to the following new policy: "All items as noted above are to be handled as previously, except that a hotel will not be declared as 'open' until 60 percent of the available rooms are rented for three consecutive months." In the case of the new hotel, management does not expect this to occur for another six to eight months. The dollar effect of the change is material.

Required:

A. Assume the role of auditor of FHL. Would you accept the change? If not, why? If so, how would it be handled in the current year's financial statements?

B. Assume, instead of auditor, the role of an accounting adviser to Funnel. Would you support management's suggestion? Why?

GALVIN DISPOSAL COMPANY

Galvin Disposal Company (GDC) is owned by the Galvin brothers. The company's main source of revenue is from waste disposal contracts with industrial firms, municipalities, and small towns. These contracts vary from one to five years in duration and stipulate that GDC will collect waste twice per week for a fee based on volume or tonnage. GDC often charges customers a monthly sum for normal volume, as stated in the contract, and an additional amount only if volume exceeds the contracted minimum fee.

Two years ago (19x2) GDC signed a five-year contract with Rose City to collect garbage in the city twice per week. The contract was obtained by competitive bidding and is for a specified minimum and maximum tonnage for each of the five years. In order to carry out the contract GDC had to buy five special trucks that were needed to fit the specialized unloading facilities at Rose City. These trucks have an estimated life of 12 years but are too specialized to be used in other contracts. Approximately 70 percent of the cash needed to acquire the trucks was obtained by GDC from an industrial finance company, which stipulated that repayment was to be over a five-year period.

GDC has had considerable difficulty with the performance of the special trucks. The total purchase price of $450,000 for the five trucks has not been paid to the manufacturer; approximately $100,000 is being withheld pending the outcome of lawsuits between GDC and the manufacturer. GDC is suing the manufacturer for inferior performance of the trucks and the manufacturer is suing GDC for the unpaid $100,000. As a result of these difficulties GDC is not certain whether Rose City will be willing to renew the five-year contract for a further five years.

Last year (19x3) GDC depreciated the trucks at 10 percent per annum (declining balance) in its accounts. The financial statements for last year do not make any reference to the contract with Rose City or disagreements with the manufacturer of the trucks. The Galvin brothers are currently wondering what should be reported in this year's financial statements (19x4).

Required:
What advice would you give the Galvin brothers about financial reporting in 19x4? Explain your recommendations fully.

GIBBINS INSURANCE LIMITED

Gibbins Insurance Limited (GIL) is regulated under a special life insurance company Act. The company is owned by the general public and its shares are traded on the Vancouver Stock Exchange. Its financial year end per the Act is December 31.

Insurance law that governs GIL does not permit the company to record its office building, furniture and fixtures, automobiles and similar long term assets on its balance sheet sent to its shareholders and filed with insurance regulators. The governing Act also specifies how reserves for losses (estimated liabilities) and unearned insurance premiums are to be computed.

For example, someone may pay $480 on September 1 for one year's life insurance. A 20 percent commission may be paid by September 30 to an agent who services the customer's accounts. The Act requires GIL to defer two-thirds of the $480 (not the $480 less 20 percent commission) on December 31. As a result whenever GIL builds up its insurance in force by attracting more customers, the income statement effect of premium revenue is delayed a year or so.

Generally the Act requires that financial statements for GIL be shown on a semi-liquid basis, so that creditors and policy holders can easily tell whether they can be paid in the event of major disasters. The reasoning is that furniture and fixtures as well as commissions to agents are not liquid assets. The Act primarily stipulates how the income statement and balance sheet should be measured and reported. It is silent about the statement of changes in financial position and notes to financial statements.

Shareholders of GIL have complained about the company's reporting. Last year GIL's financial statements contained a note: "These financial statements are prepared in accordance with insurance regulations." This note brought forth even more complaints.

Required:
A. Assume the role of financial and reporting adviser to GIL. Advise management how they can improve their financial statements to shareholders. Provide concrete advice, including examples.
B. Assume the role of auditor of GIL. What type of audit report wording would you use?

GOODALE CORPORATION

Goodale Corporation (GC) is incorporated under federal legislation and is listed on several Canadian stock exchanges. It has recently embarked on a major expansion drive and intends to double or triple its size by buying control of "suitable" companies.

Several senior executives were transferred to a new division of GC, called "Aquisitions," in the current year 19x4. They investigated opportunities in several industries in 19x4, and in particular looked closely at the operations of two companies in the hotel industry. By the year end of December 31, 19x4 the following costs had been incurred:

Costs of studying several industries, to ascertain which have the greatest potential	$ 928,600
Costs of investigating particular companies in one industry	296,300
	$1,224,900

GC's 19x4 financial statements have shown the $1,224,900 as a deferred asset. The company intends to allocate the $928,600 and further costs of this nature to the cost of companies that it buys from 19x5 to 19x7. The allocation would be based on the relative purchase price.

The $296,300 and similar costs are to be collected by industry. If a company in that industry is purchased, the costs would be charged to the acquisition price of that company. If more than one company is acquired, costs would be allocated on the basis of acquisition price. If no companies are acquired by December 31, 19x7, the amount will be expensed.

Required:

Assume the role of auditor of GC. Do you agree with the company's accounting policy? If not, what would you suggest? Why?

HAILEYBURY MANUFACTURING LIMITED

Haileybury Manufacturing Limited (HML) is owned by a father and son who are anxious to sell the company in a few years, preferably in two years when the father wishes to retire. They have decided to hire you to improve their financial statements so that the company will "be attractive" to a buyer. HML is incorporated under federal legislation. In recent years its financial statements have been given to the company's bankers and appended to the company's income tax return. Over the years several potential buyers have been interested in acquiring HML. The specific matters you have been asked about are:

1. Inventory of work in process has never been recorded by HML. Costs of work in process are expensed until the product is completed. Then finished goods inventory is debited and expenses are credited.
2. The company employs income tax depreciation (capital cost allowance) rates and methods for depreciation.
3. Where possible the company has expensed small tools rather than capitalized them, in order to postpone income tax payments.
4. Finished goods inventory excludes fixed manufacturing overhead, but includes variable overhead items.
5. The company's year end is January 31.
6. Both the father and son receive bonuses once per year in lieu of salaries.
7. HML has never prepared a Statement of Changes in Financial Position.

Required:
Advise the owners of HML.

JEWELRY PRODUCTS LIMITED

Jewelry Products Limited (JPL) is privately owned and incorporated under federal corporate legislation. Its financial year ends on December 31. The company manufactures various jewelry products for retail stores.

Management often buys several months' supply of precious stones and metals in bulk in order to have adequate quantities on hand for special orders as well as for regular production. As a general rule it has six months' supply of most items.

Two years ago, in November 19x2, it was able to acquire a four-to five-year supply of precious metal (inventory #54-107) as a result of an unusual purchase in a foreign country. JPL had a major contract at the date of the acquisition with a chain of retail stores that would buy products using metal #54-107. In 19x4 the contract accounted for 30 percent of JPL's sales. Now, in January 19x5, JPL has been informed that the major contract with the retail chain has not been renewed. Whereas existence of the retail chain contract would have used up #54-107 in 18 to 20 months, loss of the contract leaves JPL with a 15-year or more supply of #54-107 for its regular sales.

The financial statements for 19x4 have not been finalized as yet. Per the books of JPL, item #54-107 is shown at cost $890,000. If sold on the local market, #54-107 would not be worth more than $100,000 because the sale would "flood the market." However, if #54-107 is used in production over 15 or more years, the $890,000 cost probably could be recovered in the sales price of jewelry made from it.

Required:

A. Assume the role of controller of JPL. What disclosure would you give of the above in the company's financial statements for 19x4, and for 19x5?

B. Assume the role of auditor of JPL. Would you agree with the disclosure in A.

JOHNS CONSTRUCTION LIMITED

Johns Construction Limited (JCL) is a subcontractor involved in building a major Canadian project costing millions of dollars. Alleged sabotage at the construction site has delayed the project several months past the various expected completion dates for segments of the project. JCL has attributed anticipated costs of $550,000 in 19x2 strictly to the delays.

The main contractor, with whom JCL has the subcontract, is one of the largest construction companies in Canada. It has been very successful in quoting low bids on work because subcontractors have been willing to deal with the company. Newspapers and TV stations have blamed the unions and the main contractor, not the subcontractors, for the delays.

The main contractor had agreed to give JCL a bonus (not previously written into the contract) of $350,000 in 19x3 to speed up construction schedules. The eventual owner of the project – a provincial government in Canada – has to have the project completed according to the original schedule, and is willing to pay extra for on-time completion.

In 19x2 JCL filed a claim for $200,000 with the main contractor for the deficiency ($550,000–$350,000) it has encountered because of the delay. JCL also expects its costs to rise $80,000 in 19x3 for overtime premiums incurred in speeding up the work. The contract between JCL and the main contractor is vague concerning delays and financial responsibility therefor. However, the main contractor has orally stated that it has some moral obligations to work out financial settlements with subcontractors.

JCL is now in the midst of finalizing its financial statements for the year just ended, 19x2.

Required:

What accounting treatment would you give in JCL's 19x2 financial statements to the above? Why?

JONES, JONES & JONES

Jones, Jones & Jones (JJJ) are lawyers who operate as a partnership. The company has been in existence for many years and currently has about 20 partners specializing in corporate law. Some partners are what are called "capital partners" and others are "profit-sharing partners." The capital partners have contributed sufficient funds to buy various assets needed to operate the business (e.g., furnishings, working capital, etc.). Money is also borrowed from a bank in order to finance work in process and receivables. Profits are not shared equally among the partners. JJJ's financial year runs from February 1 to January 31.

The company derives its revenue by selling the services of its skilled employees and partners. Each employee working for a client keeps track of the hours spent and completes a time record once per week. When the service is completed—which may be a matter of weeks, or more than one year—an invoice is rendered to the client. Someone adds up the hours spent per employee and multiplies by the individual hourly rate for that employee or partner. All "employee" time and costs are then totalled and the total is used as a guide to billing; although, the partner in charge may decide to render an invoice that is higher than, equal to or lower than the total. Invoiced amounts are included with "accounts receivable"; and unbilled amounts are included with "work in progress" on JJJ's balance sheet. The hourly rate per employee used to calculate billed and unbilled amounts is made up of: (1) a wage cost; (2) a sum to cover various overheads, such as costs of typists, office rentals, stationery, etc.; and (3) an element of profit.

The senior partner of JJJ has approached you to ask what revenue recognition accounting principles you would recommend. Also he wants your advice on how to value "work in progress" on the company's balance sheet. In order to obtain an unbiased opinion he prefers to not tell you which accounting principles the company has followed in recent years. However, he does tell you these other facts:

1. Some clients prefer to be on a retainer basis which enables them to receive prompt service regardless of the time or day. They pay sums of $100,000 or more in February each year. They are also billed additional sums for specific services of a time-consuming nature.
2. Some clients are invoiced once per quarter on an estimated basis, which is adjusted once per year or at the end of a lengthy task such as a major law suit.

3. For income tax purposes, JJJ is allowed to expense labor costs and the various overhead costs as incurred, regardless of what accounting treatment is given to these items.
4. The Income Tax Act allows certain flexibility as to when unbilled revenue is recognized as revenue for income tax purposes. However, if Revenue Canada feels that billings are being unduly delayed, it may choose to add such amounts to revenue in a fiscal period that it deems appropriate.

Required:
Provide a response with full reasoning for the senior partner of JJJ.

KENNEDY CORPORATION

Kennedy Corporation (KC) has been owned by two shareholders for many years. In the current year, 19x4, the main shareholder, who owned 60 percent of the common shares, made an offer through KC to purchase the other 40 percent. The offer was accepted and the shares represented by the 40 percent ownership were returned to KC and are to be cancelled. When the shares were bought back by KC the former 40 percent shareholder received some cash plus low interest bearing notes payable, of KC, due in from 19x7 to 19x9. The fair market value of the cash plus notes payable is well in excess of the book value of the shares returned to KC.

Required:
Assume the role of an accounting adviser to the owner of KC.
A. How should the purchase of its own shares be recorded and reported by KC?
B. Would the entry in A be different if only cash was paid to the former minority owner?
C. How could this transaction have been simplified for KC?

LAIMON LIMITED

Laimon Limited (LL), a manufacturer, is incorporated under the laws of Canada. The company is 90 percent owned by Sam Limited (SL), which is listed on the Toronto Stock Exchange. LL has incurred operating losses for the past five years on nearly all of its major products. Executives of both LL and SL have seriously considered closing the company. However, they cannot do so easily because:

1. Several of the products have been sold under long-term contracts which have up to 10 years remaining. These contracts have severe penalty clauses if goods are not delivered as required.
2. Other manufacturers to whom LL might subcontract production will not guarantee supply and want unit prices in excess of what LL's per unit out-of-pocket costs are expected to be.
3. They feel that they have a short-term moral obligation to provide jobs in the community in which they are located.

The present (19x8) net book value of LL's buildings and machinery is approximately $40 million, of which $30 million relates to the products which have lost money for five years. Disposal proceeds on sale of these $30 million of major assets is estimated at $2.5 million today and about $800,000 if scrapped in 10 years.

Budgets have been prepared on the basis of expected revenues and out-of-pocket costs (excluding depreciation and amortization of the $30 million of assets) for the "losing" product lines and show that the company will lose money in each of the next 10 years. Losses are expected to aggregate about $8 million over the next 10 years on these products.

Officials of the company are considering the following alternatives for the 19x8 financial statements of LL and SL:

1. Writing the $30 million of assets down by $27.5 million.
2. Writing the $30 million of assets down to $2.5 million and providing a liability of $8 million (to cover the expected $8 million operating loss) in order to allow the company to break even on these unprofitable products in the next 10 years.
3. Writing the $30 million of assets down to either zero or $800,000, on the grounds that their value of $2.5 million exists only if they are sold, and not if they are used on unprofitable production.

4. Do not record any liability or write-down of the $30 million of assets.
5. Providing note disclosure of the $27.5 million figure, and the $8 million of expected losses.

Required:

A. Assume the role of the financial vice-president of LL. What would you recommend? Why?

B. Assume the role of the auditor of LL and SL. Which alternatives would you accept? Why?

LEAD BARRIER MINES LIMITED

Lead Barrier Mines (LBML) is incorporated under federal corporate legislation and its shares are listed on some major Canadian stock exchanges. As a result it must prepare quarterly (unaudited) and annual (audited) financial statements which are in accordance with generally accepted accounting principles and corporate legislation.

LBML has been in operation for just over four years producing both lead and zinc ore concentrates which it contracts to sell to refiners. It appears to have about 15 or so more years of ore if it continues to operate at a capacity of extracting 20,000 tons per day.

LBML mines the ore which includes both lead and zinc plus waste or slag. It ships this ore to a refinery which is able to separate out the lead, and the zinc, and dispose of the waste.

When the company commenced business in 19x1 it had a three-year contract with the refiner to sell its entire output. The refiner in turn had a three-year contract with a buyer who guaranteed a fixed price per ounce of refined metal. The refiner subtracted a refining cost plus profit and passed the proceeds to LBML.

LBML chose in the years 19x1 to 19x3 to recognize revenue when it sold ore to the refiner because it knew roughly how much metal would be recovered from the ore. Last year, 19x4, however, on completion of the original three-year contract, the buyer stopped acquiring zinc from the refiner. LBML thought that the situation was temporary and continued in 19x4 with the same accounting policies to be, according to the president, "consistent with previous years." By their December 31, 19x4 year end they had roughly 11 months' production of zinc in physical inventory with no buyer in sight. The refiner had not paid LBML for this zinc because the metal had not been sold.

The president now (in March 19x5) claims that the zinc will be sold at economically favorable prices either towards the end of this year, or next. He has furnished you with forecasts from the federal government's Department of Energy, Mines and Resources to support his contention that the world will have a zinc shortage in three or four years.

Although the refiner does not have a contract for the sale of the lead, sales are holding up well at favorable prices. Whereas in the years 19x1 to 19x3 cash was received from the refiner about 90 days after the ore was shipped, now and throughout most of 19x4 cash was received about 180 days after the ore was shipped. The refiner is merely storing the zinc metal, naturally not remitting any cash to LBML for it and, in fact, charging storage fees.

Required:
Assume the role of the auditor of LBML.
A. What accounting and reporting treatment would you recommend that LBML give to the above situation in its December 31, 19x4 financial statements? Why?
B. What accounting principles would you recommend that LBML use in 19x5?

LEISURE DISTRIBUTING LIMITED

Leisure Distributing Limited (LDL) has just been incorporated under federal corporate legislation. The company is owned by three salespersons who obtained personal bank loans and invested their savings in order to provide capital for LDL. The company will buy various camping and sporting goods from manufacturers and sell to the public and to clubs and other organizations from its one location, a retail store.

The owners have approached you for advice about the type of accounting principles that they should adopt. You have been able to learn the following about LDL:

1. It has leased the store for a period of five years and pays a monthly rental plus ½ of 1 percent of sales revenue.
2. Most sales (75 percent or more) are expected to be for cash or on a credit card basis. The credit card company pays 96¢ for every $1 of sales by LDL. The remaining sales are expected to come from service clubs, sports teams, and others who are slow paying and generally short of cash.
3. Salespersons are to be paid a salary plus a bonus based on net income before income tax.
4. Manufacturers allow LDL to return up to 10 percent of its purchases of undamaged goods up to 90 days after receipt. Full refunds without time limit are permitted for damaged goods if the damage occurs at the manufacturing plant.
5. LDL's policy is to allow refunds to customers for periods up to six months, if merchandise becomes defective. Some manufacturers will give refunds to LDL for defective merchandise; others will not after a period of 60 to 90 days.
6. LDL bought some display counters and furniture.

Required:
Advise the owners.

LEISUREPRODUCTS LIMITED

Leisureproducts Limited (LL) holds several exclusive wholesaling franchises in Eastern Canada for swimming pool accessories and small marine goods. The company buys from manufacturers and sells to a variety of dealers. The dealerships are generally permitted to carry competing lines.

Most exclusive franchises are for a limited period of time and permit both the company and the manufacturers to terminate the agreement under various conditions. Last year (19x2) the company lost its most profitable franchise when the original term expired and the manufacturer refused to renew it. The company thereupon arranged another franchise agreement with a new manufacturer, Hodgson-Smith Limited (HSL), a maker of outboard engines. The company acquired Eastern Canadian rights to all of HSL's product lines.

The franchise agreement between the company and HSL reads, in part, as follows:

"Hodgson-Smith Limited, the franchiser and manufacturer, has the right to cancel this agreement upon giving 90 days' notice by registered mail or courier delivery. The franchiser has the right, but not the obligation, to purchase all inventory of the manufacturer's products held by the franchisee (Leisureproducts) at invoice cost."

"...The franchiser grants a 90-day warranty to all persons who acquire its goods from the franchisee or its distributors. Such warranty covers all material and parts replacements plus labour costs. There is no other express or implied warranty..."

"Any amendment to this agreement shall not be binding on either party until signed by the president and vice-president of the franchiser and agreed upon by the franchisee..."

"Agreed upon this tenth day of October, 19x3..."

The company's financial year end is September 30. Most of the sales of HSL's products were expected in the March to July period each year. All of these sales in 19x4 were to distributorships and (except for some consignment arrangements) required cash payment within 120 days of receipt of goods.

By agreement the company may return 10 percent (by dollar volume) of goods purchased from HSL at any time up to one year from the date of purchase. This clause in the agreement became particularly useful in August 19x4 because some life preservers and similar items acquired from HSL proved to be unpopular and were returned.

About 1,500 of HSL's super deluxe outboard engines were bought by the many distributorships of LL from March to August 19x4. The selling price to distributorships was approximately $750 each and amounted to a $200 per unit gross profit to the company.

In early October 19x4 (before the September 30, 19x4 financial statements of the company were completed and audited) a major fault was discovered in several of HSL's outboard engines, and many were being returned to distributorships. Current estimates place the cost of repairing the fault at $150 to $250 per unit.

The company has given notice to HSL that it wishes to terminate the franchise agreement. HSL has agreed to the termination. As of September 30, 19x4 the company has approximately 110 of HSL's outboard engines on consignment to a few distributorships or in its own inventory. It is not known how many units are held by distributorships in their inventory or for display purposes.

Required:

A. Assume the role of an independent outsider. What accounting and reporting treatment would you recommend that Leisureproducts give to its franchise agreement with HSL and all the transactions and events related thereto in the financial statements for:

(a) the year ending September 30, 19x4.

(b) the year ending September 30, 19x5.

Support your response by reference to accounting principles, postulates, assumptions, concepts, conventions and so forth. Be specific!

B. How would your response in A differ if you were to assume the role of auditor of Leisureproducts?

LEMKE LIMITED

Lemke Limited (LL) is a construction company that builds heavy projects that take several years to complete. In 19x4 and 19x5 LL incurred large losses. Its policy is to book the entire loss on a contract at the time the amount can be estimated.

In the year just ended, December 31, 19x6, LL has incurred another large loss. In early December 19x6 it filed claims for $2 million against another contractor who performed inferior work that damaged LL's section of a project. As a result of the damage, LL incurred a major loss on the project.

As of December 31, 19x6 LL did not have reasonable assurance that the claims would be paid. Consequently, it did not record a receivable or reduce the 19x6 losses.

In February 19x7 just prior to finalization of the 19x6 financial statements, officials of LL have settled the above claims with insurers of the other company and are to receive about $1 million. LL's officials want to record this sum in 19x7, the date of settlement.

Required:

A. Assume the role of auditor of LL. Do you agree with the suggested treatment? If so, why? If not, explain your choice.

B. How might your response in A be different if you were an accounting adviser and LL did not require an audit.

MARCHANT AUTOMOBILES LIMITED

Marchant Automobiles Limited (MAL), incorporated under the laws of Canada, is 100 percent owned by its U.K. parent company. Some of the company's debt has been sold in Canada which brings the company under the jurisdiction of provincial securities commissions.

The company manufactures a wide range of automobiles which are sold to dealers which handle only Marchant automobiles. Although MAL and its dealers operate on an arm's length basis, the company will occasionally exert mild pressure on certain dealers to encourage them to buy more automobiles and to do a better sales job in their territory. Generally the sales model year runs from September to July/August of the following year.

The company's year end is December 31 but the financial statements for 19x8 have not been finalized as yet. Executives are paid a bonus based on net income and must be paid by February 15, 19x9 for the 19x8 year. It is currently early February 19x9.

Marchant manufactures only whatever dealers request. In order to provide prompt delivery to customers most dealers keep four to eight weeks' sales on hand. Unfortunately, the economy has been very slow in late 19x8 and early 19x9, and January 19x9 sales have been down 40 percent from the previous year. The company had to shut down several of its assembly plants in December and January and some are still closed. They also had to encourage dealers to order more automobiles in order to keep some manufacturing facilities in operation in December and January. As a result dealers feel that they are "overstocked."

Effective January 20, 19x9 and until March 31, 19x9 the company is advertising that it will offer cash rebates of from $200 to $500 directly to customers — not to dealers — who purchase one of MAL's automobiles in this period. MAL hopes that dealer inventories will thus drop and more orders will accordingly be placed with the company.

You are the auditor of MAL and have been approached by the company with the following proposals for accounting for these cash rebates:

1. Charge the estimated rebates to be given between January 20 and March 31, 19x9 to the year ended December 31, 19x8 because dealers are "overstocked" and still have not sold the stocks bought in 19x8, and cannot re-order until these are sold. In order to do this an estimated liability must be recorded at December 31, 19x8.

2. Charge the rebates to 19x9, as they are paid.

3. Accrue the rebates in 19x9 and charge them in 19x9 to 19x8 on the grounds that they are a prior period adjustment.
4. Charge any cash rebates paid up until February 15 (the date the financial statements for 19x8 must be finalized) to 19x8 and thereafter charge rebates to 19x9. The reasoning for this alternative is that by February 15 most dealers would have on hand only automobiles which were bought in 19x9.

Required:
Assume the role of auditor for both 19x8 and 19x9.
A. Which of the above alternatives listed by the client would you accept for the audited financial statements? Which treatment would you recommend to your client? Why?
B. What other accounting and reporting issues can you identify? Give your recommendations.

McDONALD FOREST PRODUCTS LIMITED

McDonald Forest Products Limited (MFPL) is incorporated under corporate legislation of British Columbia. MFPL is relatively small in the industry, but its common shares are traded on some of the stock exchanges. Generally its net income is in the $3 million to $4 million range each year.

For several years it has held a common share interest in a public company, Bayshore Finance Limited (BFL). As of December 31, 19x3 MFPL's financial statements showed its investment in BFL at cost of $460,000 (market value $650,000). During 19x4 BFL went into receivership and its common shares stopped trading. Financial analysts have stated that both the preferred and common shares of BFL are worthless. The receiver in bankruptcy has not yet issued an official report on BFL and, because of the complexities involved, may not report fully for another year.

In early 19x4 MFPL bought another $100,000 of common shares of BFL. Shortly thereafter several of BFL's loans to clients were discovered to be worthless. Several creditors of BFL forced the appointment of a receiver to wind up BFL.

The controller has prepared MFPL's financial statements for the year ended December 31, 19x4. One of the assets is titled "investments," and included therein is $560,000 for the common shares of BFL. The controller included the sum on order from the president who stated that "The receiver has not yet reported. We do not know how much we will receive when BFL is wound up."

Required:

Assume the role of auditor of MFPL. What disclosure would you require in the 19x4 financial statements in order to issue an unqualified report? Why?

MERCANTILE PRINTING LIMITED

Mercantile Printing Limited (MPL) is owned by three brothers who started the business 20 years ago. MPL has grown steadily and in 19x5 revenue was $22 million.

MPL has one large printing plant which handles a variety of printing jobs: books, catalogues, road maps, telephone directories, etc. Business tends to be seasonal with two-thirds of the sales volume in the warmer six months of the year.

Most of the company's capital requirements have been internally financed by successful operations. However, $5 million is owing to a federal government lending agency, and up to $2 million tends to be owed to a bank at peak season. The company's year end is December 31, by which time receivables are low.

In order to balance annual production activity, MPL signed a five-year contract with the local telephone company to print several telephone books annually for neighboring regions. In 19x5, the third year of the contract, revenue was about $4.5 million from the telephone books.

MPL has not finalized its accounts for the past year, 19x5. It has just (January 19x6) been informed by the telephone company that changes are to be made to amalgamate and reduce the number of telephone books. This is contrary to the contract with MPL. The telephone company says that as compensation a new five-year contract will be written, with expected revenue to MPL being about $2.1 million in 19x6. Moderate increases can be expected in future years.

At commencement of the first five-year contract, MPL bought special equipment at a cost of $7.2 million to produce the telephone books. This special equipment is used for only a few other jobs, generating about $2 million revenue annually.

Required:

What financial accounting and reporting would you give to the above in the year ended December 31:

A. 19x5?

B. 19x6?

MILLER METALS LIMITED

Miller Metals Limited (MML) is owned by three companies, with each holding one-third of the common shares. Two of the three owners of MML are companies whose shares are listed on major Canadian stock exchanges. The other owner is a privately incorporated company.

MML operates two mines which produce gold, silver, copper and minor quantities of other metals. The company has a contract with a refiner who accepts the ore concentrates from MML, refines the concentrates into metals and ships them to MML's customers. The usual processing time from ore shipment date by MML to receipt of refined metal by MML's customers is four months. Customers are required to pay cash on delivery of the refined metals.

MML sells to customers on three bases:

1. Prices and quantities are fixed on negotiation of a contract, which can be four to eight months prior to delivery of the refined metal.
2. Quantities are fixed on negotiation of a contract, which can be four to eight months prior to delivery, but prices are specified to be "current world prices" as of a specified date close to the expected delivery date.
3. Prices and quantities are to be determined on the date of delivery of the refined metal.

Generally accepted accounting principles for a company like MML allow inventories of concentrated ore awaiting refining and delivery to be reported at net realizable value, called NRV (estimated selling price of the refined metal less estimated refining and selling expenses). This accounting principle (NRV) is widely used by those companies that can (1) estimate the likely quantity of metal that can be recovered from the ore concentrates, and (2) sell the majority of their refined metal at prices fixed prior to delivery of ore concentrates to the refiner. In practice in the past the use of NRV has tended to work well because the companies have had between four to six weeks of hindsight before their financial statements have to be finalized. That is, financial statements are usually not issued to shareholders until one to two months after the financial year end. By then, temporary metal price movements at the year end can be clarified as to any trend. MML has reported its inventory of ore concentrate awaiting refining at NRV for the past several years. The NRV for the inventory that has been sold for "current world prices" at time of delivery tends to recognize some or all of the price change between December 31 and the date of finalizing the financial statements.

In the year just ended (December 31, 19x7) selling prices of metal had been fluctuating considerably more than in prior years. Also a noticeable upward price movement was occurring in spite of the fluctuations. In the first six weeks of 19x8 metal prices increased steadily and in mid-February 19x8 were 20 percent above those that existed at December 31, 19x7. As of the year end date MML had more than the normal quantity of ore concentrates in its inventory account because it had been producing at capacity to meet demand. (In actuality, of course, the ore concentrates were being delivered to, or were at, the refiner.) However, in view of the recent price fluctuations MML had chosen to sell only 60 percent (instead of the usual 75 percent) of the ore concentrate inventory at December 31, 19x7 at fixed metal prices. Thus, MML faced a more complex valuation problem for inventories at December 31, 19x7 than it had in its previous several years. The 19x7 financial statements had to be finalized in two days and sent to the printer. Thus the reporting problems had to be resolved quickly.

Required:

A. Assume the role of the chief financial officer of MML. Explain what reporting you would give to the inventory of ore concentrates at December 31, 19x7.

B. Assume the role of a prospective buyer of the one-third of MML's shares that are held by the privately incorporated company. Would you agree with the reporting treatment described in A? Why?

MITCHELL CANADA LIMITED

Mitchell Canada Limited (MCL) is 70 percent owned by a publicly-held U.S. corporation and 30 percent by a variety of Canadian shareholders. MCL manufactures several lines of machinery which are sold throughout Canada.

In mid-year MCL's parent sold its small machine subsidiary in the U.S. after it had encountered several successive years of losses. As the U.S. company provided research advice for MCL's small machinery division, MCL became concerned about the economic viability of its division. Recently the division has been very successful, but this is primarily because it has made machines designed in the U.S. at a major cost of development to the parent.

Towards the end of the year MCL decided to sell its small machinery division. A Canadian subsidiary of a U.S. parent became interested and offered $8 million cash for MCL's small machinery division. This amounted to $2,650,000 in excess of book value. However, the sale is not automatic and has to be approved by the Canadian government, which is likely to take four to six months to reach a decision. This means that the sale would not be effective until about April 1, 19x4 which is after the issuance of financial statements for the current year ended December 31, 19x3.

MCL's vice-president of finance grew concerned about financial reporting for the current year when it became known publicly that MCL wished to sell its small machinery division. Sales volume started to drop because of the uncertainty about future servicing of machinery. Also, in December 19x3, another company, primarily Canadian-owned, expressed interest in buying the division for $7 million. As a result some feared the Canadian government might not favor the sale for $8 million. The president of MCL signed a formal sales agreement dated December 1, 19x3 for the $8 million 10 days before the offer of $7 million was received.

The vice-president is also concerned that additional costs might have to be recorded in the current year. The first four months (January to April) are usually unprofitable for the small machinery division. In 19x3 the losses amounted to $450,000 in January to April, and prior to the sale the same amount could be incurred in 19x4. About $400,000 of severance pay will be required on sale, and another $180,000 in legal costs are likely to be incurred.

Required:

Assume the role of accounting adviser to MCL. What advice would you give to the vice-president of finance about the current year's reporting? Be specific.

MURPHY PROPERTIES LIMITED

Murphy Properties Limited (MPL) is incorporated under the laws of New Brunswick. It is privately owned by two families.

Most of MPL's properties were acquired many years ago and are now worth five or more times their book value. MPL has large cash and short-term security balances but little retained earnings. The owners do not want to buy more assets in MPL; instead they want cash to invest individually.

MPL's lawyer has pointed out that dividends may be paid out of appraisal surplus under MPL's act of incorporation. Thus, the owners have asked you, their auditor, if it would be acceptable to appraise their properties in order to increase appraisal surplus, and then to pay dividends.

Required:
Advise the owners of MPL.

NEWLIFE LIMITED

Newlife Limited (NL) is incorporated under federal legislation. Its common shares are widely held across Canada, although it only trades over-the-counter. Its fiscal year ends on July 31.

During 19x3 one of NL's two main products was discovered to have defects. Many of the products were returned to NL by customers for full refunds. A few customers sued NL. This caused a large drain on NL's financial resources and position. As a result, in 19x4 NL went into receivership.

By July 31, 19x5 the receiver had managed to pay, or otherwise renegotiate with, many of the creditors who had forced the receivership on NL. Although business operations were now profitable, it was expected that financial affairs would take eight to 10 months to be fully straightened out.

Approximately $5,250,000 in legal, accounting and receivership fees have been charged to income in the year ended July 31, 19x5. About $3.5 million pertains to receivership duties incurred in the 19x5 fiscal year. For example, some debt agreements had to be rewritten and the division that produced the defective product had to be closed.

The remaining $1,750,000 represents costs that are expected to be incurred in the year ended July 31, 19x6. About $750,000 probably will relate to final winding up of the defective product division including sales of its fixed assets and settlements of outstanding lawsuits. The other $1 million is the estimated cost of legal and receivership fees expected to be performed in the 19x6 fiscal year in extracting NL from its receivership state and returning it to the control of the owners.

Required:
Assume the role of auditor of NL. Is the company's accounting treatment in the year ended July 31, 19x5 acceptable to you? If so, why? If not, why not?

NORTHERN GROCERS LIMITED

Northern Grocers Limited (NGL) is owned by three business persons. Previously the three operated their own separate stores but decided to amalgamate, by incorporating NGL a year ago, January 1, 19x1, under a Provincial Companies Act. Shares were granted to each of the three persons in proportion to the estimated current cost of their stores at the date of amalgamation, less any liabilities. The main creditors of the company are a bank (loan of $800,000) and three mortgage companies (total mortgages payable are $1.1 million).

You have been hired to assist the company's accountant in preparing financial statements for the year ended December 31, 19x1. In particular, you have been asked to give your recommendations about the following matters.

1. Store 1 has always used FIFO costing of inventories, Store 2 has used weighted average, and Store 3 has used FIFO for meats and produce, and weighted average for grocery items. NGL management wonders whether any change is necessary, and if so to what bases of accounting for inventories of grocery, meats and produce.

The following data is available for each store for 19x1:

	Store 1		Store 2		Store 3	
	Meat and Produce	Grocery	Meat and Produce	Grocery	Meat and Produce	Grocery
Opening inventory:						
FIFO	$ 2,000	$48,000	$ 3,100	$61,500	$ 5,180	$70,110
LIFO	1,800	42,500	2,900	54,700	4,740	65,190
Weighted Average	1,900	45,000	3,000	56,200	4,900	68,330
Closing inventory:						
FIFO	$ 2,200	$49,165	$ 3,315	$64,960	$ 5,570	$75,175
LIFO	1,850	44,120	2,900	56,950	4,840	68,200
Weighted Average	2,140	47,915	3,180	60,100	5,225	73,235

2. A fourth store, Store 4, will be opening in early 19x2. As of December 31, 19x1 the following expenditures associated with Store 4 had been accumulated by the company's accountant in a "Suspense" account, awaiting year end clearing out to other ledger accounts:

a. The building in which Store 4 is located was acquired for $400,000 on October 1, 19x1. Cash of $100,000 was paid, and a mortgage of $300,000 was obtained. By December 31, 19x1 repayments on the principal of the mortgage amounted to $10,000 and interest of $12,000 had been paid. The entire $22,000 was debited to the Suspense account.

b. Although renovations to the building were occurring from October 1 to December 31, 19x1, a portion of the building was rented. The $3,000 revenue to December 31, 19x1 was credited to the Suspense account.

c. Renovation costs of the building in October, November and December 19x1 amounted to $112,450, and were debited to Suspense.

d. A parking lot beside the building was paved at a cost of $22,055, all of which was debited to Suspense.

e. Property taxes of $3,000 for October 1 to December 31, 19x1 were debited to Suspense.

f. Depreciation expense on the building of $5,000 for October to December 19x1 was charged to Suspense.

g. Costs of training the new managers and clerks for Store 4 in December 19x1 amounted to $2,600 and were debited to Suspense.

h. Advertising costs of $3,500 announcing the forthcoming opening of Store 4 were incurred in December 19x1 and debited to Suspense.

i. The president of NGL is paid $60,000 per year. He believes that one-tenth of his 19x1 efforts related to selecting a site for Store 4 and supervising renovations. The company's accountant charged $6,000 to Suspense.

Required:

Advise the company's accountant on the above matters, explaining how each item should be treated in the 19x1 financial statements.

PRECIOUS METALS INC.

Precious Metals, Inc. (PMI) is a refiner of precious metals and produced the latter in various forms for jewelers and coin clubs. From time to time, it is necessary for PMI to borrow certain precious metals from banks or other refiners and suppliers to fulfill their commitment to customers. Although the terms of these borrowings may vary, the normal terms call for PMI to repay "in kind" (i.e., to repay the bank or suppliers in the same quantity of the precious metals as was originally borrowed).

In July 19x3, PMI borrowed 25,000 ounces of gold and 100,000 ounces of silver from the International Bank of Canada. The price of gold at the date of borrowing was $400 an ounce and silver was $15 an ounce. The entry recorded in the books of PMI at that time was:

	DR.	**CR.**
Inventory of borrowed gold	$10 million	
Inventory of borrowed silver	1.5 million	
Due to International Bank of Canada		$11.5 million

At October 31, 19x3, PMI's fiscal year end, the price of gold was $600 an ounce and silver was $35 an ounce. At fiscal year end, PMI had not repaid any of the precious metals borrowed in July.

Required:

Assume the role of auditor of PMI. What is the minimum accounting and reporting treatment that you would insist on for 19x3? Why?

PRENTICE OIL LIMITED

Prentice Oil Limited (POL) was incorporated many years ago under Alberta corporate legislation; its head office is situated in Calgary. The company is currently engaged in preparing its financial statements for the year ended December 31, 19x4.

In September 19x4 POL made an offer to the shareholders of Williams Gas and Oil Limited (WGOL) to acquire all of their common shares. The offer was $50 cash per share or two shares of POL for every share of WGOL. Just prior to the offer WGOL's shares were being traded for $44 to $46 per share, and POL's shares were selling between $24 and $25 per share. The offer expired on December 15, 19x4.

When the offer closed POL had acquired about 85 percent of the 5,000,000 outstanding common shares of WGOL. Shortly after POL made its offer, one of its exploration wells proved to be successful. This caused the price of the common shares to rise from around $25 per share to between $34 and $38 per share. As a result 4,000,000 shares of WGOL were acquired by issuing 8,000,000 shares of POL. At the time of issue POL's common shares had a book value of $12 per share. Another 250,000 shares of WGOL were acquired for $50 cash per share. Most of these were bought when POL's common shares were trading around $25 per share.

By December 31, 19x4 POL common shares were trading for $39 to $40 per share. WGOL's shares did not trade in the week ending December 31, 19x4, but one lot of 100 shares traded on January 7, 19x5 for $47 per share.

Required:

A. Assume the role of vice-president of finance of POL.
   (i) As of December 15, 19x4 what amount would you record in the books of POL to reflect the purchase of shares in WGOL? Why?
   (ii) Give the appropriate journal entry in POL's books to reflect the information in A.

(iii) How would you report your investment in WGOL in the financial statements of POL for the year ended December 31, 19x4? Why?

B. Assume the role of a shareholder who sold 10,000 shares of WGOL to POL and received 20,000 shares of POL in exchange. What journal entry would you make on your books? Why?

QUEEN CITY DRUGSTORES

Queen City Drugstores (QCD) commenced business about two months ago, with one store in a new shopping mall outside of town. The store is owned by J. Amernic, a pharmacist. He hopes to build up sufficient volume so that he eventually will be able to sell the store to one of the drugstore chains, or become a franchisee. As a franchisee he can still operate the store but, for a fee, will benefit from lower purchase prices of inventory, and national advertising.

QCD needs additional funds to finance a larger inventory and to complete a section of the store that will sell stationery, school supplies, Christmas goods and various seasonal items. The owner has approached you, the local banker, with a financial statement for the first six weeks of operations (to February 28, 19x1). He states that the accounting methods are tentative and are based on advice received from a friend.

You examine the financial statement, ask some questions, and learn the following:

1. QCD has a five-year lease for the store in the new shopping mall. The monthly rental is to be negotiated once per year for the following 12 months, but cannot increase more than 15 percent per year. QCD has an option to lease the store for another five years.

2. Inventory is purchased from a large wholesale drug company. QCD receives volume discounts for most of its purchases, but these discounts are calculated once per year after QCD's year end.

3. QCD paid $70,000 to decorate the store and add partitions prior to opening. The financial statements show that this cost is being amortized at 1 percent per month.

4. Mr Amernic is charging a salary of $2,000 per month to QCD. The store's net loss for the first six weeks is $3,790.

5. Inventory is being costed on an average cost basis, using the retail inventory method. The method that QCD is using treats the store as one unit and an average mark-up is computed for all goods in the store. A physical inventory was not compiled at February 28, 19x1.

6. A cash register that records sales by type of item was bought for $24,000. The cost of this register is being depreciated over 10 years on a straight-line basis.

7. A considerable amount of advertising material, costing $3,000, was printed for distribution in neighboring rural areas. About one-third has now been distributed, but the financial statements at February 28, 19x1 show an asset of $3,000.

8. QCD will allow local merchants to buy on credit as long as payment is made within 30 days. Thereafter interest is to be charged at 2 percent per month.

9. QCD had a "store-opening sale" in early February, and gave a 10 percent price reduction on certain items. The price reductions on items that were sold were charged to "Opening Costs" and are being amortized over 24 months.

Mr Amernic would like your advice on the "appropriateness" of the accounting principles for all parties, but especially for lenders. He wants to ask you for a loan when the financial statements are finalized.

Required:
Advise Mr Amernic.

REEL ESTATES LIMITED

Reel Estates Limited (REL) is a privately owned company which operates 12 apartment buildings in Toronto. These buildings are registered in REL's name but are heavily mortgaged. REL's source of revenue is rentals, and costs include interest expense, taxes, depreciation, repairs and maintenance and similar items.

Mammoth Enterprises Corporation (MEC) also operates some apartment buildings in addition to being engaged in various other ventures.

MEC's common shares are traded on the Toronto Stock Exchange.

REL and MEC have agreed to trade two apartments buildings, with each giving up one and getting one, currently valued at $6 million each. The cost less depreciation of the one on REL's books is $2.9 million; whereas, the cost less depreciation on MEC's books for the apartment building that they wish to give in exchange is $3,960,000. No cash will be exchanged; the switch will be a pure barter arrangement; by luck both buildings happened to have almost the same mortgage liability of $2.6 million.

The president of REL has asked you to explain how the barter should be accounted for and reported, and why.

Required:
A. Prepare your response to the president of REL, giving full explanations of your reasoning.
B. How would your response differ if MEC had asked for advice?

SCRUMPTIOUS BREAD

Scrumptious Bread (SB), a proprietorship, operates two bread shops in metropolitan Toronto. About 10 varieties of bread and buns are baked on the premises and sold only to retail customers.

SB is thinking of expanding its operations by baking bread for small grocery stores. In order to do this it needs additional funds to acquire delivery trucks and finance accounts receivable and raw materials such as flour. A local bank has agreed to consider making a loan to SB but first the bank wants to see a set of financial statements. To date SB has not kept sophisticated records and has tended to operate on a cash basis of accounting. (Income tax authorities apparently did not notice that cash basis accounting was being used because they did not ask the owner for information.)

You have been asked by the owner of the company, Mr Gilbert, to prepare financial statements of SB for each year since it commenced, and in the process of doing this learn the following:

1. The ovens in the two stores were acquired in 19x1, on commencement of the business, for $42,000 each. Installation costs amounted to $1,200 each.

2. Each store operates in leased premises on 10-year leases which were signed in 19x1. Monthly rental is $300 in one store and $540 in the other. If leases were signed today the rental cost would be 50 percent higher.

3. Partitions, signs and similar items costing $2,200 for each store were needed to ready the stores for the opening of business in 19x1.

4. SB has a contract with a flour mill that makes weekly deliveries, for which cash must be paid. Once per year in July the mill grants a rebate depending on the volume of flour bought by SB in the past year ended March 31. SB's financial year ends on December 31.

5. Sugar and other ingredients for bread-making are bought every six weeks or more in order to obtain quantity discounts.

6. Several members of Mr Gilbert's family work in the stores on a part-time basis. The cash records do not show any payments to members of the family, although cash was paid to them.

7. One of the stores has a one-bedroom apartment above it, that is occupied by a daughter and son-in-law of the sole owner. The couple work in the store at night and on weekends and do not pay rent on their apartment. A fair rental value would be $250 per month.

8. Some members of the family have loaned SB money and received periodic interest payments at 5 percent per annum. Bank interest rates currently are 14 percent.

9. Earlier this year (19x4) two cash registers were acquired on an installment plan which requires the store to pay $200 per month for 18 months. The registers could have been bought for $1,400 each.

10. The shopping centres in which the stores are located assess an improvement fee once per year, usually in summer. In 19x3 this amounted to $120 in one location and $290 in the other. The maximum annual charge for improvements is $400 per location.

11. The stores have never been visited by auditors who check the unemployment insurance deductions or workmen's compensation payments.

12. The owner feels that he has established $10,000 of goodwill in his community.

Required:
How would you treat the above in the financial statements of SB for each of the four years ended December 31, 19x1 to 19x4.

SEASIDE RESORTS LTD.

Seaside Resorts Ltd. (SRL) owns two resort hotels in the Caribbean. The company is incorporated under the Canada Business Corporations Act, and all of the shareholders and major creditors are located in Canada.

One of the resort hotels has been owned for many years. The other (second) was built to the company's specifications and opened in September 19x4. The company's year end is June 30, and it is now July 19x5. The financial statements for the year ended June 30, 19x5 have not yet been finalized.

The peak tourist season in the Caribbean is December 15 to April 15, when the rates are roughly double those of the remaining part of the year. Some Caribbean countries have experienced political and social unrest in recent years, and this sometimes affects the volume of tourist travel and length of stay. Whereas occupancy is over 90 percent in the peak months, it drops to under 40 percent for one-half of the off-season months.

SRL has decided to review its accounting priniciples thoroughly in view of the opening of the new hotel:

1. Previously depreciation has been on a straight-line basis. However, the company believes that, because its second hotel is in a new location for tourists, sinking fund depreciation should be used. Sinking fund depreciation charges are low in the first few years and increase each year over the useful life of the asset. SRL believes that it will take several years to build up very profitable operations at the second hotel's location.

2. Advertising costs for the second hotel have been heavy and the company proposes to capitalize and amortize these on a straight-line basis over five years. Management feels that advertising is an integral part of their investment in the hotel business.

3. In view of expected initial low occupancy at the second hotel, management proposes that operating costs, except for depreciation and advertising, should be capitalized as "pre-opening costs" until such time as break even is attained on a cash flow basis (cash revenue less cash operating costs). Then, "pre-opening" costs would be amortized on a straight-line basis over three years. "Revenues" received prior to cash flow break even are to be deducted from "pre-opening costs."

4. Two senior executives spent nearly all of their time in the year ended June 30, 19x5 at the new hotel site. Their combined salaries are $100,000 per year. SRL is proposing to capitalize these costs as part of the

building cost because the time was spent supervising construction, ensuring that last minute alterations were made, and training staff.

5. In view of recent fluctuations in prices, the company wishes to switch from FIFO to LIFO for charging inventory to cost of goods sold.

6. SRL intends to recast last year's financial statements so as to use the new set of accounting principles. In order to do so some approximation of the inventory at July 1, 19x3 and 19x4 is necessary.
SRL wishes to introduce these principles for the year ended June 30, 19x5.

Required:

A. Assume the role of auditor of SRL and state which of the company's proposed accounting changes you would accept and still give an unqualified audit opinion for the year ended June 30, 19x5. Why?

B. Explain why you would not accept the principles not mentioned in A.

STOLLAR FURNITURE STORES

Stollar Furniture Stores (SFS) was formed many years ago by the Stollar brothers. The company has been fairly successful and last year (19x3) had a net income of $90,000 for the year ended December 31. One of the brothers, M. Stollar, died early December 19x4; and financial statements are being prepared at the date of his death to settle his estate and satisfy the company's banker. It is expected that a large portion of M. Stollar's share of the business will be sold to the surviving brother, I. Stollar, who will have to borrow to finance the purchase of additional ownership of SFS.

M. Stollar had always handled the preparation of financial statements of SFS. Thus, I. Stollar, in conjunction with the firm's recently-hired public accountants, has been experiencing some difficulties in deciding how to account for some items, the most important of which are:

1. No provision had ever been made by M. Stollar for slow moving or old inventory stock. Items over two years old usually have been reduced in price until sold. This year I. Stollar wishes to write down inventory over six months old by 20 percent and all items over one year old by 50 percent.

2. In October 19x4 the city expropriated some land which the company bought in 19x2 as a site for a future factory. The land was carried on the books at cost of $220,000, and the city paid this sum "plus $27,000 for carrying charges and property taxes" as a "deposit until the agreement is finalized." The agreement will not be finalized until 19x5 when the property is appraised. SFS thus does not know how much additional payment it will receive but expects anywhere between $30,000 and $80,000.

3. SFS owns some common shares in a public limited company. The shares are carried in the accounts at $37,000. At the date of M. Stollar's death the selling price of the shares was $22,500 but the shares would now sell for $25,800.

M. Stollar's wife has never liked I. Stollar's wife. Hence, there is little likelihood of settling the accounting issues by friendly negotiation.

Required:

Assume the role of an accounting adviser to SFS. What recommendations would you make? Why?

SWEENEY LIMITED

Accounting Adviser (AA): (picking up telephone) "Hello, Will Tailor speaking."

Controller of Sweeney Limited (CS): "This is Stu Ardship, Will. Can you help me with a problem?"

AA: "Sure Stu. What is it?"

CS: "Our board of directors want us to put something in this year's annual report about the effects which inflation and price changes are having on the company's profits.... To be honest with you, I'm not much up on the subject. I know that there are several alternatives around, but they've always baffled me.... I prefer the good old days when we did everything one way and no one asked questions about my reports. We did our work, filed the reports, and that was that. Now that people want to use financial statements they keep asking for changes."

AA: "Does the Board want something in the financial statement package, or just a paragraph or two elsewhere in the annual report?"

CS: "They want something in the financial statement package—maybe audited, maybe not, depending on what the auditors are willing to agree to—plus they will refer to it elsewhere in the annual report."

AA: "How have inflation and changing prices affected the company?"

CS: "The price of our common shares has dropped [the shares are listed on the Toronto Stock Exchange], even though profits have gone up. Our manufacturing volume [the company makes small appliances] is about steady, but selling prices have gone up a little to offset cost increases. Wages are about in line with industry averages. Costs of replacing machinery [built in the United States] have doubled in five years, and raw materials used in the manufacturing operations are up 20 to 80 percent in the past few years."

AA: "Who is the Board trying to reach with any message in your annual report?"

CS: "Government, I suppose—for income tax relief and so they will control inflation. Also, the Board is annoyed that our share price has dropped. We need funds for expansion.... We've got to tell the stock brokers that everything is under control in the company."

AA: "Is it under control?"

CS: "Well now, that's an interesting question, isn't it? Aside from needing more cash to run the place—we haven't gone bankrupt have we—I guess we are O.K."

AA: "So, what would you like me to do?"

CS: "Tell me about these ideas called general price-level accounting and current value and whether they fit our situation. I need something concrete to show the Board at their next meeting."

Required:

Assume the role of AA:

A. Explain the different alternatives to historic cost to Mr Stu Ardship. What does each accomplish?

B. What should the company do? What would you recommend?

THOMAS TOYS

Thomas Toys (TT) was recently formed to manufacture and distribute some new toy inventions of the founder, A. Thomas. Thomas invested a large sum of his own money to commence operations and borrowed about $100,000 from a bank to finance working capital needs.

A special machine, costing $40,000 to build, was needed to make one toy, "The Incorrigible." Thomas doubts that he can ever use that machine again for other toys, although some parts worth about $4,000 can be salvaged at any time over the next four years. Estimated production volumes, selling prices and out-of-pocket costs (excluding depreciation) for The Incorrigible are:

	Production and Sales Volume	Selling Price Per Unit	Out-of-pocket Production and Selling Costs
19x1	100,000 units	$3.00	$0.40
19x2	100,000 units	2.00	0.40
19x3	100,000 units	1.00	0.40
19x4	100,000 units	0.50	0.40
19x5	Zero	Zero	Zero

Thomas has been told that he ought to prepare a set of financial statements to attach to his income tax return, and for his banker. He has heard that he ought to consider a depreciation policy or method—especially for the machine which makes The Incorrigible. He has come to you for advice.

Required:
What detailed advice would you give Thomas concerning his accounting problem with The Incorrigible-making machine?

TORONTO BUILDER INC.

Toronto Builder Inc. (TBI) is a wholly-owned subsidiary of Ontario Real Estates Co. Ltd. (ORE) which in turn, is 51 percent owned by Can Properties Ltd. (CPL). All companies are privately owned. TBI's main operations are design and construction of buildings, whereas both ORE and CPL are engaged in selling, leasing and management of properties.

19x4 was a booming year for the real estate market in Canada. TBI completed the construction of an office building at a cost of $20 million in early 19x4 and sold it to Mr X in mid-19x4 for $25 million. Mr X was a foreign investor from one of the oil rich Middle East countries and was unrelated to any of the above companies. The entire proceeds were paid in cash, of which $15 million was financed by a bank loan to Mr X.

Due to the inconvenience of managing the building himself and for other reasons, Mr X leased the entire building to CPL. Both parties agreed that:

1. the lease would be for 10 years;
2. the rental payment would be $500,000 per annum; and
3. the lease could be renewed for a further five years.

The building was to be managed by ORE. TBI did not guarantee this lease.

In 19x4, TBI included the $5 million gain on sale of the building in income. Overall, net income for 19x4 was $18 million.

Required:

Assume the role of auditor of TBI. Evaluate the accounting for these transactions and indicate the minimum reporting treatment that you would insist on for 19x4. Why?

WEINTROP INSURANCE BROKERS LIMITED

Weintrop Insurance Brokers Limited (WIBL) was incorporated on March 1, 19x4 to acquire the common shares of Kaiser Limited (KL), an insurance agency. KL is presently owned equally by J. Weintrop and the estate of C. Bychance. WIBL is owned solely by Mr Weintrop. His shares of KL are to be transferred to WIBL at fair market value of $1.2 million. With the aid of a bank loan and other savings Mr Weintrop will buy shares owned by the estate of C. Bychance. The actual mechanism involves having Mr Weintrop deposit the proceeds of the bank loan and his savings into WIBL, and then having WIBL buy shares in KL from the estate of C. Bychance for $1.2 million. Mr Weintrop will receive common shares of WIBL for his shares in KL and the proceeds of the bank loan plus his personal savings.

The net tangible assets of KL amount to $180,000 at cost and fair market value. The worth of KL is derived from its customers and their willingness to buy insurance through it. KL receives a commission annually for insurance that it places with various insurance companies.

Mr Weintrop has been asked to furnish the bank with quarterly financial statements of WIBL, prepared in accordance with generally accepted accounting principles. The bank does not necessarily want audited statements. You, a public accountant, have been hired to assist Mr Weintrop and to prepare financial statements for the three months ending May 31, 19x4.

Required:
Assume the role of the public accountant for WIBL. What would the balance sheet of WIBL look like on March 1, 19x4 assuming that all of the shares of KL are purchased on that date? Explain your reasoning.

WILLIAMS ESTATES
(A PARTNERSHIP)

Williams Estates (WE) is owned by the Williams family. Despite frequent advice to the contrary, the founder refuses to incorporate the company. He also has very rigid rules on the transfer of ownership interest (or ownership share of the partnership) within the family.

The company's banker has requested a financial statement for the year just ended. The following issues arose during preparation of the statements, and your advice has been sought:

1. Generally the company buys land from farmers, obtains rezoning, installs utilities and other necessities, and sells the land to home builders. This year no land was sold to builders; hence, overall "revenue" of the company is well below last year. The founder is considering capitalizing interest on funds borrowed to acquire the land. He also believes that property taxes should be added to the cost of land.
2. WEL builds apartment blocks by contracting out much of the construction to subcontractors. Usually the apartments are rented by WEL in order to provide cash flow. This year occupancy is well below last year. The founder of the company is considering the following:
   a. not recording depreciation on unrented apartments;
   b. capitalizing interest on borrowed funds on unrented apartments; and
   c. capitalizing interest on borrowed funds on apartment buildings still under construction.
3. The market value of one apartment building has declined significantly because it is located in a suburban district that is suffering economically because the one industrial plant in the area closed down. The founder wants to ignore the decline.
4. One apartment complex was renovated during the year at a cost of $200,000. Costs of the renovation are currently debited to the asset account, on the advice of the founder.

Required:
Give the requested advice, explaining your reasoning clearly.

WILLIAMS ESTATES LIMITED

Williams Estates Limited (WEL) is owned by the Williams family. The founder has very rigid rules on the transfer of shares to other family members. Generally he conducts business with a handshake and dislikes written contracts.

The company's banker has requested a financial statement for the year just ended but did not specify that an audit was necessary. The following issues arose during preparation of the statements, and your advice has been sought by the owner of WEL:

1. Generally the company buys land from farmers, obtains rezoning, installs utilities and other necessities, and sells the land to home builders. This year no land was sold to builders; hence, overall "revenue" of the company is well below last year. The founder is considering capitalizing interest on funds borrowed to acquire the land. He also believes that property taxes should be added to the cost of land.

2. WEL builds apartment blocks by contracting out much of the construction to subcontractors. Usually the apartments are rented by WEL in order to provide cash flow. This year occupancy is well below last year. The founder of the company is considering the following:

   a. not recording depreciation on unrented apartments;
   b. capitalizing interest on borrowed funds on unrented apartments; and
   c. capitalizing interest on borrowed funds on apartment buildings still under construction.

3. The market value of one apartment building has declined significantly because it is located in a suburban district that is suffering economically because the one industrial plant in the area closed down. The founder wants to ignore the decline.

4. One apartment complex was renovated during the year at a cost of $200,000. Costs of the renovation are currently debited to the asset account, on the advice of the founder.

Required:
Give the requested advice, explaining your reasoning clearly.

Section III:

Intermediate and Advanced Level

ADANAC TRANSPORTATION CORPORATION

Adanac Transportation Corporation (ATC) is incorporated under a Provincial Companies Act and is listed on the major Canadian stock exchanges. It has borrowed extensively over the past two decades and has several restrictions on its debt to equity ratio and on retained earnings balances that must exist after any dividends are declared. It issues quarterly financial statements as well as an annual report to shareholders and creditors.

A block of shares (representing about 24 percent of the voting shares) of ATC were recently acquired by your client Kennedy Corporation (KC). Since the remaining 76 percent of the shares are widely held KC had, in effect, obtained control of ATC's board of directors. The board appointed you auditor for the 19x5 financial year, that ends on February 28, 19x5.

During the course of the audit for 19x5 the following matters come to your attention:

1. ATC's main source of revenue (over 90 percent in some years) is from its fleet of ships which transport grain and other cargo in Hudson's Bay and the Great Lakes. As a result of freeze-up in winter revenue is seasonal. Most of the ships are idle three to five months of the year. The only revenue the ships might earn would be a storage fee for holding a cargo of grain over winter for early delivery in the spring when the ice breaks up.

2. The balance of ATC's revenue is from a small fleet of trucks which are licensed to carry general freight between locations in northern Manitoba. Much of this source of revenue is also seasonal because of the climate problems in the North. The senior officers of ATC directly own 25 percent of the truck line.

112

3. Depreciation on the ships has traditionally been recorded only in the months when the ships operate. In the quarter ended February 28, 19x5 the only depreciation that has been recorded is on office, selling and trucking equipment, plus adjustments as noted below.

4. Overhaul work on the ships is carried out during winter and charged to a "provision for overhaul." The "provision" was set up in the previous operating months by debiting expense as the ships were used to earn revenue. Annual painting costs are expensed as incurred. Any balance in the "provision" account is credited or charged to expense after freeze-up in early winter.

5. Some of the ships are leased, with options to purchase them after 10 years at the market price prevailing then. ATC is required under the lease agreement to pay for all insurance, maintenance and other operating costs. In addition ATC must guarantee that the market value of the ships does not fall below a specified figure, as a result of neglect of maintenance and repairs. ATC expenses lease payments as they are incurred.

6. In accordance with the union contract, employees who have been with ATC for over 10 years are entitled to a pension based on years of service with the company. Payments to the pension plan trustee are expensed as paid.

7. One license to operate trucks between three towns in northern Manitoba cost ATC $45,000. Although the five-year license expires on December 31, 19x8 no amortization has been recorded.

8. A variety of management bonuses are based on income before income tax and are computed and paid annually. The bonuses, which are material in 19x5, have been accrued as of February 28, 19x5 and are to be paid by April 30, 19x5.

9. Administrative and office costs (excluding depreciation and bonuses) are estimated prior to commencement of the year and the estimated annual costs are allocated to each month on a formula basis tied to estimated revenue. For example, July would be charged with a sum calculated as follows:

$$\frac{\text{Estimated July revenue}}{\text{Estimated annual revenue}} \times \text{estimated administrative and office costs}$$

Any adjustments between estimated and actual are credited and charged to the month of February.

10. A 23-day strike in May 19x4 caused a decline in revenue. No depreciation and similar allocated costs were charged during the strike period.

Required:

What accounting and reporting treatment would you recommend be given to the above in the 19x5 annual financial statements? Why?

ARCTIC EQUIPMENT LIMITED

Arctic Equipment Limited (AEL) is listed on the Toronto Stock Exchange and was incorporated under the laws of Canada several years ago. Its financial year ends on December 31.

Approximately 60 percent of its sales are to the federal government and represent specialized pieces of equipment designed for arctic life and exploration. The balance of its sales are to a few public companies, such as large integrated oil companies.

Contracts with the federal government are generally on a cost-plus basis whereas contracts with other companies are usually fixed price agreements, often obtained by competitive bidding. The reason for this difference is that most government contracts involve experimenting with various designs and testing them under severe weather conditions. The government is willing to pay for experimenting, testing and modifying designs. Patent rights remain with AEL. Generally, non-government contracts are for fairly standard-type equipment which has previously been manufactured for the government or others and tested. However, in a few situations AEL will bid on contracts quoting fixed sums even though some experimental work must be conducted in order to build effective equipment.

Last year (19x4) in October the company submitted a large bid (#432R) of $35 million (almost one-quarter of its recent annual sales) to a major oil company to produce a unit virtually identical to one which it previously built in early 19x4 for the federal government, who were charged $33 million in 19x4. Costs of the government contract were:

Design and testing	$12 million
Materials and manufacturing labor	11
Direct Overhead	4
General Overhead	2
	$29
Profit	4
Billed to government	$33 million

Estimated costs of the oil company unit (#432R) are:

Testing	$1 million
Materials and manufacturing labor	12
Overheads	7
	$20
Profit	15
	$35 million

On January 2 this year (19x5) AEL received official confirmation that it was the winning bidder on the oil company contract. AEL had heard unofficially from the oil company in late December that it was the winning bidder. Work commenced in late January; the contract is expected to take approximately 20 months to complete.

It is now early February 19x5 and you are the company's auditor attempting to finalize the accounts for the year ending December 31, 19x4. Officials of the company have presented the following proposals to you concerning contract #432R:

1. "A profit of $11 million ought to be recorded on contract #432R in 19x4 because this sum is a fortuitous gain—arising because a company is willing to pay us for developmental costs which we will not have to incur. That is, our profit on contract #432R is $15 million instead of $4 million because of the almost identical nature of the job. Consequently, the extra $11 million is earned when we are awarded the contract; and this in effect was in the year just ended."
2. "Alternatively, if you cannot accept 1. above, we will record the $11 million in 19x5, plus any other profits accrued on a percentage-of-completion of the remaining $4 million estimated profit."

3. "If it is absolutely necessary, we will record the $15 million profit on a percentage-of-completion basis. . . . We have great needs for funds from the public to promote expansion and are not interested in overly conservative accounting procedures. Our formula for costs is to be based on $31 million costs (i.e., design and testing would be shown at $12 million per the government contract, not $1 million, and other costs would be $19 million). Hence, we should record an immediate 11/31 of $15 million when we receive word that we are low bidder. That is, $11 million of the $31 million is a cost which we do not have to incur. The design work is already complete and we will be paid for it."

Required:

A. Assume the role of auditor of AEL:
   (i) What accounting procedure would you recommend for contract #432R? Why? Explain thoroughly.
   (ii) How much revenue would you be prepared to record in 19x4, and in 19x5, (assuming costs actually incurred in 19x5 were $15 million of the $20 million) before you would qualify your audit opinion? Why?

B. Assume the role of an accounting consultant to AEL. What would you recommend? Why?

BAXTER RESOURCES LIMITED

Baxter Resources Limited (BRL) is privately owned and incorporated under Ontario legislation. It has several divisions, one of which is an operating mine, another is a heavy equipment distributor, and others which are engaged in financing, manufacturing and retailing. The founder of BRL believes in having a "balanced portfolio." Hence, despite protests from his sons and daughters, the founder of the company requires BRL to hold a large amount of government and corporate bonds.

Until the year ended October 31, 19x6 BRL had not been audited. A review of the company's accounting policies showed that they follow what they call "exchange accounting" for the bonds. That is, if one federal government bond is sold and another federal government bond is purchased with most or all of the proceeds, no gain or loss is recognized on the bond that is sold. The same principle applies when provincial bonds are "traded" for other provincial bonds, or corporate bonds are "exchanged" for other corporate bonds. Gains and losses would be recognized if one class, such as corporate bonds, was "traded" for another class, such as federal government bonds.

The company's reasons for not recognizing gains and losses on "equal exchanges" is that the risk has not changed. They reason that by trading, BRL is only exchanging one coupon cash flow for another, and that yields are unchanged.

Required:

Assume the role of auditor of BRL. Would you accept the company's "exchange accounting" treatment as being in accordance with GAAP?

BETTY BOUTIQUES LIMITED

Betty Boutiques Limited (BBL) is incorporated under federal corporate legislation. Last year (19x2) its financial statements were not consolidated but included BBL's one subsidiary, Paula Shoppes Limited (PSL), at cost. PSL, acquired earlier in 19x2 by BBL, did not live up to expectations and by its December 31 year end in 19x2 was being offered for sale.

In the spring of 19x3 BBL changed the merchandise line in PSL to make it closer to that of its parent company. This had a dramatic effect on sales of PSL and increased the worth of the company by 100 percent or more. By December 31, 19x3 management of BBL was considering merging the two companies or selling PSL. In BBL's December 31, 19x3 financial statements, PSL was carried at cost.

In late 19x4 PSL's operations were wound up and became a branch of BBL. The assets less liabilities of PSL were recorded at amounts well in excess of the "investment in PSL" on BBL's books.

Financial statements of BBL are generally used for income tax purposes and sent to the company's five shareholders and the bank. In 19x4 they will be audited for the first time. The auditor has raised the question of how the excess of assets less liabilities of PSL over the cost to BBL should be reported in the 19x4 financial statements.

Required:

Assume the role of an adviser to the auditor of BBL and recommend an appropriate reporting treatment, giving reasons.

BRENNAN AIRLINES LIMITED

Brennan Airlines Limited (BAL) is privately owned by the Brennan family. BAL operates a charter air service plus a few scheduled flights between four towns in one Canadian province. Its financial year ends on December 31.

Until recently it owned eight small aircraft. In October 19x3 it acquired the assets of a bankrupt aircraft dealer who bought, rebuilt and sold used airplanes. The bankrupt company had six usable aircraft plus an extensive stock of spare parts. The assets of the bankrupt company were acquired for well below market value.

BAL has been able to lease two of the six aircraft to an industrial company, but the lease date does not commence for six months (June 1, 19x4) and then it extends for five years (to May 31, 19x9). Another two of the six aircraft will be put into charter services, but the remaining two plus many of the spare parts will be "stored" for use in future years. BAL is applying for rights to have scheduled service between other towns in the peak summer periods. If rights are granted the two aircraft in storage could be used as early as 19x4.

The acquisition of the bankrupt company was financed by a term bank loan. It is hoped that this loan can be repaid in full in four years.

The charter business tends to be seasonal and cash flows vary considerably from month to month. Most of the revenue is generated in the May to September period.

Required:

A. Explain in detail how BAL should account for the acquisition of the bankrupt company in its December 31, 19x3 financial statements.

B. What accounting issues may arise in years subsequent to 19x3 as a result of the acquisition? What accounting and reporting treatment might be given at the appropriate date?

CALIFORNIA CORPORATION

California Corporation (CC) is a large company that is generally described as a real estate developer. It acquires farm land and real estate projects needing refurbishing, and either holds them for a while or sells them when they are fully developed or rented. Some of the properties are currently rented at less than their full potential under leases that expire in two to three years. On termination of the leases the value of the properties is expected to increase 30 to 40 percent because they will be modernized, and rental revenues can be increased substantially. One large reputable company has an option to rent two of CC's costly buildings at the higher rental rates as soon as the current leases on the buildings expire and modernization occurs. Costs of refurbishing the buildings are expected to be much less than what is likely to be received in additional rental revenue.

The ownership of CC has recently changed and you have been appointed auditor for the current year, ended December 31, 19x3. Two events have come to your attention.

1. New owners and management have had their entire "properties" portfolio (land, buildings under construction and rental property) appraised at their "highest and best use." This means that the values are calculated as the net present value of rental revenue, less operating expenses, that likely will be received when the property is fully developed or modernized, and rented or leased. Management has recorded the "highest and best use" values in its books and on its financial statements.

2. The former president and vice-president were dismissed in early January 19x4 and were paid severance pay of $1.4 million. This sum was composed of:

Bonus plan	$ 600,000
Unfunded pension benefits	680,000
Severance, of six months' salary	120,000
	$1,400,000

The bonus plan payment was based on a "phantom stock plan." The plan pays management, whenever it wishes, for a percentage of any increase in CC's retained earnings. For example, the plan may grant a bonus to the president, to be based on 1 percent of any increase in retained earnings between the date that the option is granted and the date that the president exercises his option. The reason that such an approach is employed is because CC's shares do not trade publicly. Hence, no market price exists that can be used for stock option plans.

The pension payment arises from a "phantom pension plan" that is not funded. The "plan" is arranged to pay executives 5 percent of their average annual salary times their number of years of service, plus interest at 10 percent per year, as a lump sum on their retirement. If they have been employed by CC for over 10 years they receive a payment calculated on the same basis on termination, for any reason, prior to retirement.

The new management of CC has accrued the entire $1.4 million in 19x3.

Required:

Assume the role of auditor of CC. State how the transactions and events should be treated in the 19x3 financial statements in order to avoid a qualified auditor's report.

CARTER CORPORATION

Carter Corporation (CC) is privately owned by one family, and incorporated under Manitoba legislation. CC holds a 40 percent interest in the common shares of Portage-Main Limited (PML) and thereby exerts significant influence. CC also owns all of the cumulative preferred shares of PML. In its financial statements for the years ended June 30, 19x3 and 19x4 CC reported PML on the equity basis.

During the year ended June 30, 19x5 PML did not declare any of the quarterly dividends on the cumulative preferred shares. At June 30, 19x5 $100,000 of preferred dividends of PML were in arrears. Net income of PML during its 19x5 fiscal year was $312,500.

Required:

Assume the role of an adviser to the owners of CC. How should CC's investments in PML be accounted for and reported in the year ended June 30, 19x5? Why?

CHALCOPYRITE LIMITED

Burro Limited (BL) owns 15 to 20 percent of the issued common shares of many companies in the mining industry, including Chalcopyrite Limited (CL), Tailings Limited (TL) and Slagg Limited (SL). Shares in BL, CL and TL are listed on Canadian Stock Exchanges and the three companies have recently been issuing quarterly reports. Shares of SL are traded over-the-counter. All four companies have December 31 year ends.

Chalcopyrite owned 30 percent of the issued common shares of an unrelated company, Granite Limited. In June 19x6 CL signed the following written contract:

1. The shares in Granite were sold to Slagg Limited for $1,850,000 with payment due March 1, 19x7.
2. In the event that Slagg failed to make the payment on time, CL would receive 132,135 shares (market value $1,850,000 in June 19x6) of Burro, which were owned by TL. The cost of the Burro shares to Tailings was $1,175,000, and represented 2 percent of the issued shares. Pursuant to the agreement TL deposited the shares of Burro with a trustee.

The Granite shares cost CL $2,320,000. CL needs cash in 19x7 to finance exploration activities scheduled for that time.

The 19x6 annual financial statements were not finalized as of March 1, 19x7. On March 1 Slagg failed to make the required cash payment, whereupon Tailings acquired the shares of Granite and the trustee released the shares of Burro to CL. The market price of the shares of Burro had declined steadily since June 19x6 and as of March 1, 19x7 were being traded for $10 per share. As of December 31, 19x6 the Burro shares were trading at $11 per share.

In late April 19x7 CL sold the shares of Burro for net proceeds of $1,315,000. The financial statements of CL for the year ended December 31, 19x6 were to be finalized and printed on March 20, 19x7. Hence, the hindsight was not available at that time.

Required:
Assume the role of the chief financial officer of Chalcopyrite Limited. What disclosure would you give in the annual financial statements of the company for 19x6 and 19x7? Explain fully.

COMMERCIAL HELICOPTERS LIMITED

Commercial Helicopters Limited (CHL) is incorporated under federal corporate legislation. Its financial year ends on December 31. CHL's common shares are traded over-the-counter in several Canadian provinces. The company also has a sizeable amount of long-term debt.

CHL operates a fleet of helicopters (aircraft) which it either leases annually to industrial companies or rents on an hourly, weekly or monthly basis complete with pilots. Each aircraft has to be overhauled after a specified number of hours of flying. Sometimes two overhauls might occur in one financial year because work is completed over the winter when use of the aircraft is minimal (i.e., an overhaul for 19x8 could occur in January 19x9 and one for 19x9 might occur in December 19x9). Whenever the aircraft are overhauled they are, in effect, "brand new" because new parts are added. While overhauls occur for engines and related parts only and not for the air frames or structure of the aircraft, the first represent about 80 percent of the original cost of a machine.

The company has asked you whether they should be depreciating the original cost of a helicopter as well as charging the income statement for annual overhauls. Also they wonder whether it is fair to charge the cost of two overhauls for some machines in one year.

Income taxation officials have stated that overhaul expense may be charged only when incurred, and capital cost allowance (income tax depreciation) on original cost of machines is 40 percent, on a declining balance basis.

Required:

Assume the role of an accounting adviser to CHL. What accounting and reporting treatment would you recommend? Why?

DAVIS OIL AND GAS LIMITED

Davis Oil and Gas Limited (DOGL) was incorporated on January 2, 19x3 under federal corporate legislation. The company is owned by a small group of investors.

During 19x3 DOGL entered into several joint venture agreements that were formed to drill for oil and gas in various parts of the world. Drilling occurred in 19x3 in Canada, Australia and Spain. As of December 31, 19x3 none of the test wells had proven successful. Approximately $1.1 million had been expended by DOGL on unsuccessful drilling ("dry holes") and another $296,000 had been spent on drilling that is still in process. These sums are regarded as "intangible drilling costs" and exclude fixed assets and working capital of the joint venture.

Officials of DOGL are wondering how they should account for the $1,396,000 in the 19x3 financial statements. They have heard that the $296,000 could be shown as an asset because it is not yet known whether the drilling will be successful. However, they are not sure whether to capitalize or to expense the $1.1 million.

When they entered into the joint ventures they fully realized that some would be successful and others would not. Overall they believe that the cost of drilling will be much less than revenue from the few successful wells. Otherwise, they would not have chosen to drill and invest in the oil and gas industry. Thus, they believe that sound arguments exist for capitalizing the $1.1 million and expensing it over revenue from successful wells. They might refine their accounting somewhat by using three capital accounts: one for Canada, one for Spain and one for Australia. Costs incurred in each country would then be amortized only over the revenue from their successful wells in that particular country.

The officials have heard of GAAP and think that it may require expensing the $1.1 million in 19x3. They have heard that accountants believe that "research" costs should be expensed because there is not sufficient certainty that profitable operations will result. However, they are not sure that drilling is the same as research.

Required:
Assume the role of an adviser to officials of DOGL. What are the arguments in favor of capitalizing the $1.1 million ("full cost" method) in total, and by country or region, as well as expensing it ("successful efforts" method)? What do you recommend? Why?

DENHAM LIMITED

Denham Limited (DL) is incorporated under corporate legislation of Alberta. On November 10, 19x5 its board of directors met and approved the following:

1. A business combination with Ross Limited (RL), which is also incorporated under Alberta legislation. The business combination qualifies as a pooling-of-interests. DL is to issue its shares to the shareholders of RL, and RL will become a 100 percent owned subsidiary of DL. Shares of DL are to be issued at $30 each, but the book value per share of RL's assets is between $9 and $10 each. The combination is to be effective November 28, 19x5 and all shares are to be exchanged as of this date.

2. Effective November 29, 19x5 200,000 shares of DL are to be issued to a 100 percent owned subsidiary of DL. The subsidiary intends to hold these shares for a few months and then may sell them to senior management of DL at the then prevailing market price.

3. A common share dividend of the new DL was declared on November 10, 19x5 to shareholders of record on November 30, 19x5. The dividend is $1 per share and is to be paid on December 15, 19x5.

Required:

Assume the role of chief financial officer of DL. How would you report the above in the financial statements of DL for the year ended November 30, 19x5. Consider both the consolidated and unconsolidated statements.

DONAMAR CORPORATION

Donamar Corporation (DC) was incorporated under federal legislation on January 2, 19x5 to acquire Apple Limited (AL) and Banana Inc. (BI). The acquisitions occurred in January 19x5 and resulted in AL becoming 100 percent owned by DC and BI being 95 percent owned by DC. BI has a 90 percent owned subsidiary, Cherry Limited (CL). DC is owned by the general public.

DC paid $6 million for 95 percent of BI, which had a book value and fair value of $3.5 million ($3,325,000 for 95 percent) at the time. DC paid $1 million for AL, whose book value and fair value was a negative $100,000 on the acquisition date. Thus, consolidated goodwill on the date of acquisition was $3,775,000 ($1.1 million plus $2,675,000).

Shortly after AL was acquired, DC invested $300,000 in AL by purchasing previously unissued common shares. DC then sold all of its shares in AL to CL and received 100,000 special preferred shares of CL in exchange. The special preferred shares have only two rights: (1) to a dividend of $400,000, and (2) once the $400,000 dividend has been paid the shares may be redeemed for $10,000. The reason for this unusual arrangement is to use up large income tax losses in AL.

After CL had acquired all of the shares of AL the two companies were amalgamated into a "new" CL. The income tax losses of the "old" AL were used to offset 19x5 taxable income of CL. Before the year end of December 31, 19x5 CL paid the $400,000 dividend to DC and redeemed the special preferred shares for $10,000.

As a result of the transactions several accounting and reporting problems arose. Management of DC asked its internal accountants to provide recommendations, and they arrived at three, different possibilities:

1. Since AL no longer exists the carrying value on DC's books of $890,000 ($1.3 million less $410,000) should be expensed in 19x5, possibly as an extraordinary loss. This would mean that, on a consolidated basis, $890,000 of goodwill would no longer exist.
2. Increase DC's investment in BI by $890,000.
3. Increase DC's investment in BI by $1,290,000 ($1.3 million less $10,000) and record the $400,000 as a windfall gain arising from utilization of a previously unrecorded income tax loss carry forward.

Required:
Assume the role of auditor of DC. Which of the three accounting and reporting methods would you be willing to accept? Why?

ENCHANTED FOREST PRODUCTS LIMITED

Enchanted Forest Products Limited (EFPL) is incorporated under the laws of Nova Scotia and its common shares are traded on several Canadian stock exchanges. EFPL is an integrated forest products company with logging, lumber and transportation divisions plus three subsidiaries 60, 65 and 70 percent owned respectively.

EFPL holds all of its timber lands, most of which were acquired 30 or more years ago, on a freehold basis. It is therefore responsible for reforestation of harvested lands and protection against insects and fire. EFPL expects to have a perpetual yield from the forests, which should replenish themselves over 60-to 80-year periods. All reforestation and protection costs are expensed in the year that they are incurred.

In 19x4 EFPL sold a large portion of its freehold timberland, carried on its books at $4 million, to the 60 percent owned subsidiary for $50 million, which was the estimated market value at the time. The timberland had originally cost $9 million but had been depleted for accounting purposes, in accordance with company accounting policies, at a rate of 2 percent per year. The 2 percent is a conservative average that assumes that timber acquired with the land will be harvested over a 50-year period. EFPL recorded the gain on sale of the timberland as an extraordinary item in 19x4.

In 19x5 EFPL re-acquired the same lands from the 60 percent owned subsidiary for $56 million, which was the estimated market value at the time. EFPL paid the subsidiary $15 million cash and issued it a debenture for $41 million. Income tax authorities told the company that depletion for income tax purposes must be based on the $4 million book value when the land was sold to the subsidiary, and not the $56 million.

The president of EFPL has stated that he wants to base depletion in 19x5 and future years on the $4 million figure. The company's controller has stated that depletion has to be based on the $56 million. The president, however, has argued with the controller that it is "ridiculous to charge reforestation costs of $3 million per year on this land as well as over $1 million in depletion. The trees are growing, not disappearing."

EFPL's fiscal year ends on December 31.

Required:

A. Assume the role of an accounting adviser to EFPL. What accounting treatment would you have given to the timberland sale in 19x4, repurchase in 19x5, and related reforestation and depletion issues? Why?

B. Assume the role of auditor of EFPL. If the president's views are incorporated into the 19x5 financial statements of EFPL would you qualify your audit report?

GRAMMAS FOODS

Grammas Foods (GF) operates seven health food stores in a large city. Its owner, Sandy Grammas, started the business with one store in a shopping plaza and gradually added stores as he became aware of potentially good locations throughout the city.

For some time now Sandy has been aware that his stores cover too wide a geographical area and that supplying each store and visiting each is becoming more and more costly. He has therefore seriously thought about selling two of the stores that are well away from the five others located in the northeast part of the city. Unfortunately, these two are the first ones he opened and are often the most profitable. The two stores presently contain the following assets:

Inventory	$86,000
Leasehold improvements, less amortization of $60,000	40,000
Equipment, net of accumulated depreciation	30,000

Annual revenue for the two stores is around $400,000, gross profit is about $100,000 and operating expenses are $60,000 or so.

This week Marigold Grocers Limited (MGL), another, much larger, health food chain, offered GF three MGL stores in the northeast part of the city for the two GF stores. No money is to be exchanged, just leases, employees and other assets at each store are to be "traded" on an equal basis. MGL's officials state that the book value of the tangible assets in the three stores is $220,000 and that a fair value would be around $350,000. MGL is owned by approximately 50 investors.

Sandy Grammas estimates that it would cost him $6,000 to alter the three new stores to fit the color scheme, name and so forth of his other stores. He is tending towards accepting the offer from MGL, and has come to you to clarify how he might account for the transaction.

Required:

A. What advice would you give Sandy? Why? (Be specific!)
B. How would your advice differ if MGL had asked you?
C. If Sandy accepted the offer from MGL how should he account for the asset exchange?

GRAUL EXPLORATIONS LIMITED

Graul Explorations Limited (GEL) is incorporated under federal corporate legislation. Its shares and a small amount of debt are held by many owners across Canada.

GEL was approached three years ago by a prospecting syndicate of 12 persons who had discovered an economic ore body. An agreement was reached between GEL and the syndicate to develop the mine, to be called Mein Mine (MM). The agreement called for GEL to incur various expenditures that are preliminary to setting up successful operations, and for which GEL would receive substantial ownership of MM.

As a result of uncertainty about both company and income tax law (statute revisions were under consideration by provincial and federal governments at the date of signing of the agreement) the parties chose not to incorporate MM until the uncertainty diminished. GEL thus recorded expenditures on behalf of MM in GEL's books and claimed many of them as deductions in computing its income. These expenditures fell into three categories: (1) salaries of GEL's employees who were working primarily on MM's development; (2) various public relations outlays designed to encourage a provincial government to build a railway into the site of the mine and to finance development of a town nearby; and (3) exploration and construction at the site of the mine.

To GEL's surprise a large percentage of the above expenditures were permitted for federal and provincial income tax purposes. However, a few were disallowed. Thus, GEL was able to lower its income tax by claiming MM's expenses.

The syndicate also incurred some costs but these were mainly salaries, and were not claimed for income tax purposes. They remain on the personal books of one member of the syndicate and are shown as an asset. Various costs of financing the prospecting crew that discovered the ore and of registering ownership of the surrounding land were long ago expensed by a major owner of the syndicate.

This month the uncertainty decreased substantially. Consequently, MM was incorporated as a limited company. According to the agreement between GEL and the syndicate, various expenditures to date are to be tallied and used in deciding relative ownership interests of MM. Common shares are then to be distributed, giving the syndicate control because it found the ore.

A chief financial officer has been hired by MM. He is to be both a controller and treasurer and will have to negotiate financing for MM. After examining the situation he has asked your advice on what the opening balance sheet should look like.

Required:

Advise the chief financial officer. Be specific and give full reasons.

HANNA CORPORATION LIMITED

Hanna Corporation Limited (HCL) is incorporated under federal corporate legislation and listed on a major Canadian stock exchange. It operates various small wholesale warehouses and retail store chains throughout Canada.

During the year just ended December 31, 19x6, HCL disposed of one wholesale chain to a new company owned by several members of HCL's management team. The wholesale warehouse chain represented 40 percent of the assets and liabilities of HCL and contributed about 50 percent of the revenue and net income in 19x5.

The management of HCL used about 60 percent of the proceeds of sale of the chain to declare a dividend to the common shareholders of HCL. The remaining 40 percent of the proceeds was used to redeem HCL's preferred shares.

The sale became effective October 1, 19x6. Between then and December 31, 19x6 about 20 percent of HCL's purchases of goods for retail sale were acquired from the recently sold warehouse chain.

One of the terms of sale requires the buyers of the new wholesale chain to pay HCL additional consideration if income before income tax exceeds a specified amount over the next three years. The additional consideration is to be paid annually on January 31 commencing in 19x8. The payment will be based on income before income tax of the new wholesale chain for the previous year ended September 30. In the three months ended December 31, 19x6 the new wholesale chain made substantially more net income before income tax than the amount specified in the purchase and sale agreement.

Required:

What accounting and reporting treatment would you give to the foregoing in HCL's financial statements for the year ended December 31, 19x6. Be specific.

HERAUF LIMITED

Herauf Limited (HL) is incorporated under federal corporate legislation. The company is in the money-lending business, and through a 100 percent owned subsidiary, Smith Limited (SL), leases automobiles to companies and individuals.

HL's primary source of revenue (excluding income from SL) is derived by financing individuals' purchases of automobiles. An automobile dealer will sell a new or used vehicle subject to a finance company agreeing to accept the credit status of the customer. For example, if the automobile is sold for a $5,000 equivalent cash price, the customer has to sign a note for $5,000 plus a finance charge of, say, $1,800 for a total of $6,800. The customer then agrees to pay roughly $190 per month for 36 months. HL issues a cheque to the automobile dealer for about $4,750; the remaining $250 is held back until the customer repays the full $6,800. In the event that the customer defaults and the automobile is repossessed and sold for less than the outstanding receivable at the time, the $250 is used in full or in part to offset any loss.

HL's primary accounting problems relate to the handling of unearned revenue ($1,800 in the above example), valuation of receivables, valuation of repossessed automobiles and expensing of costs. HL's main costs are for credit checks on prospective customers, making sure that the auto-mobiles are insured by customers, collecting receivables monthly, and han-dling of interest expense. The company borrows money from banks but also borrows large sums by selling debt payable (one, three, five or 10-year notes) to the general public. Often there is a cost of issuing this debt—advertising, discounts and so forth.

SL has similar but not identical problems. It acquires automobiles directly from manufacturers and leases them for 24, 36 or 48 months to individuals or companies (lessees). The lessee pays for insurance, licences, gas, oil, washes and minor tune-ups. Generally, but not always, the lessee guarantees the resale price. For example, a $6,000 automobile may have an expected resale value of $2,000 at the end of four years. If it sells for less than $2,000 (because of damage or other defects) the lessee must pay any deficiency.

SL must decide how to record revenue from the leases and how to record various costs such as advertising, interest, extraordinary repairs in excess of the manufacturer's warranty, office, and so forth.

Required:

Assume the role of an accounting adviser to HL and SL. What accounting principles, policies and procedures would you recommend for them? Why? Explain fully.

ISLAND MANUFACTURING LIMITED

Island Manufacturing Limited (IML) is privately owned and incorporated under a Provincial Companies Act. It has borrowed large sums of money from a bank this year and has been requested by the bank to have an audit. Its financial statements have not been audited in prior years.

Three years ago, 19x5, the company's board of directors signed a bonus contract with its senior management. Both the directors and management wanted an incentive plan, but because the company's shares were not traded on a stock exchange, bonuses were set as a percentage of net income. The plan provided for the appointment of an arbitrator in the event that management and the board could not agree on accounting principles used in the computation of net income.

As a result of having a first audit, several issues have appeared which have brought forth a disagreement between the auditors (who have generally, but not entirely, been supported by the board of directors) and management. You have been hired as the arbitrator. Net income, before considering the following issues, for 19x8 is $265,000. A 40 percent income tax rate may be assumed.

1. IML has always recorded bad debts and warranty costs as they are incurred or paid. The auditors want to record year end allowances totalling $85,000. Most of this is for expected warranty costs.

2. IML has used declining balance depreciation in prior years. The auditors believe that straight-line depreciation is "more appropriate." Straight-line depreciation in 19x8 would be $32,000 in excess of declining balance amounts.

3. The company has always used direct costing in its manufacturing operations. The auditors want the company to switch to absorption costing. In 19x8 this adjustment would lower income by $26,500.

4. IML has always expensed any alterations and repairs to equipment which cost $10,000 or less. The auditors want to capitalize alterations. The effect on 19x8 is not significant, being less than $1,000, but a change could affect other years' net incomes.

5. A long-term receivable which is due in 19x13 on sale of land was recorded in 19x8 at its face value of $200,000. The auditors want to discount the receivable because it is non-interest-bearing.

Required:

Assume the role of arbitrator and advise the parties to the dispute. (Give your recommendations with reasons.)

JOPLIN DISTRIBUTORS LIMITED

Joplin Distributors Limited (JDL) is federally incorporated and is listed on major Canadian stock exchanges. Its financial year ends on December 31.

Until October 1, 19x5 JDL owned 80 percent of Halifax Enterprises Limited (HEL). On this date it acquired the remaining 20 percent of the issued common shares. JDL and HEL are in similar businesses, involving the manufacture and distribution of fishing equipment.

HEL incurred losses for income tax purposes in the years ended December 31, 19x2, 19x3 and 19x4. JDL was unwilling, until 19x5, to invest in modernizing HEL's operations because the minority shareholders would not agree to furnish additional funds. Without the modernization future losses were expected. In the 19x4 financial statements of both JDL and HEL no accrual was made for income tax savings which could arise from utilizing income tax loss carry forwards.

On November 1, 19x5 the management of JDL was informed that if it wound up HEL into JDL the income tax losses of HEL could be utilized. Management of JDL thus decided to wind up HEL in the next four months. The following costs and losses of HEL are expected as a result of the wind-up of one of HEL's two manufacturing facilities:

Operating losses: to December 31, 19x5	$200,000
: in early 19x6	120,000
Disposal of fixed assets	195,000
Severance pay	150,000
Cancellation of leases and contracts	40,000
Miscellaneous	25,000

In addition, modernization of the remaining plant, planned for 19x5 and 19x6, will cost $1.8 million. During modernization no production is possible. Hence, employees will be employed at "unproductive work" at a cost of $100,000. Various fixed costs (insurance, property taxes, interest, etc.) of $85,000 will be incurred during the modernization period.

Required:
How should JDL account for the acquisition and wind-up of HEL in its December 31, 19x5 financial statements? Why?

KAISER AND SON

Kaiser and Son (KAS) manufacture furniture in an old factory in an older part of a large city. The firm has been in business for 60 years and has been very profitable. KAS was formed by F. Kaiser who operated it for 38 years before retiring and turning over management to his son, M. Kaiser.

The daughter of M. Kaiser recently graduated from university. She convinced her father after much debate that KAS should diversify into real estate. She arranged for the purchase of land and a small 14-year-old building in the heart of the downtown core but on a less used street. The purchase price was $1.2 million and was financed with $200,000 cash and a 20-year mortgage bearing interest at 10 percent per annum. The mortgage is repayable in equal amounts which include both principal and interest. The present plan is to rent the building under the leases now in existence as long as the tenants wish to stay. The building is 100 percent occupied with leases expiring at various times in a three- to seven-year period. The land was appraised on the purchase date at $200,000 and the building at $1 million. Land values are expected to increase in future years.

Gross rental revenues currently are $220,000 per year, and out-of-pocket operating costs (maintenance, property taxes, heating, etc.) are about $70,000 per year. Ms. Kaiser believes that rental revenue can be raised to offset any future cost increases so that an average annual net cash flow of $150,000 per year can be expected over the next 20 years.

The depreciation policy for accounting purposes had not been given much thought until after the acquisition, but now it is of some concern to the firm. It had been assumed that the firm would depreciate the building on a straight-line basis just as it does its old factory building. Initial calculations assumed a 20-year life with no building value at the end of that time. However, calculations on this basis indicate that the investment in the building will contribute nothing to income in the first year:

Rental revenues	$220,000
Less:	
Out-of-pocket operating costs	70,000
Interest on mortgage	100,000
Depreciation	50,000
	$220,000

In fact, M. Kaiser observed astutely, "This thing is costing us income this year because we had to cash some marketable securities and increase our bank debt to find the $200,000 cash payment."

Yet, judging from the projections, as the years go by the investment will appear to become more and more profitable, as interest on the mortgage declines. (See Schedule A.) "It sure seems strange," said M. Kaiser "but I don't see what we can do about it."

Ms. Kaiser had an answer: sinking fund depreciation. "They're all doing it!" she said. She then proceeded to explain how sinking fund depreciation would work:

"In buying this property we really are buying a stream of future cash revenues and the purchase price should be viewed as the present value of this stream. In our particular case, in return for the $1 million building portion of the purchase price we are receiving estimated net cash receipts (before interest) of $150,000 each year for the next 20 years. This represents about 13.9 percent return on our $1 million investment before taxes. To put it another way, the present value of this 20-year 'annuity' of $150,000 per year at 13.9 percent is our cost of the $1 million. Depreciation for Year 1 is logically the loss in value of the assets—that is the decrease in its present value. This can be calculated as follows:

Present value at beginning of Year 1 (cost)	$1,000,000
Add interest at 13.9 percent	139,000
	1,139,000
Less estimated net cash receipts	150,000
Present value at end of Year 1	$ 989,000

Depreciation for the first year is therefore $11,000 ($1,000,000 less $989,000)."

Schedule B shows the depreciation calculation and its impact on net income, ignoring income taxes, for the entire 20-year period. Said Ms. Kaiser: "You can see that this sinking fund method, using an internal rate of return of 13.9 percent, results in a constant return on investment before mortgage interest charges. The accelerating depreciation factor effectively counterbalances the declining interest on the mortgage. Thus, sinking fund depreciation is perfectly logical because it amortizes the entire building systematically over its useful life."

M. Kaiser was not overly pleased with his daughter's sinking fund depreciation method. He was particularly concerned because it would be inconsistent with the straight-line basis used on the factory building. Ms. Kaiser replied, "Dad, just change your depreciation method on the factory."

M. Kaiser and his daughter agreed to seek outside advice to settle their argument.

Required:

A. Is sinking fund depreciation appropriate for the firm? Explain fully.

B. Assume that the firm has an annual audit because their bankers request such. As auditor what recommendations would you make to Ms. Kaiser and her father? Why?

Schedule A

KAISER AND SON

Building–Impact on Income Assuming Straight-Line Depreciation

	1	2	3	4	5	6
	Projected revenue (net of operating	Mortgage interest	Depreciation (5 percent	Net income before tax	Net book value of building at beginning	Before Tax return on investment as percent of net
Year	expenses)	expense	Straight-line)	[1-(2&3)]	of year	book value
1	$150,000	$100,000	$50,000	$ 0	$1,000,000	0
2	150,000	98,254	50,000	1,746	950,000	.2%
3	150,000	96,334	50,000	3,666	900,000	.4%
4	150,000	94,220	50,000	5,780	850,000	.7%
5	150,000	91,896	50,000	8,104	800,000	1.0%
6	150,000	89,340	50,000	10,660	750,000	1.4%
7	150,000	86,528	50,000	13,472	700,000	.
8	150,000	83,436	50,000	16,564	650,000	.
9	150,000	80,032	50,000	19,968	600,000	.
10	150,000	76,290	50,000	23,710	550,000	.
11	150,000	72,174	50,000	27,826	500,000	.
12	150,000	67,644	50,000	32,356	450,000	.
13	150,000	62,662	50,000	37,338	400,000	.
14	150,000	57,184	50,000	42,816	350,000	.
15	150,000	51,156	50,000	48,844	300,000	.
16	150,000	44,526	50,000	55,474	250,000	.
17	150,000	37,232	50,000	62,768	200,000	.
18	150,000	29,208	50,000	70,792	150,000	.
19	150,000	20,384	50,000	79,616	100,000	.
20	150,000	10,700	50,000	89,300	50,000	178.5%
	$3,000,000	$1,349,200	$1,000,000	$650,800		

Schedule B

KAISER AND SON

Building–Impact on Income Assuming Sinking Fund Depreciation
at (Approximately) 13.9 Percent Over 20 Years

Year	Projected revenue (net of operating expenses)	Mortgage interest expense	Depreciation	Net Income before tax	Net book value of building at beginning of year	Expected return on investment before tax and interest	Before tax return on investment as percent of net book value
1	$150,000	$100,000	$11,000	$39,000	$1,000,000	13.9%	3.9%
2	150,000	98,254	12,530	39,216	989,000	13.9%	3.9%
3	150,000	96,333	14,270	39,396	976,470	13.9%	4.0%
4	150,000	94,220	16,250	39,530	962,200	13.9%	4.1%
17	150,000	37,232	89,100	23,668	431,900	13.9%	5.4%
18	150,000	29,208	101,500	19,292	348,800	13.9%	5.5%
19	150,000	20,384	115,600	14,016	247,300	13.9%	5.7%
20	150,000	10,700	131,700	7,600	131,700	13.9%	5.8%
	$3,000,000	$1,349,200	$1,000,000	$650,800			

Schedule C

KAISER AND SON

Building–Impact on Income Assuming Sinking Fund Depreciation
10 Percent Over 20 Years

Year	Revenue (net of operating expenses)	Mortgage interest expense	Depreciation (Sinking fund -10 percent)	Net income before tax	Net book value of building at beginning of year	Before tax return on investment as percent of net book value
1	$150,000	$100,000	$17,460	$32,540	$1,000,000	3.2%
2	150,000	98,254	19,206	32,540	982,540	3.3%
3	150,000	96,333	21,126	32,540	963,333	3.4%
4	150,000	94,220	23,240	32,540	942,208	3.4%
5	150,000	91,896	25,564	32,540	918,968	3.6%
6	150,000	89,340	28,120	32,540	893,404	3.6%
7	150,000	86,528	30,932	32,540	865,284	3.8%
8	150,000	83,436	34,024	32,540	835,352	3.9%
9	150,000	80,032	37,428	32,540	800,328	4.1%
10	150,000	76,290	41,170	32,540	762,900	4.2%
11	150,000	72,174	45,286	32,540	721,730	4.5%
12	150,000	67,644	49,816	32,540	676,444	4.8%
13	150,000	62,662	54,798	32,540	626,628	5.1%
14	150,000	57,184	60,276	32,540	571,830	5.7%
15	150,000	51,156	66,304	32,540	511,554	6.4%
16	150,000	44,526	72,934	32,540	445,250	7.3%
17	150,000	37,232	80,228	32,540	373,316	8.7%
18	150,000	29,208	88,252	32,540	292,088	11.1%
19	150,000	20,384	97,076	32,540	203,836	16.0%
20	150,000	10,700	106,760	32,540	106,760	30.5%
	$3,000,000	$1,349,200	$1,000,000	$650,800		

LAUGHLIN PIPELINE LIMITED

Laughlin Pipeline Limited (LPL) is incorporated under a special Act of one Canadian province. Its common shares are privately held. LPL gathers oil from wells in a small region and transports it to a larger pipeline. In order to finance LPL, many long-term bonds were issued. Some of them were issued in Canada and others were sold in the United States. As a result of the U.S. sales of bonds LPL has had to file financial reports and statements with the Securities and Exchange Commission (SEC) in the U.S.

Last year, 19x5, all of the remaining U.S. dollar bonds were redeemed. This year, 19x6, LPL does not propose to file its financial statements with the SEC. As a result, it is thinking of amending some of its accounting principles away from U.S. practice, which it had chosen to simplify its dealings with the SEC, towards Canadian practices.

In prior years LPL has repurchased some of its own bonds payable for two reasons:

1. A few of the many different series of bonds were issued under terms that require LPL to repurchase each year 5 percent of the face value of that series, and to hold the bonds in a sinking fund.
2. Rising interest rates have lowered market values of the bonds making them attractive to buy, particularly because LPL no longer needs to borrow to finance its operations.

Until December 31, 19x5 LPL has deferred all gains and losses on the repurchase of the bonds and amortized them on a straight-line basis over the remaining life of that particular series of bonds. For 19x6 and subsequent years it proposes to record as current operating income any gain or loss on bonds required to be purchased as a sinking fund under the terms of that issue. Other gains or losses on repurchased bonds that are not cancelled by LPL are to be deferred and amortized on a basis that provides a constant yield to maturity of that series. If bonds are to be cancelled the gain or loss would be recorded as operating income in the year in which the directors choose to cancel the bonds.

LPL believes that its situation is unlike that of most industrial firms which are frequently borrowing funds from the public. LPL needed money to build one large project that is unlikely to be replaced. In this sense the company could have a limited life.

Required:

Assume the role of an investor in LPL. Do you agree with the company's proposed accounting policy for bonds for 19x6?

LEASE-A-CAR LIMITED

Lease-A-Car Limited (LACL) has just been incorporated under federal corporate legislation. At the present time there are four owners. If the business proves to be successful, in five to 10 years attempts will be made to make it a publicly-owned company with its shares or bonds being sold through an underwriter.

Each of the four owners has invested $100,000 and a further $400,000 potential maximum bank loan has been arranged. The four owners have given personal guarantees to the bank, and have pledged forthcoming accounts and lease agreements receivable as collateral.

LACL's business operations are fairly simple. LACL has made arrangements with the major automobile manufacturers to buy automobiles at the same price as is charged to new car dealers (who, in turn, sell to the public). LACL makes a small down payment and finances most of the purchases through large finance companies. For example, a $7,000 car might be financed as follows:

Down payment (5 percent)	350
Portion to be financed	$6,650
	$7,000

LACL will then sign a note payable with the finance company for $6,650 plus interest charges of, say, $2,000 for three years. They then pay under what is called a balloon payment plan of $150 per month plus a balloon payment at the end of three years of $3,250 (i.e., $6,650 plus $2,000 less 36 months' payments of $150 per month).

LACL does not actually purchase a car until a customer has been located and has signed a three-year lease. (The company also signs one- and two-year leases, and therefore arranges different balloon payment plans with its finance company.) Using the above situation as an example, the company would ask the customer (lessee) to sign a three-year lease at, say, $220 per month. The lessee would pay for gas, oil, washing, licenses, damages, insurance and similar operating costs.

LACL expects that the balloon payment at the end of the three years will approximate the resale price of the car ($3,250). If this is correct, LACL's gross cash receipts per month are $220 and its cash outlay to the finance company is $150. Its initial cash outlay is $350 plus any costs of locating a customer (advertising, personal contract, etc.). Also it has monthly costs of receiving and paying cash, payrolls to meet and so forth. On top of all this, the company incurs expenditures to rent office and sales space, furnish the offices, advertise the opening of the company, buy office supplies and make the company operational. Very little business activity is expected in the first three to six months.

Required:
You have been appointed auditor of LACL. You have been asked by the president of LACL to recommend suitable accounting principles and policies for the company and explain the benefits and limitations of the principles which you have chosen.

LEMON CORPORATION

Lemon Corporation (LC) was incorporated under federal legislation many years ago. Its financial year ends on December 31. LC issued convertible preferred shares to the general public in 19x1. The company's main operations are the purchase, sale and lease, through wholly-owned subsidiary companies, of various real estate properties.

In 19x1 LC adopted a policy of recording most of its real estate assets at appraisal values. Generally, these appraisal values exceed cost, or cost less accumulated depreciation. When the appraisals were recorded by LC, no recognition was given to the fact that the excess of appraisal over book value (or undepreciated capital cost) was not deductible for income tax purposes. The appraisals were recorded at their "gross" values. Depreciation each year was based on the new "gross" appraised value. Deferred income taxes were recorded on the difference between depreciation based on historic cost and reported capital cost allowance times the current income tax rate.

In November 19x4, the current year, two of the appraised real estate properties were sold at a gain on appraised value of $1.3 million (a material amount). The income tax applicable to the sale amounts to $2.1 million, leaving a net loss of $800,000.

Also, in December 19x4, LC abandoned its attempt to buy the common shares of a public company. Its offer to shareholders of the public company was resisted by the public company's management. The cost of the unsuccessful attempt (mainly legal, accounting and travelling) amounts to $850,000. LC intends to make an offer for another company in 19x5.

Management of LC has asked your advice on how to report the two transactions above in its 19x4 financial statements.

Required:

A. Advise management.

B. Assume that the two transactions occurred in the third, instead of the fourth, quarter of 19x4. Would your response given in A differ for reporting in the company's third quarter report to preferred and common shareholders? Why?

LIGHTENING ELECTRONICS LIMITED

Lightening Electronics Limited (LEL) was incorporated under federal corporate legislation many years ago. Prior to incorporation it operated as a partnership with three partners. The same three people plus their families now own all of the shares of LEL. Financing of expansion that has taken place over the years has mainly been made possible through internal generation of funds plus bank borrowings, mortgages and medium term loans from government agencies.

LEL's sales volumes and profits have been dropping steadily in the past five or more years because of strong competition from imported goods, and technological improvements. The company now finds itself with several problems and unsettled issues as it prepares to finalize its financial statements for the year just ended, December 31, 19x2.

1. The company's one manufacturing plant was closed for three months because of a strike. The president has suggested that depreciation of

$300,000 not be charged during this period, and that other costs of maintaining the plant during the three months ($145,000) be deferred, and amortized over the next three years. The president contends that such a procedure is logical because supervisory personnel used the period of the strike to reorganize the main assembly lines and re-locate some equipment to make the plant more efficient. The cost of this reorganization was $160,000, including wages of the supervisors.

2. Funds generated from operations were negative in the past two years and amounted to minus $147,000 (tentatively) in 19x2 and minus $32,000 in 19x1. The company has never included a Statement of Changes in Financial Position in its financial statement package.

3. During the strike, the vice-president of personnel was fired because he sided with striking employees during a demonstration and physical fight between the strikers and security guards hired by LEL. The vice-president has filed a lawsuit for wrongful dismissal and breach of contract, and is seeking $200,000 in damages. At this point the company's lawyers want to settle out of court but have not indicated a figure that they feel is reasonable. The vice-president had two and one-half years remaining on a contract calling for $55,000 per year plus profit bonuses.

4. LEL has applied for patents on a new smoke detector that it has been working on for four years. The president has estimated that the cost of developing this patent is $260,000 and wants to capitalize the sum and retroactively adjust prior years' income for costs "wrongfully charged to expense."

5. The company is still attempting to negotiate the terms of a bank loan of $2 million which was supposed to be repaid by March 15, 19x3, but upon which no payments have been made.

6. During 19x2 LEL sold its warehouse next door to the manufacturing plant on a sale and leaseback arrangement. The president wants to include a profit on sale of $81,000, currently credited to buildings, in ordinary revenue. The lease calls for rentals over 20 years sufficient to yield the buyer 12 percent.

7. The company has held Canadian manufacturing rights to two products for 10 years that expire on April 1, 19x3. So far the U.S. holder of the rights has not renewed the agreement. In 19x2, 18 percent ($435,000) of LEL's sales revenue was from these products whereas in 19x1 it was only 11 percent ($298,000).

8. As of now (February 1, 19x3) unfilled orders amount to $202,000 at retail.

You have recently been hired as controller and vice-president of finance of LEL. You have been instructed to improve financial controls and reporting.

Required:

Assume the role of controller and vice-president of finance of LEL. What disclosure and accounting treatment, if any, would you give in the 19x2 financial statements to the above? If any of your suggested disclosure differs from the president's wishes what arguments would you make to the president to support your recommended treatment?

MARBLE INSTALLATIONS LIMITED

Marble Installations Limited (MIL) an engineering contractor and consulting firm is incorporated under federal corporate legislation. MIL engages a firm of chartered accountants annually. Generally the accountants prepare unaudited financial statements; but, audited statements are prepared whenever ownership changes occur, which usually is every three or four years generally at other than year end dates. MIL uses its unaudited annual financial statements to accompany its income tax return and also gives them to the company's bankers.

A standard ownership agreement has been drawn up by MIL. Important employees are allowed to buy shares in MIL at estimated fair value at the date of purchase. They must sell the shares back to the major owners of the company when they leave or die. Repurchase price is the original price paid plus or minus any change in book value per share during the ownership period.

A 15 percent owner has decided to leave MIL effective at the company's year end of December 31, 19x2 and the auditors have been called in to prepare audited financial statements. During the course of their audit, the following information and transactions are encountered:

1. A long-term contract was "completed" in December 19x2 but "clean-up" costs at the site usually take two to three months and could amount to $30,000 including severance pay.
2. Typically, warranty costs are expensed when incurred but for contract 2-08 an accrual of $40,000 was made in 19x2 for repairing a default which became noticeable in December 19x2.

3. In 19x2 the loss for income tax purposes is expected to well exceed the taxable income in 19x1 and taxes paid to date in 19x2 will be refunded. MIL has limited its credit to the income statement in 19x2 to the amount of 19x2 tax installments to be refunded.
4. MIL itself insures for the first $50,000 of liability and fire losses. In early January 19x3 a fire destroyed some materials that it had at a construction site. The loss is expected to be over $50,000.
5. An engineering defect was discovered in January 19x3 on contract 1-05 which extends over a three-year period from May 19x1. MIL employs the percentage of completion basis of recording income on long-term construction contracts. The defect is expected to cost $65,000 to repair and this eliminates the overall profit expected on contract 1-05.
6. During 19x2 the company decided to change its basis of recording bonuses to executives from a cash basis, paid after the year end, to an accrual basis. About $30,000 is involved.

Required:
Assume the role of auditor of MIL. How would you handle the above transactions and information? Explain thoroughly.

NATIONAL COMMUNICATIONS LIMITED

National Communications Limited is incorporated under the laws of Canada and is listed on a major stock exchange. Its shareholders have approved splitting off a portion of the company in order to comply with federal government regulations. The new company, Central T.V. Limited, will be issuing approximately 70 percent of its voting shares to the general public within six months of its incorporation, which will be well into the next fiscal year (19x5). Federal authorities have specified that a minimum of 40 percent of the voting shares of Central must be sold to the general public.

The financial vice-president of National has suggested the following procedure for accounting for the organization of Central in the current fiscal year (19x4):

1. All individual assets and liabilities are to be recorded on the opening balance sheet at fair market value.
2. Goodwill is to be recorded at a value which results in the opening equity being at a sum agreed upon by two underwriters as the fair market value of the company.
3. Any gain on the "spin-off" of Central is to be an extraordinary item in National.

Required:

A. As auditor of National, and the likely auditor of Central, would you agree with the proposals of the financial vice-president?
B. As an accounting adviser to National and Central what accounting treatment would you recommend?

NATURAL STEEL LIMITED

Natural Steel Limited (the company) is federally incorporated. Its common shares and debentures are held by the general public in Canada.

Recently, steel mills such as Natural have been seriously criticized for increasing their selling prices of steel. Management has decided to embark on a publicity campaign in order to explain to the public and their customers that the company is not making an adequate return on investment. In addition, management wishes to emphasize their approach by restating some of their major assets (inventory, plant and equipment) to replacement cost on the current year's (19x4) financial statements.

Replacement cost is being estimated by looking at such sources as Statistics Canada price indexes, suppliers' price lists and costs of competing machinery. In some instances appraisers are being asked to give valuations for specialized machinery.

Management wishes to incorporate the replacement cost of inventory and long-term assets directly into the audited financial statements for 19x4. They have asked your advice, as auditor, as to how this might be accomplished. In particular, they have asked these questions:

1. Should deferred income taxes be recorded on the difference between replacement cost and net historic cost book value?

2. Where should appraisal and "write-up" credits be recorded: (a) in income; (b) as an extraordinary item (which they do not like); or (c) in the equity section of the balance sheet?
3. What note disclosure is required in the financial statements for 19x4, and 19x5?
4. Will the audit report be of standard form with no qualifications?
5. Are there any serious income tax implications to recording at replacement cost?

They do not wish you to restrict your response to the above questions if you have other pertinent matters to call to their attention.

Required:
Assume the role of auditor of the company and provide written advice.

NORTHERN EXPLORATIONS LIMITED

Northern Explorations Limited (NEL) is listed on the Toronto Stock Exchange. Its common shares are widely held across Canada.

Last year NEL acquired all of the outstanding shares of Southern Resources Limited (SRL) for cash plus shares of NEL. At that time SRL was somewhat unproven as an exploration company but held important exploration rights and land. Purchase price of SRL was approximately $12 million. Tangible assets less liabilities were about $2 million; hence, some $10 million of the purchase price was allocated to "land and exploration rights" on the consolidated balance sheet of NEL.

Shortly after acquisition of SRL, NEL loaned SRL $2 million to further explore a particular property. When initial ore test results proved favorable a further $4 million was loaned by NEL to SRL to commence developing a new mine ("Eve Mine").

Towards the middle of the current year (19x5) metal prices dropped sharply. This caused SRL to terminate some construction contracts for developing the mine; contractors were paid $1.2 million in severance pay. Including an estimated $6 million (60 percent of the original $10 million allocated to land and exploration rights) initial cost, a total of $13.2 million had thus been invested in this new mine. SRL showed $4.9 million in unamortized preproduction costs plus $2.3 million in mine assets on its balance sheet and the remaining $6 million arose on consolidation.

Management of SRL has stated that it will re-examine the feasibility of continuing development of the new mine in 19x6, and perhaps earlier if metal prices improve. Meanwhile, it proposes to transfer the $4.9 million and $2.3 million to an account called "Investment in Eve Mine" for its year end 19x5 balance sheet presentation. The quarterly report of NEL for the third quarter of 19x5 contained a brief comment: "Further development work at Eve Mine has been discontinued pending improvement of ore and metal prices."

Required:

Assume the role of auditor of both NEL and SRL. Consider A and B below independently.

A. What recommendations to management of NEL would you make with respect to reporting the investment in Eve Mine on the audited financial statements of NEL at the end of 19x5. Why? Support your position by referring to accounting and auditing "principles."

B. Suppose NEL insisted that the $13.2 million be shown as "Investment in Eve Mine" on the year end consolidated balance sheet of NEL, without further explanation. What would you do? Why?

OLYMPICS BROTHERS

Olympics Brothers (OB) operated four logging camps in Eastern Canada prior to their recent sale to Mammoth Corporation (MC). The terms of sale were carefully spelled out in a contract that stated that the selling price was to be $2.5 million in excess of "owners'" equity reported in the audited financial statements at December 31, 19x8. The contract was made binding by transfer of a deposit from MC to OB prior to December 31, 19x8.

Preparation of the financial statements for 19x8 proved to be more difficult than in previous years because of cost and selling price fluctuations towards the end of the year. Traditionally, OB sold its logs to two different users — one of whom used the logs (saw logs) for making lumber and the other for making paper (pulp logs). Selling prices of pulp logs were generally well below prices of saw logs used for lumber.

However, because of a recession in 19x8 the reverse occurred and prices of saw logs dropped dramatically, being well below pulp log prices. In 19x5 to 19x7 roughly 70 percent of OB's logs were sold as saw logs.

Cost of OB's log inventory at December 31, 19x8 was well in excess of net realizable value. After some lengthy discussion between OB and its auditors, agreement was reached that net realizable value was to be based on January 2, 19x9 prices for pulp logs, less a selling or disposal allowance of 5 percent. The auditors' report on OB's 19x8 financial statements was dated January 20, 19x9.

The drop in log prices forced OB to curtail production at two of its logging camps in 19x8. OB has always employed unit-of-production depreciation. As a result depreciation charges in 19x8 were considerably lower than in previous years. In spite of the curtailment OB still had four month's sales in its inventory at the end of 19x8.

When OB's audited 19x8 financial statements were presented to officials of MC the latter raised serious objections to the effect on owner's equity of the depreciation charges and inventory valuation. Since the purchase-sale agreement between OB and MC provided for appointment of an arbitrator in case of disputes, the two parties have approached you to settle the disagreement over selling price of OB to MC. Your opinion is to be binding on both parties.

Required:
Write a brief, well-reasoned report giving your opinion, which is to be binding on both parties.

OSMOSIS PIPELINE LIMITED

Osmosis Pipeline Limited (OPL) was incorporated many years ago under federal corporate legislation. Its common or voting shares are owned by several oil companies. However, OPL has issued 25-year debentures to the general public and is therefore classified as a public company. It must issue quarterly reports to debenture holders according to terms included in the prospectus offering the debentures to the public. The annual reports must be in accordance with generally accepted accounting principles and be audited.

OPL buys oil from various small producers, transports it long distances by pipeline and then sells it to large refiners. About 16 years ago the company signed several 20-year contracts with each of the small producers to acquire all of their output. Purchase prices were set for the first 15 years of the contract and the last five years were to be at negotiated prices agreed to between the small producers and OPL. The contracts have a standard clause which states that an arbitrator will choose the price if the parties fail to agree. The decision of the arbitrator is binding on both parties. Different arbitrators could be appointed for each contract. Settlement prices would be retroactive to the beginning of the 16th year, January 1, 19x6.

Late in the 16th year of the contracts (19x6) it became clear that the company would not reach agreements with any of the small producers. As a result various arbitrators were appointed. It is now February 19x7 and OPL is trying to finalize its accounts for the year ended December 31, 19x6. All through 19x6 it paid the small producers at 19x5 rates, according to the terms of the original contracts.

At this point only one arbitration award has been released, and it is for an unusual case involving a very small producer. The award calls for an 8 percent increase over 19x5 prices until the end of 19x7 and a further 10 percent increase for 19x8, 19x9 and 19x10.

Selling prices of oil are set independently of purchase prices paid by OPL, although the company tries its best to match contract quantities and lengths so that it may make a fair profit. OPL is partially regulated by a government body, but the regulation involves price changes for both producers and refiners in addition to those negotiated in contracts between OPL and others.

Required:

Assume the role of financial vice-president of OPL. What accounting and reporting treatment would you recommend for the above situation for your 19x6 financial statements? Explain fully. What about 19x7?

PARK ESTATES LIMITED

Park Estates Limited (PEL) is owned by the Park brothers and their families. PEL is primarily a real estate development company which owns investment and speculative properties throughout Canada. It buys raw land and develops it over a five-to 10-year period into residential housing (single or multiple family dwellings), shopping centres, office buildings and so forth. On some occasions it will enter into real estate joint ventures with another developer, usually in a situation where it owns exactly 50 percent of the venture company.

Five years ago, PEL and an independent company, Row-Green Enterprises Limited (RGEL), incorporated a joint venture, Turner Cliffs Limited (TCL). PEL owns exactly 50 percent of the outstanding shares of TCL, with the balance being held by RGEL. They each invested $1 million at the time of incorporation and bought 1,000 acres of land in Tumbledown Cliffs, British Columbia. Since incorporation, another $1.2 million has been invested in TCL to pay property taxes and to make a few improvements to the land. A recent appraisal indicates that the value of the land is $5 million. Since the land is the only asset in TCL and liabilities are negligible, this means that TCL as a company has an appraised net worth of $5 million.

RGEL is listed on the Toronto Stock Exchange. It frequently issues debentures and shares to the public.

RGEL has offered to buy PEL's 50 percent share in TCL through an exchange of assets and liabilities. RGEL will transfer title to three properties which it presently owns (having an appraised value of $3.6 million) for the 50 percent ownership of TCL. These properties are mortgaged for $1 million and the mortgages will be assumed by PEL if the exchange occurs. PEL's management understands that RGEL bought the three properties many years ago at a cost of $700,000 or so. Nevertheless, these managers believe that the three properties are good investments and are therefore inclined to enter into the transaction with RGEL. The legal title to one property of the three, with an appraised value of $600,000, would not be transferred for another year but a contract can be prepared by lawyers now to make the arrangement legally enforceable.

Before completing the transaction they have decided to seek additional legal and accounting advice just to be certain that everything is satisfactory and meets their desires.

Required:

A. Assume the role of an accounting adviser to PEL. What advice would you give them on how they might record the transaction if they entered into it and completed it? Why?

B. If you were the auditor of PEL how would you advise the company? Same as in A, or otherwise? Why?

C. Would your answer in B differ if you were the auditor of RGEL? Must the two companies adopt the same basis of accounting for this transaction? Why?

PARKINSON LIMITED (A)

Parkinson Limited (PL) was incorporated under federal legislation many years ago. During the year just ended, December 31, 19x5, PL was privately owned.

PL has two divisions, separately incorporated. One operates in Canada and the other, a 100 percent owned subsidiary of the Canadian company, is situated in a foreign country. The two divisions do not sell or buy goods from each other and operate only within the country in which they are located. Both divisions were commenced by the owners of PL, hence no goodwill on consolidation exists and no other consolidation adjustments are necessary.

The recent net incomes, consolidated and for the Canadian division, are as follows:

	Consolidated	Canadian Division
19x5	$8,700,000	$4,700,000
19x4	8,700,000	4,490,000
19x3	8,700,000	4,350,000

The net income figures for the Canadian division are not reported in PL's consolidated financial statements. However, you were able to obtain them because PL is seeking a loan from you.

PL translates the financial position and operating results of its foreign subsidiary by using the current exchange rate method. The currency exchange rates between Canadian dollars ($) and the foreign currency (F.C.) were as follows for PL's income statement transactions:

19x5	1 F.C. =	$0.75 Canadian
19x4	1 F.C. =	0.95 Canadian
19x3	1 F.C. =	1.15 Canadian

Management of PL wants you to lend the company $10 million for a 10-year period. At this point all you know about PL is what is shown in the foregoing paragraphs.

Required:
Analyze the above information and give your tentative observations about the financial operations and possible prospects for PL.

PARKINSON LIMITED (B)

Background information on Parkinson Limited (PL) is provided in the (A) portion of the case. In the year ended December 31, 19x6 PL "went public" by issuing common shares to Canadian residents. As a result PL's management is having to prepare its first annual report to public shareholders.

You have been asked to assume the role of adviser to management concerning the type of information about PL that shareholders would like to see included in the annual financial statements for 19x6.

During 19x6 1 F.C. = $0.70 Canadian and the consolidated income of the two divisions was approximately $8.7 million. Net income of the Canadian division in 19x6 was $5,130,000.

Required:
What financial reporting would you recommend to ensure that shareholders can become aware of the circumstances that you have identified in the A and B portions of the case. Be specific, giving detailed examples.

PEACEFUL GARDENS CORPORATION

Peaceful Gardens Corporation (PGC) is incorporated under provincial legislation. It is owned by five families. PGC's principal business is the operation of cemeteries and land speculation related thereto. That is, it sells cemetery plots, but also will sell excess land, or excess locations, to builders who wish to develop a subdivision of semi- or fully-detached homes.

PGC holds several options on land which it wishes to, and must, acquire to ensure continuity and growth of the organization. In order to finance these acquisitions it will have to sell shares or debt or both to the general public within two years, the beginning of various expiry dates for the options. Whereas it has previously been able to select accounting principles suitable for a limited objective, it now has to rethink its policies.

Its business operations consist primarily of the following types of transactions:

1. It usually buys undeveloped land from farmers, and holds onto the land until it is needed for a cemetery, or an attractive offer is made by a builder. Sometimes the land is subdivided (roads, sewers, etc. are installed); generally it is not. During the period PGC holds the undeveloped land, it must pay property taxes, interest on borrowings made to buy the land, etc.

2. It sells cemetery plots and locations to individuals or families as needed, or several years in advance. These advance sales are made on two bases:
   a. full receipt of cash is requested (for which a discount is allowed).
   b. a 25 percent or more deposit plus annual payments is required; interest is charged on any unpaid balance.
   Various costs are incurred on unsold plots (maintenance, etc.).

3. Maintenance of the cemeteries. The sale price includes what PGC calls "perpetual care" — which means that grass is cut, weeds removed, border flowers kept neatly and so forth for 100 years or more, or as required under legislation affecting cemeteries. A portion of the perpetual care price must be invested to provide annual funds to maintain the plots.

Officials of the corporation have approached you for advice on the accounting principles which they should select for the company for the next several years. They wish complete reasoning in support of your advice.

Required:

A. Give the requested advice.

B. Draft *two* accounting policy notes which the company would use on its financial statements to explain the principles which you have recommended in A.

PHILIPS INVESTMENTS LIMITED

Philips Investments Limited (PIL) is, in effect, owned by one person. The company was originally incorporated to minimize or defer income tax payments for the owner. Since incorporation, activities of PIL have expanded largely as a result of the owner's ability to obtain bank loans to finance a variety of investments. The bank has asked to see audited financial statements for the year just ended January 31, 19x6.

Two of PIL's largest investments are in common shares of other companies. In neither case does PIL own more than 5 percent of the outstanding common shares of these companies. During the year just ended both of these companies offered shareholders the opportunity to receive more common shares (a stock dividend or stock reinvestment plan) in place of a cash dividend. PIL requested a stock dividend from both companies.

PIL's owner is now wondering how to account for these stock dividends in the financial statement being prepared for the company's bankers. Are the dividends income, or reductions of investment cost? The owner is concerned because there are some arguments in favor of each method:

1. Shareholders in the same companies who chose to receive cash would be treating the sums received as dividend income.

2. If PIL treats the dividends as dividend income it results in showing a net income but no corresponding liquid asset is received.

3. For income tax and other purposes PIL occasionally wants to pay cash dividends to the owner. Without the cash and sufficient retained earnings that is not possible.

Required:

A. Assume the role of accounting adviser to the owner of PIL. What do you recommend? Why?

B. Assume that you are PIL's auditor. Which method(s) would you accept for the audited financial statements? Why?

PLANET LIMITED

Planet Limited (PL) publishes daily newspapers in several cities and towns in Canada. It is a public Canadian company, traded on several Canadian stock exchanges. Net income after income tax was $5.1 million in 19x5. Management is proud of its increasing profit trends; the company has sustained a 10 to 15 percent annual net income increase for the past five years.

PL has decided to set up a company (Mag Ltd.) to produce a glossy weekly magazine. Mag will begin operations on January 1, 19x7. A great deal of thought and detailed planning has gone into the magazine including market surveys, economic studies, etc. One detailed forecast indicates that Mag will lose significant amounts of money in the first few years. To be precise, a $1 million loss is expected in the first year, $800,000 in the second and approximately break even in the third year. From then on steadily increasing profits are expected.

Mr Chester, controller of PL, phoned you, an accounting consultant, to explore some of the accounting considerations. Mr Chester explained that they viewed the "start-up losses" as part of the necessary investment in this project. "As long as we are able to keep to our budget," he said, "there could obviously be no impairment in our investment in Mag."

Mr Chester said that another accountant had told him that Mag would have to recognize the full losses in its statements. Mr Chester was genuinely upset. "But that just doesn't make economic sense," he complained. "That kind of accounting would discourage people from making sound investments like this. Accountants are becoming a bunch of technicians. Put the rule books aside for a minute and look at the economic substance of this thing."

Next day, Mr Chester phoned back with another idea. "It is those fixed costs in the Mag forecasts that are really causing our problem. Much of that is depreciation on the presses and other fixed costs. We are covering the cash outflows and variable costs right from the first and our projections indicate that ultimately we will earn a very handsome return on our fixed costs. Why can't we just write enough depreciation to reduce

Mag to a nil profit situation in the first two years? Isn't that what they do in the apartment rental industry?"

Required:

A. Assume the role of the accounting consultant. Recommend an accounting treatment which could be justified to the company's auditor and be satisfactory to officials of Mag Ltd.

B. Assume the role of auditor of PL and of Mag Ltd. What accounting and reporting treatment would you be willing to accept without having to qualify your auditor's report because one or both companies was not following GAAP?

PLEASANT MINES LIMITED

Pleasant Mines Limited (PML) is owned by a syndicate of wealthy families in British Columbia. Its operations have proven to be very unusual. Underground ore is usually mined by sinking one vertical shaft into the earth and rock to the depth of the ore, and building various horizontal passageways underground so as to bring out the ore. Often the shaft is sunk into low grade ore or rock capable of supporting tunnels and passageways without fear of cave-ins. The cost of getting a mine to economic production levels is generally capitalized as an asset and amortized over the expected tonnage of ore to be removed from the mine. Most mines, prior to attaining economic production levels, credit revenue received from sales of incidental amounts of ore removed in building a shaft and passageways to the cost of developing the mine.

In order to speed up production so as to meet contractual obligations requiring quick delivery of ore, PML chose to sink two shafts directly into the richest part of the ore body. This meant incurring a $1 million additional cost of reinforcing each shaft and underground passageways. However, as a result of this mining method they were able to withdraw $19.8 million of ore in the space occupied by the main shafts and main passageways between the shafts.

During the first year of developing the mine the following expenditures and receipts resulted:

Outlays for sinking shafts and building main passageways (includes $1 million mentioned above)	$17.2 million
Outlays for subordinate passageways to ore bodies	2.6 million
Revenues from ore found in main shafts and passageways	19.8 million
Revenues from ore extracted from subordinate passageways	2.2 million

By the end of the year the mine was obviously operating at economic production levels. The foregoing results somewhat perplexed the accountant and he is seeking your advice on how to prepare an informative income statement and balance sheet.

Required:
What advice would you give the accountant? Explain fully.

PORTAGE LIMITED

Portage Limited (PL or the company) was incorporated under federal corporations' legislation many years ago and was privately owned until January 20, 19x2. On this date approximately 75 percent of its voting shares were acquired by Main Limited (ML), a publicly-owned company. Both ML and PL are in the same line of business, manufacturing small appliances. As a result both have similar types of assets. PL's year end is November 30, ML's December 31.

Until November 30, 19x2, PL depreciated its fixed assets on a declining balance basis using the maximum rates permitted for income tax purposes (these ranged from 5 to 30 percent per annum). ML has always depreciated on a straight-line basis of 2½ percent per annum for buildings and 10 percent per annum for all other fixed assets.

ML's consolidated financial statements for the year ended December 31, 19x2 included the exact sums shown on PL's balance sheet at November 30, 19x2 and PL's revenues and expenses for the period from date of acquisition to November 30, 19x2. PL did not prepare an income statement from November 30, 19x1 to the date of acquisition by ML. ML merely included 314/365 of all revenue and expense accounts of PL in its consolidated income statement for 19x2.

Effective for the years ended in 19x3 both PL and ML have changed their auditor to a larger firm. This was done on the advice of ML's underwriters.

The chief financial officer of ML wants to alter PL's basis of recording depreciation to that used by ML, as follows:

1. Depreciation for 19x3 and subsequent years is to be based on the original cost of assets, but using ML's straight-line basis and rates.
2. If PL had always been using the straight-line basis and rates mentioned in 1, its accumulated depreciation at November 30, 19x2 would be $1.6 million lower (a material amount on PL's financial statements). This "excess" is to be transferred out of accumulated depreciation into a separate account and "amortized" on a straight-line basis against the depreciation computed in 1. The amortization would be in 19x3 plus the remaining average six-year life of the assets.

Required:
Assume the role of the new auditor of PL and ML. Comment fully on:
A. the accounting practices suggested for the years ended 19x2 and proposed for 19x3; and
B. any other accounting or reporting issues which require attention. Give supported recommendations.

PORTION MINING LIMITED

Portion Mining Limited (PML) is incorporated under federal corporate legislation and listed on the Toronto Stock Exchange. The company is in effect a holding company with a dozen mines, all of which are 100 percent owned, separately incorporated, companies. Two years ago the company closed the operations of two of the mines. According to the laws of the provinces in which the mines are located particular environmental "clean up" steps were necessary. Managers of the two separate mines made some attempts to comply with the laws, which were somewhat vague, and the clean up costs were charged to operations at that time, 19x1.

About one and one-half years after the mines were closed a public outcry caused a revision of the laws in order to make some provisions clearer so that enforcement was possible. Also "new" provisions were added. The mining companies claim that the provisions are new, the government states that they merely clarify previous intent. Both the revisions for clarity and the so-called new provisions have retroactive clauses covering the period affecting the two mines.

Three months ago a mine inspector set forth what had to be done in order to comply with the law. The company has estimated the cost of compliance as follows:

Clarifications of previous law	$2 million
"New Laws"	3 million
Total cost (a material sum to PML)	$5 million

The following conversation occurred in January 19x4 between PML's vice-president of finance (VP) and its controller (C) concerning the financial statements for the year ended December 31, 19x3:

C: "Should we accrue the $5 million estimate in 19x3's financial statements? If so, where do I show the debit?"

VP: "No. Why should we? Our profits are low enough already. We can do the clean up over the next two years. We'll expense as we pay. Who knows, the mine inspector may take pity on us and the costs could be less."

C: "But the $5 million relates to 19x3 or previous years. At least I think it does. The law became effective in 19x3 so we have to accrue in 19x3, don't we?"

VP: "The law became effective in 19x0—at least the original part which was clarified in 19x3 was effective then...Say, maybe we should charge the $5 million to 19x1, the year of closing the mines."

C: "We can't. The $3 million relates to new laws and this is a change of circumstances."

VP: "The government says the entire change in 19x3 merely clarifies the 19x0 law."

C: "They have to say that so the law can be made retroactive."

VP: "Yes, I guess so."

C:	"We can't claim the $5 million for income tax purposes in 19x3 can we?"
VP:	"I don't think so. Only when we incur it."
C:	"What do you want me to do?"
VP:	"Now you've got *me* confused."
C:	"What should I say to the auditors when they ask? They'll ask, you know."
VP:	(Sigh) "I know. Why don't you phone them now and argue for expensing on a pay-as-you-go basis. If they don't buy that, then argue for a retroactive charge to 19x1. Tell them you can't see the difference between this and an income tax reassessment. We made our best estimate in 19x1..."
C:	"The mine inspector's letters say that we tried to get around the law as it existed in 19x1, and would have been 'caught' for at least $2 million if he hadn't been short of staff to inspect..."
VP:	"Phone the auditors and argue as I said."
C:	(Sigh) "O.K."

Required:
Assume the role of auditor of PML. Give your response with full reasoning.

RADIO GAAP LIMITED

Radio GAAP Limited (RGL) operates two radio and two TV stations in Canada. The voting shares are held by four business persons. However, RGL has sold bonds to the general public across the country. As a result it requires audited annual financial statements for the creditors.

The controller of RGL is attempting to finalize the accounts and prepare financial statements for the year ended December 31, 19x2. During 19x2 approximately $100,000 at suggested retail price ("cost" $20,000) of advertising time was taken up by local newspapers, not owned by RGL, under barter arrangements. These barters involved agreements with the newspapers to trade RGL advertising in the newspaper for advertising about the newspaper on the radio. In most circumstances radio advertising about the newspaper occurred at times when no other advertisers had bought "commercial time" from the station.

The controller is uncertain how he should record these barter transactions and seeks your advice. At present no journal entries have been made.

Required:
Assume the role of auditor of RGL. What advice would you give the controller? Explain your reasoning.

REVAMP LIMITED

Revamp Limited (RL) is incorporated under federal corporate legislation. Its operations are currently being restricted by management to one Canadian province, primarily for political reasons.

RL has two divisions: (1) waste disposal services; and (2) general trucking and delivery. Both operations are heavily subsidized by either or both the provincial government and local governments. All voting and ownership shares in RL are privately held by a small group of business people.

RL's subsidies are paid quarterly by the various governments. The company prepares an unaudited quarterly report showing the volume of services provided, and within 60 days of receipt of the report by the government body concerned, RL is sent a subsidy cheque. Subsidies for waste disposal are based on a formula that weighs miles travelled by the trucks, hours worked by employees and tons of waste carried. Subsidies for general trucking are limited to specific routes, such as between one town and another in the northern part of the province.

In addition to the specific subsidies noted above, the waste disposal division is eligible for a general subsidy of 50 percent of any deficiency in "target profit." "Target profit" is defined in the agreement between RL and the provincial government in these terms: "15 percent of disposal division assets including working capital, ignoring any income taxes and the subsidy... All accounting procedures are to be in accordance with generally accepted accounting principles." Hence, if profit is only 10 percent of divisional assets, the subsidy is 2½ percent of divisional assets.

In order to receive any general subsidy RL must open its books to annual audit by a provincial government auditor.

Until recently RL has not applied for a general subsidy. However, because of several factors (a new union contract and the closing down of a mine and portions of a company town serviced by RL) the company is expecting a poor year with low profits or possibly losses. RL has been forced to borrow heavily from a local bank. Although RL has never had audited financial statements before, the banker would now like the company to have an audit.

The changed circumstances have encouraged management to rethink its accounting principles. In particular, it is considering the following for the current year:

1. Altering its depreciation policy from the declining rates that it has used for income tax purposes to straight-line depreciation.
2. Reporting subsidies in the year or period of activity (accrual basis) instead of when received.
3. Spreading management bonuses over each quarter instead of making an annual accrual.
4. Amortizing discounts on debt payable over the life of the debt instead of making a lump sum write-off to income, which it made three years ago.
5. Recognizing revenue when the service is performed instead of when cash is collected.
6. Crediting proceeds on disposals of depreciable fixed assets to accumulated depreciation instead of to fixed assets.
7. Some assets are common to both divisions and have never been shown as belonging to either. Management proposes to split them for accounting purposes using relative sales dollars in each division each year.

You have obtained the audit of RL and have been asked to give concrete advice on each of the seven proposed changes noted above. Management is expecting well-documented reasoning for each situation.

Required:
Give the requested advice.

SALTSPRAY MINES LIMITED

Saltspray Mines Limited (SML) is owned equally by two companies, both of which are listed on major Canadian stock exchanges. SML was incorporated about 15 years ago to mine copper in British Columbia, primarily at one site.

Five years ago in 19x2 SML sold the mining rights to another site to Gibralter Limited (GL). The reason for this was that the ore body was not large enough to support a permanent mill which would sort the rock from the ore concentrates. GL owned a portable concentrator mill in the vicinity and bought the mining rights because it expected profitable results. The terms of purchase and sale were:

1. No down payment; 60¢ per ton of ore mined and sold; plus annual payment of $25,000.
2. GL has the option of abandoning the property on January 1 of any year if the selling price of copper is less than costs of mining and refining.
3. The maximum amount that GL would have to pay to SML would be $2 million.
4. The agreement is silent on who would pay for costs of restoring the environment at the end of the mining operation.

By December 31, 19x2 (when SML first had to account for the sale to GL) some hindsight was available to show that GL had mined and sold 200,000 tons of copper and had paid a total of $145,000 to SML. An additional 100,000 tons had been mined but not sold. SML decided to compute a selling price of the site by discounting expected cash payments by GL at 6 percent and arrived at a figure of $1,750,000 as the sale price. Since this site was carried at a cost of $150,000 on SML's books, a gain on sale of $1.6 million was reported by SML in 19x2.

SML is currently preparing its financial statements for the year ended December 31, 19x7. A receivable from GL now stands at $802,000. In the past three years copper prices have been low and GL has not been actively mining at the site. GL expects prices to rise in the next three to nine years and has not chosen to abandon the site to SML. However, GL's financial position has weakened and it has not yet made the $25,000 annual payment to SML. GL currently has 500,000 tons of concentrated copper mined but not yet sold to a smelter that will refine it into copper because selling prices are thought to be too low. A bank has loaned GL $200,000 on the security of this unsold tonnage.

Required:

A. How would you account for the agreement with GL in SML's 19x7 financial statements? Assume the role of (i) the chief financial officer of SML, and then (ii) the auditor of SML if you feel that the auditor would have a different viewpoint and position from the chief financial officer.

B. *Without* using hindsight, how would you have accounted for the agreement with GL in SML's financial statements for 19x2?

C. Would your response in B have differed if SML was not incorporated? Why?

SCHANDL LIMITED

Schandl Limited (SL) is incorporated under federal corporate legislation and its common and preferred shares are listed on a major stock exchange. It is required under stock exchange rules to issue quarterly financial statements and to follow timely disclosure policies. Recently the company has been criticized by several groups for not giving more than "minimum disclosure"—at least these are the words chosen by the critics to describe the company's attitude.

The audit committee of SL's board of directors called a joint meeting with the senior officials of the company, and here is a partial text of the meeting:

Chairman of Audit Committee (CAC): "All of us have read the criticisms of the financial policies and practices of the company noted in the newspaper and letters to the company. The purpose of this meeting is to see whether our policies are justifiable and sensible under current circumstances. In brief, here is a listing of the major criticisms made by outsiders:

1. Our last annual report (for 19x4) was marked down by judges in the annual reports contest for:
   a. Failing to consolidate our 100 percent owned South American subsidiary and for using the equity basis of reporting.
   b. Showing our investment in a 25 percent owned company on the cost basis instead of using equity reporting.
   c. Giving the minimum disclosure on product line profitability instead of complete income statements and balance sheets for each division.

2. Some financial analysts are critical of the following:
   a. Failure to amortize goodwill that has been on our books for years.
   b. Failure to quote market values for minority investments in private companies whose shares are not traded.
   c. Our "tendency," on acquiring common share investments in other companies, of allocating large portions of the excess of purchase price over net book value to the consolidated land account.
   d. Failure to give product line breakdowns of assets, income and so forth.

Vice-President of Finance of SL (VPF): "We do not consider that any of the criticisms are valid."

CAC: "Who's the 'we' you are referring to."

VPF: "Myself."

Treasurer of SL (TSL): "Just a minute. If we are going back to the security markets every couple of years in order to sell debt or equity we can't be indifferent towards those who might want to buy our securities ....And at times we are more than indifferent; we are almost hostile. People don't like uncertainty."

VPF: "Let me take the criticisms one by one. What's the difference between consolidation and equity accounting? Who cares? In my opinion analysts are interested in cash flows, not accrual accounting; equity figures are as good as consolidation figures. We can't give full product line breakdowns because we have joint cost problems. Besides, how do you decide what constitutes a division or segment? Our subsidiaries sell to each other and this gives us transfer pricing difficulties. The old goodwill is from 30 years ago. Why should we charge income for something which is not a current operating cost? How can you quote market values when you don't know them? Our auditors certainly would not accept guesses."

CAC: "If you can't do all of the things you mention, how do you manage the company? Maybe some of the private companies should be sold..."

VPF: "How many people are complaining? Maybe our competitors are raising the queries so as to get useful information from us."

TSL: "I thought that you just finished saying that the information was *not* useful."

President of SL (PSL): "Just a minute. What we need is an impartial, outside opinion...."

Required:
What would you recommend? Why? Be specific.

SEYMOUR MANUFACTURING LIMITED

Seymour Manufacturing Limited (SML) was incorporated under federal legislation many years ago. It was owned by the Seymour family until earlier this year, 19x1, when it was sold to two brothers. The brothers hope to expand the company's operations by doubling the size of the manufacturing plant.

SML produces custom-made furniture as well as some standard lines of tables, chairs and desks for use in offices and homes. It has one manufacturing plant with an on-site "factory direct to consumer" shop. Most of its sales (approximately 90 percent last year) are to retail stores, developers and office supply retailers.

The two brothers have hired you to advise them as to the suitability of the company's financial accounting policies. On examination of the company's financial records and reports you learn the following:

1. SML has never had its financial statements audited.
2. Custom-made furniture is costed on a job order basis using actual direct material and labor plus an overhead charge based on direct labor cost. A 25 percent mark-up to cover selling, administrative and other costs is added to arrive at selling prices. The sales manager, who intends to stay with the company and its new owners, sometimes decreases the 25 percent rate to meet competition.
3. The standard lines are produced and stockpiled whenever the plant does not have sufficient custom work. In the past the inventory increase has been financed by the bank, which also lends money on SML's accounts receivable. Standard lines are costed on a process-standard cost-absorption costing basis. Sometimes this cost is reduced to net realizable value.
4. Custom-made furniture is not started into production unless a 20 percent down payment has been received from the customer. Revenue normally

is recognized on receipt of cash, which is usually 30 to 45 days after delivery. A few custom-made goods are sold "on customer approval" and may be returned within the 45 days. The 20 percent deposit is not returned to customers who send back the merchandise, unless SML has erred in the specifications. Any returned goods are sent to an auctioneer for disposal.

5. Standard lines are sold at current market rates as decided by the sales manager and customer. Revenue is recognized on shipment and is generally received in cash about 90 to 120 days later. The company has not recorded an allowance for bad debts, and writes off receivables only when they are over one year old.

6. SML obtained a forgivable loan from the government in 19x0 because the company qualifies on the basis of providing employment in an economically-depressed region. The loan is forgivable in 10 equal installments extending through to 19x9 as long as it maintains a specified size of work force. This number was maintained in 19x0 and 19x1. The company shows the full loan outstanding on its December 31, 19x1 balance sheet.

Required:
Advise the two brothers, giving full reasons.

SHAW BROTHERS BUILDERS' SUPPLY

Shaw Brothers Builders' Supply (SBBS) was formed several years ago by two brothers, C. Shaw and S. Shaw, who with their immediate families now own the company. SBBS consists of three retail stores which stock a variety of plumbing, sheet metal and hardware items.

In the year just ending, 19x2, sales are expected to be close to $1 million and net profit, ignoring any income taxes and before any year end adjustments, will be about $150,000. As a result of some unusual economic conditions, the valuation of year end inventories could present some difficulties.

1. Overall net realizable value of inventories exceeds the $700,000 cost by 15 to 20 percent. Total assets are $1.4 million.

2. The Shaw brothers expected a shortage of a line of hardware and invested $130,000 in this line about mid-year, anticipating a huge profit on sales over the following 12 to 15 months after purchase. Unfortunately, the shortage did not materialize and SBBS now has seven to eight years' sales of the line on hand. Net realizable value over the next seven to eight years is expected to exceed cost by only a few dollars.

3. S. Shaw owns 100 percent of a company, S. Shaw and Daughters (SSD), that sells some important sheet metal items to SBBS. The manufacturing equipment in SSD is old and inefficient and the goods are generally becoming too costly for SBBS to buy. For years SSD has sold to SBBS at cost plus 10 percent. Lately the average purchase price to SBBS is about $11 per unit. Seventy percent of SSD's cost is variable. Yet, SBBS now could buy the same units from others for $6 per unit and sell for a mark-up of $33\frac{1}{3}$ percent on cost. At the year end about 10 percent of inventory of SBBS will be made up of purchases from SSD.

4. SBBS has a commitment to buy $100,000 worth of hardware at an average price of $5 per item. The supplier has had a six-month strike which just ended, but the goods will arrive shortly after the year end. In order to meet customer demand SBBS had to order from an alternate supplier and after filling the orders still has $18,000 in inventory with an average price of $6 each. Replacement cost from a new supplier trying to get established in the market is $4 each with prompt delivery promised.

5. SBBS has sales commitments for $80,000 (5,000 items at $16 each) of plumbing materials. The usual supplier has gone bankrupt and it now seems as though the items will have to be acquired at a premium price of $18 each. Selling costs are $1 each.

Required:

Assume the role of an accounting adviser to SBBS, and give your recommendations on the above.

SMOOTH LIMITED

A: "An asset that still has capital cost allowance [CCA — depreciation deductible for income tax purposes] left is worth more than one with zero CCA left. Right?"

B: "So what?"

A: "Then we should acknowledge this fact in the financial statements."

B: "What fact? You mean from the company's point of view, and not from the view of somebody who wishes to buy the asset?"

A: "Right. From the company's or its owners' points of view."

B: "I don't disagree with disclosing facts, but I do disagree with your idea of disclosure."

A: "You mean using a deferred income tax account or tax allocation?"

B: "Yes. Why don't you show the asset net of its income tax effects? Or, why not disclose the unused CCA in a note to the financial statements? Maybe you could disclose by CCA categories such as 20 percent, 30 percent and so on."

A: "Accountants don't record assets net-of-tax. It's too cumbersome and probably has little information content. As far as note disclosure is concerned, this is poor disclosure because people don't read notes to financial statements."

B: "Who says that people can't read or won't read? Have you ever heard of the efficient market hypotheses?"

A: "That's a bunch of nonsense. I can think of dozens of situations where people haven't understood financial statements. The user wants an income figure. You can't derive a proper income figure if everything's in a note. It's ludicrous. Do you want analysts to start quoting a new statistic—financial statement footnotes per share? What about capital maintenance? How is the company maintaining its capital? Footnotes don't tell you!"

B: "You have a point about some users and capital maintenance. But what does this have to do with CCA?"

A: "We must recognize when CCA exceeds accounting depreciation or vice versa, and similar accounting versus income tax timing differences. These must be recorded in the income statement."

B: "Why must they?"

A: (Sigh) "I've just told you why. To help the reader."

B: "You could help the reader more by disclosure. Why don't you also discount income tax effects to present value?"

A: "Accountants don't discount, except in rare situations."

B: "Maybe this is one of those rare situations."

A: "Maybe you're just being unreasonable today."

Required:

A. Describe the different accounting treatments which could be given to accounting and income tax timing differences.

B. What accounting treatment would you recommend in the following situations, assuming that you alone could set accounting policy for Canada:

1. General purpose financial statement for a large public company.
2. An audience that could be regarded as an efficient market.
3. A small, privately-held limited company.

SOUTHERN MINES LIMITED

Southern Mines Limited (SML) is incorporated under the corporate law of British Columbia. Its common shares are traded on the Vancouver Stock Exchange, and are widely held throughout Western Canada.

SML's mine and ore concentrators are in the northern part of the province. The concentrates are shipped by rail to southern B.C. where they are refined into various metals. By agreement with a mining sales organization, the metals are sold at world metal prices as soon as they are refined. The time from shipping ore concentrates to receipt of proceeds of metal sales is roughly four months.

When the sales proceeds, less refining and selling costs, are received from the mining sales organization, cost of sales is charged and inventory is credited. Inventory costs include all direct production costs but not depreciation of mining assets, amortization of deferred development costs (i.e., costs to get the mine in a state where ore could be mined), and depletion of mining properties (i.e., costs of development not included in deferred development costs).

Deferred development costs and mining properties are amortized on a unit-of-production basis. Tons of estimated recoverable ore are used as the base for setting amortization rates; and annual amortization charges are dependent upon tons of ore mined in the year.

Mining assets are depreciated on either an annual straight-line or a declining balance method over 10 to 20 years. For example, the annual depreciation charge for mobile equipment is 10 percent straight-line of original cost.

In the year which is just ending, March 31, 19x5, the company had the first of what it believes will be a series of labor problems which might extend over the next decade. The strike this year lasted four months and greatly affected revenue and income for the company, lowering income by 50 percent. Other strikes are expected, but not for two or more years.

Officials of the company are now concerned about the accounting and reporting principles that they previously adopted and are currently using. Company officials expect metal prices to fluctuate in the near future. They are concerned about the company's ability to find new ore at different locations. For example, they wonder whether they can finance exploration costs for a new mine. They are also concerned that circumstances may have changed since their accounting principles and policies were selected. For instance, should straight-line depreciation be charged during a strike?

Required:

A. Identify the accounting and reporting principles that the company is currently using, and indicate those that appear to be appropriate and why you think so.

B. Recommend new principles in those cases where you believe they are more appropriate for SML. Provide reasons.

ST. DENIS SOFTDRINKS LIMITED

St. Denis Softdrinks Limited (SSL) is incorporated under the laws of Canada, and is listed on the Alberta Stock Exchange. SSL's prime source of revenue is from the sale of "brand name" soft drink concentrates to bottlers and canners that are independently-owned companies. These "independents" buy only from SSL.

Traditionally, SSL has recognized revenue at the point when concentrate is sold to these bottlers. One month prior to this year end (December 31, 19x6), SSL announced that in one month (January 1, 19x7) the price of concentrate would increase. As a result, the bottlers made very heavy purchases in December 19x6. Historically, December sales represent 5 percent of annual sales, but this year they were 11 percent, a material difference.

SSL's accounting staff propose to defer the profit on what they consider to be the additional sales this year, 19x6. It is the company's belief that 19x7 sales will be reduced because the bottlers are overstocked with concentrate. They feel certain about the overstocking because they claim that they have close relations with each bottler. Failing acceptance of the profit deferment by SSL's auditors, the company wishes to treat the additional sales as consignment sales, with realization to occur either in 19x7 or when the bottler sells to his customer. Failing acceptance of the two above procedures, the company wishes to record revenue on all concentrate sales at the point when independent bottlers sell to their customers.

Required:

A. Is either (i) deferment of December 19x6 sales or (ii) consignment treatment or (iii) revenue recognition for SSL at the point when the bottlers sell in accordance with generally accepted accounting principles for SSL? Explain fully.

B. Assume that you are SSL's auditor. What viewpoint would you adopt? Why?

SWITCH LIMITED

Switch Limited (SL) is incorporated under federal corporate legislation. Controlling ownership (60 percent) of the company recently changed, and this has brought forth a review of some of the company's accounting principles, policies and practices. In particular, officials of the company are considering the following:

1. Previously whenever a long-term depreciable asset was sold, the proceeds of sale would be compared to net book value and a gain or loss would be recorded. If the sum was thought to be material it would have been reported separately; otherwise, it would have been grouped with other expenses. The company now wishes to credit proceeds on sales to the fixed asset account, unless no more assets of that category exist, in which case the former procedure would be used.

2. SL's officials are examining the life of all fixed assets to see whether some should be extended for depreciation accounting purposes. In addition depreciation is to be changed from declining balance to straight-line. Both of these situations are to be handled retroactively for accounting purposes.

3. The company has renegotiated some leases that were previously of the "operating" category so that it can acquire the assets for a bargain price at the end of the leases. The vice-president of SL wants to capitalize the leases retroactively and depreciate the assets on a declining balance basis from the date they were leased.

4. Bad debts provisions previously have been reported as an expense but in future are to be deducted from revenue.

5. Sales outside of Canada have previously been reported on receipt of cash from purchasers. In future they are to be credited to sales revenue on the date of shipment. All sales outside Canada are sold in the currency of the buyer.

SL's other voting shares (40 percent) are held by several investors. The shares are not listed and trade periodically over-the-counter in Ontario and British Columbia. The new majority owners hired a new firm of public accountants to do their audit for the current year.

Required:
Assume the role of the new auditor of SL:

A. Give your recommendations on how each of the above should be handled in the company's financial statements in the year of "change."
B. Which of the treatments noted in A would require a consistency qualification in the auditors' report?

TAYLOR PIPELINE LIMITED

Taylor Pipeline Limited (TPL or the pipeline) is a public company incorporated under federal legislation. TPL operates a feeder system which gathers natural gas from several fields owned by different companies, brings it to a central location and then transports it to a large pipeline. TPL charges fees to the companies that want to transport their natural gas as follows:

1. There is a basic fee per month regardless of the quantity of gas transported.
2. In addition there is a fee per million cubic feet transported in excess of a contracted minimum quantity.

The total sum is invoiced monthly about 10 days after the month end.
TPL has been granted a monopoly by the government and, as is typical in such cases, is regulated by a government agency. From time to time, as costs rise, TPL applies to the government agency for permission to raise its fees for transporting gas. Often, but not always, the companies that are having their gas transported oppose the amount of fee increase. The agency hears arguments from all parties and chooses a fee to be charged until the next application and hearing. Usually the agency lets the pipeline apply the new rate to several prior months. For the purpose of setting fees, the agency allows the company to earn a "competitive" rate of return on its "rate base." This rate base includes the net book value of fixed assets.
TPL's main asset is the pipeline, including contracts giving it a right-of-way for 50 or more years. Operating costs are incurred for pumping stations, helicopter inspection of the feeder lines, head office expenditures and so forth. Maintenance costs are expected, but are at irregular intervals. The agency allows depreciation to be included in operating costs.
The pipeline expects throughput to increase over the next 20 years.

Additional small feeder lines will have to be built and some will have to be abandoned as supplies are exhausted. However, the main pipeline is of sufficient size that it will not have to be duplicated significantly. Engineers estimate that the main pipeline will last between 40 and 60 years.

TPL financed some of its assets by selling bonds to insurance companies. These companies and the government agency desire an annual financial report from the pipeline.

Required:

Assume the role of controller of TPL. What accounting and reporting principles or practices would you recommend for the pipeline company? Explain thoroughly indicating how your recommendations meet the company's needs.

THORNTON TRANSPORTATION LIMITED

Thornton Transportation Limited (TTL) operates a fleet of trucks which haul general freight in several regions of Canada. Over the years, TTL has acquired several other trucking companies in order to obtain their government licences to haul freight between various towns. In July 19x3 TTL acquired 40 percent ownership of Amernic Freightlines Corporation (AFC). The other 60 percent of AFC is held by another company, which is owned by a small group of businesspersons who have ownership interests in several companies in different industries. TTL is owned by the Thornton family.

AFC has been in operation for five years and has been expanding rapidly, adding freight storage buildings in several towns and small cities. These additions are primarily financed by debt and AFC follows the practice of capitalizing interest charges during the construction period. It also defers all other, what it calls, "pre-opening costs" (property taxes, insurance on partially-constructed assets, etc.) until the building is considered "open" — which AFC regards as 90 days after the building is first used. These pre-opening and capitalized interest charges are amortized on a straight-line basis over five years. TTL expenses these types of costs when they are incurred directly by it.

AFC was able to acquire many spare parts for its trucks and the equipment this year (March 19x3) by buying the assets of a bankrupt company. These assets were acquired at prices well below fair market value. In a different transaction (May 19x3) AFC bought some used trucks that have not proven to be satisfactory and have been taken out of service. Management of AFC is considering writing up the value of the spare parts and crediting this sum to the trucks that were taken out of service.

Required:

A. Assume the role of accounting adviser to AFC. What would you recommend?

B. Assume the role of accounting adviser to TTL. How would you account for the 40 percent ownership of AFC, including the transactions described, in TTL's financial statements for 19x3?

TIESSEN COFFEE CORPORATION

Tiessen Coffee Corporation (TCC) was incorporated many years ago under federal corporate legislation. It is publicly owned with its shares being traded on several stock exchanges in Canada.

During January 19x5 TCC was charged along with four other coffee importers and distributors with conspiring to fix wholesale prices of some types of coffee in Canada from 19x1 to 19x4. The company is in the process of finalizing its financial statements for the year ended December 31, 19x4 and is wondering how to handle the charge.

The action has been brought under the Combines Investigation Act. TCC denies the charges. Officials of the company know that few charges under this Act have resulted in convictions. However, costs of defending the companies that have previously been charged tend to be large.

The company's solicitors believe that the evidence against TCC is thin and that there are good technical defences against the charges. Traditionally, fines levied under the Act have not been major.

Nevertheless, one of the companies jointly charged with TCC has just issued its 19x4 financial statements. Note 7 states: "The company has been named as a defendant in an action brought under the Combines Investigation Act (Canada). The company intends to offer defences against the charge. In the opinion of the company's solicitors it is too early to predict an outcome to the charge or to estimate costs or possible fines." The auditors' report accompanying the financial statements is qualified, and states in part: "subject to the outcome of the charges described in note 7 to the financial statements,...accompanying financial statements ...present fairly..."

Required:

Assume the role of auditor of TCC.

A. What reporting would you expect that officials of TCC would want to give to the charge in their 19x4 financial statements? Be specific!

B. What would you do?

WATERHOUSE PROTECTION SYSTEMS

Waterhouse Protection Systems (WPS) operates under a franchise granted by a U.S. corporation, Protective Systems Incorporated (PSI). WPS has exclusive rights in Ontario for a line of fire alarms, sprinkler systems and burglar protection devices. WPS is owned by James and John Waterhouse. In the past they have received financial support from one of the large banks in Canada.

The franchise agreement with PSI requires that all sales and installation be conducted by WPS using approved procedures. WPS is expected to grow gradually.

PSI has been in operation for close to 10 years and has been able to improve its products every year so that they are now very well received by prospective customers. The usual terms of sale by PSI to its customers, excluding its franchisees, involve signing a five-year renewable contract. For example, $2,000 of equipment, which has a cost to PSI of about $1,200, may be installed on a customer's premises. A down payment of anywhere from $200 to $1,000 or more would be requested. The balance would be payable over the five years to yield about 18 percent interest per annum. For a small service charge per annum the contract could be extended for another five years. This entitles the customer to free servicing of the equipment including replacing faulty parts for the entire 10 years, and not just for the first five years. PSI has discovered that over 90 percent of the customers renew. Usually about 60 percent of the $2,000 selling price represents equipment, the title to which remains with PSI. The balance is labor, unrecoverable installation supplies, overhead and profit from installations.

WPS has been in operation for six months and seems to be doing well. It is handling contracts and service exactly as prescribed by PSI, and therefore expects much the same experience and success rates with customers and equipment.

The bank has requested a financial statement for the first six months of operations. WPS's owners are suddenly faced with the problem of choosing suitable accounting principles for the company. WPS's operations include: selling contracts at down payments varying from 10 percent to 60 percent; financing the balance over five years at 18 percent interest per annum to WPS; buying the equipment and supplies from PSI; installing the leased equipment; servicing and repairing the equipment; and collecting cash.

Information obtained by WPS from PSI indicates that servicing and repair costs are about 5 percent of equipment, not total contract, costs in the first five years and 15 percent in the second five years. However, service revenue in the second five-year period is in excess of PSI's servicing and repair costs. At the end of 10 years the equipment either has to be replaced or, if still in good condition, is often sold to the customer for a small sum (5 to 10 percent of costs of equipment). WPS does not give a further five-year service contract, which would extend the contract to 15 years, because the equipment is not thought to be very reliable beyond 10 years. However, it will provide some repair work at cost plus profit to WPS.

Required:
Advise the owners of WPS which accounting principles they should employ, and why.

WESTERN STEEL SUPPLY LIMITED

Your client, Western Steel Supply Limited (WSSL), is a public company listed on the Alberta Stock Exchange. WSSL has two divisions: steel warehousing and fabrication. The steel warehousing division buys large quantities of steel from Canadian and foreign steel mills and sells it in much smaller quantities to a variety of companies. The fabrication division cuts and shapes the smaller sizes of steel to customer specifications.

The warehousing division is a high risk operation. A large variety of sizes and qualities of steel must be stocked in order to supply customers. Steel mills tend to produce some sizes and types to specifications only two or three times a year and do not stock production. Thus, future needs must be anticipated fairly accurately by WSSL with orders placed so as to avoid overages and shortages. Costs of buying from overseas markets can be high mainly due to transporation costs.

The fabrication division's assets are mainly machinery. All the inventories that are needed are bought from the warehousing division as required. Customers tend to pay the current cost of steel plus processing costs for fabricated items. However, one-third of the fabrication division's sales come from jobs obtained by competitive bidding.

In recent years steel prices have been fluctuating widely. This has resulted in wide net income variations caused by: (1) selling steel below or significantly above, replacement cost; (2) overstocking prior to price declines; (3) high sales of previously written down inventory; and (4) major swings in volume, caused both by having or not having inventory when customers request it, and by general variations in country-wide economic activity. The president of WSSL believes that shareholders have not been given an adequate picture of the state of the business. He also feels that his company is being overtaxed and is paying income tax on its capital investment.

In order to better communicate with shareholders and to try to attract attention to "income tax inequities" the president wants a major revamping of financial reporting for the coming year, which ends on December 31, 19x3. He appointed a committee to make proposals to him and chose one that he believes suits his needs. The proposal has now been sent to you (in September 19x3) for official assessment on two bases:

1. Its acceptability to you, in your role as the firm's auditor.
2. Its technical soundness in terms of WSSL's needs and the president's desires.

Proposal

1. Certain replacement cost figures will be presented in conjunction with, or as a separate column alongside, the GAAP figures.

2. The standard auditors' report will contain a third paragraph, as follows:

    We have also examined the income statement and statement of changes in financial position prepared on a current cost basis. In our opinion the information and results are presented fairly in accordance with the accounting policies described in Note 2.

3. Note 2 will be worded somewhat as follows:

    "Replacement cost accounting policies. *Inventories* are reported at the lower of replacement cost or net realizable value. Any write-ups or write-downs of inventory are credited or charged to a replacement cost capital reserve account. Replacement cost of inventories is computed as follows:

    a. Items on order: at current prices quoted by suppliers.

    b. Items frequently ordered: at the estimated cost of the next order.

    c. Items not included in A or B: at the previously known replacement cost, plus 1 percent inflation per month.

    Long-lived assets are reported at the lower of discounted value of the services to be rendered by that asset or estimated replacement cost as quoted by suppliers. Whenever replacement costs are not available, estimates are made by reference to the components of the asset. Labor components are indexed by labor wage indices and material components are indexed by industrial goods indices. When appropriate indexes are not available, the implicit price deflator of the Gross National Expenditure is to be used. Any write-ups or write-downs, net of accumulated depreciation, are credited or charged to a replacement cost capital reserve account.

    Income tax expense is based on the income taxes that are currently payable, plus the discounted present value of amounts estimated to be payable in future years as a result of timing differences between income tax legislation and replacement cost figures. Inventory allowances allowed by income tax legislation are shown as reductions of income tax expense.

    Deferred income tax includes timing differences as noted in the previous paragraph plus the non tax deductible element of differences between replacement cost of long-lived assets and original cost of the asset.

    Accounts receivable less accounts payable This sum as of the beginning of each year is indexed by the Consumer Price Index. Any difference between the indexed sum and the year end balance is charged or credited to a replacement cost capital reserve account.

Debt payable is indexed by the Consumer Price Index and the differences between year end and indexed beginning-of-year figures (net of additions or redemptions) is debited to a replacement cost capital reserve account."

4. Income statement format will be:

Year ended December 31, 19x3

	Replacement cost policies	Generally accepted accounting principles
	(figures are illustrative only)	
Sales		
Cost of goods sold at replacement cost	$1,000	$1,000
Gross profit at replacement cost	700	700
Adjustment to GAAP	300	300
Gross profit		160
Selling and administrative expense, excluding depreciation		460
Cash flow	210	210
Depreciation	90	250
Income (loss) before income tax	120	90
Income tax	(30)	160
Net income (loss)	65	75
	$ (95)	$ 85

5. The other financial statements will have a similar double column design.

Required:

A. As requested by the president, evaluate the company's proposal.
B. Suggest a reasonable alternative that you feel would meet with the approval of the president. Explain the advantages and disadvantages of your proposal.

WHELAN FARMS LIMITED

Whelan Farms Limited (WFL) is owned by the Whelan family. The company is incorporated under the laws of Canada, and has an annual audit to satisfy principal creditors.

WFL has several divisions: (1) eggs; (2) dairy; (3) vegetables; and (4) other. In the year ended, 19x6, the dairy division disposed of a large portion of its land to Stawinoga Homes Limited (SHL), a large real estate developer. The terms of sale were that WFL would receive 20,000 shares of SHL (with a current market value of $10 each) plus a cash amount of $400,000 on signing the agreement. The balance of the cash amount was to be paid in accordance with the following:

1. 30 percent of the acreage would be turned over to SHL and subdivided within 12 months, and a further 20 percent cash ($800,000) would be paid to WFL at that time;
2. The remaining 70 percent of the land can be used by WFL for a rental of $1 per year, until needed by SHL. WFL can let its cows roam the land, and use a barn as long as it builds a fence costing $6,000, which becomes the property of SHL;
3. The 70 percent acreage will be subdivided by SHL not earlier than four years from now, and not later than six years hence.
4. Payments of $400,000 will be made every six months by SHL commencing five years hence until the remaining purchase/sale price is fully paid. Interest on the unpaid balance does not commence for five years and is at the rate of 10 percent per annum.

In view of the complexity and unusual nature of the transaction, the accounting adviser to the company has been advised by income taxation experts that income taxes will be assessed on this transaction on whatever basis the company chooses for its audited accounts.

Required:
A. Assume the role of an accounting adviser to WFL. How would you record the agreement with SHL in the 19x6 and 19x7 financial statements? Why?
B. Assume the role of WFL's auditor. What accounting treatments in 19x6 and 19x7 would you be willing to accept? Why?
C. Assume the role of financial vice-president of SHL. What accounting and reporting treatment would you choose for 19x6? 19x7?

WHOLESUM GRAIN TERMINAL

Lac Du Bonnet Flour Mills Limited (LFML) is a private company incorporated under the laws of Saskatchewan. LFML manufactures and distributes flour products and exports grain. The company has been approached by four other companies and has been asked to participate with them in a partnership, Wholesum Grain Terminal (WGT).

WGT would be formed to rebuild an existing grain terminal near Vancouver that is presently owned by the federal government. The federal government would grant ownership to the partnership on the condition that $100 million be spent on rebuilding the terminal. The five partners require a modern terminal in order to be able to ship large quantities of grain to China and the Soviet Union.

The partnership agreement is to be structured on a limited partnership basis with LFML having unlimited liability and the other four having limited liability as silent partners. A provincial government is willing to loan the partnership $50 million, on the condition that they have a first mortgage on the terminal, but that no guarantees are required from the five partners.

LFML is a "partner" in several incorporated joint ventures that own grain terminals. They have always accounted for these by the proportionate consolidation method. LFML would own only 20 percent of WGT but would be paid a management fee to cover the unlimited liability and general management of WGT. Overall, WGT is expected to only break even or have a minimum of net income because storage and other fees will be set on a break even basis.

LFML has several large bank loans with numerous restrictive covenants that require between a minimum and maximum debt to equity ratio. If LFML included their proportionate share of assets and liabilities of WGT on their audited balance sheet a contravention of the terms of the restrictive covenants would result. They are therefore proposing to their auditors that the investment in the WGT partnership be handled on the equity or cost basis as "Investment in WGT." If this treatment is not acceptable they will not be able to enter into the partnership agreement.

Required:
Assume the role of auditor. What response would you give to your client LFML?

ZIPAIR LIMITED

Zipair Limited (ZL) was incorporated under federal corporate legislation on January 1, 19x2 as an "amalgamation" of three small regional charter services. All three were privately owned, hence common shares of ZL are closely held by about 10 people.

ZL intends to apply to the Canadian government for licenses to operate scheduled air services between various remote regions. It has made arrangements with aircraft manufacturers and a chartered bank to provide financing for three small aircraft. ZL hopes to obtain the licenses and aircraft in late 19x3.

The following accounting problems arose in 19x2:

1. Eighteen aircraft and parts were acquired on January 1, 19x2 when the three charter companies merged to form ZL. In addition, a large quantity of spare parts was obtained. Shares in ZL were issued for the fair value of these assets. Previously two of the companies had expensed their spare parts and had depreciated aircraft at high income taxation rates.

2. ZL maintains public liability insurance on its charter operations but does not insure its aircraft against loss or damage.

3. The "amalgamating" companies still have some unsettled income tax problems which will affect asset values for income tax purposes in ZL.

4. At the end of the summer ZL decided to close down several "unprofitable" charter bases (i.e., where aircraft are located). These closures are expected to reduce revenue by 15 percent. Some aircraft previously stationed at these bases will be sold and others will be relocated.

Required:

A. Assume the role of chief financial officer of ZL. How would you record and report the above transactions or effects?

B. Assume the role of a banker. Which of the above effects or transactions would be of interest to you? Why?

Section IV:

Comparing Two Companies

COMPARING TWO COMPANIES

The cases in this book deal with particular problems or sets of problems affecting portions of one company, or one company and its affiliates. At some point instructors may desire to broaden the viewpoint of students by dealing with an entire company situation, or even better, by comparing two companies.

This section reproduces the financial statements and accompanying information for two companies, Falconbridge Nickel Mines Limited and Noranda Mines Limited. Both companies provided shareholders and interested persons with more information in their 1980 Annual Reports than we have reproduced in this section. For example, both companies prepared schedules on how inflation has affected them. Overall, though, Falconbridge provided a more extensive amount of disclosure.

When studying the financial statements of the two companies, students may wish to consider the following types of questions:

1. Even though both companies conformed their reporting to GAAP, is it possible to compare the two companies and obtain informative results? Why?
2. Are the objectives or purposes of financial accounting and reporting likely to be the same for the two companies? Why?
3. What do the financial statements of *each* of the two companies tell you? What does the financial statement package of *each* company not tell you? (For example, if you were a prospective investor what else would you want to know?) Consider each financial statement and schedule when responding. (For example, what did you learn from reviewing the Consolidated Statements of Changes in Financial Position?) Be specific in stating how particular pieces of information were judged to be useful, and for what purpose(s).

4. Are the two companies using the same or different accounting principles? List any differences. Why might the principles differ?

5. Are the two companies in the same industry? Would changes in economic conditions affect them the same way? What factors would have the greatest effects on the incomes of each? Which company faces the most risks?

6. What are the common shares (or capital stock) of each company selling for today, according to your newspaper? What might have occurred in each company since these financial statements were published to explain any change in share price?

7. What major issues would the management and corporate accountants of each company have to face when trying to capture the essence of their financial activities and position in annual financial statements and accompanying schedules?

8. What data in each report do you not understand? Explain your confusion: is it caused by terminology, phrasing, lack of knowledge, or what?

9. If you were responsible for preparing the financial statement package for each company, what would you do differently from what each company has done? Why?

Accounting Policies

BASIS OF PRESENTATION OF FINANCIAL STATEMENTS

The accompanying financial statements are prepared in accordance with accounting principles generally accepted in Canada and include, on a consolidated basis, the accounts of Noranda Mines Limited (the Company) and all of its subsidiaries. The Company together with its subsidiaries is referred to as Noranda. Noranda's interests in associated companies in which it has significant influence but not majority share ownership are accounted for on the basis of cost plus Noranda's equity in undistributed earnings of such companies since the dates of investment. The difference between the cost of the shares of associated companies and the underlying net book value of the assets is amortized over the life of the assets to which the difference is attributed. Other long-term investments are carried at cost less any amounts written off.

Certain subsidiary and associated companies own shares in the Company. The Company's pro rata interest in the carrying value of such shares has been deducted from shareholders' equity. Similarly, the Company's earnings per share have been calculated on the number of shares outstanding after reduction for such intercompany holdings.

TRANSLATION OF FOREIGN CURRENCIES

Foreign currency assets and liabilities of the Company and its subsidiaries and associated companies are translated into Canadian dollars as follows: working capital at exchange rates prevailing at the end of the period; fixed and other long-term assets, long-term debt, and depreciation provisions on the basis of historic rates of exchange; revenues and expenses (other than depreciation) at average rates during the period. Exchange translation gains and losses from these procedures are included in consolidated earnings.

INVENTORIES

Mine products are valued at estimated realizable value and other inventories at the lower of cost and market.

FUTURES CONTRACTS

From time to time, the Company owns futures contracts for the purchase or sale of metals and currencies not related to production. These contracts are not reflected in the Company's accounts, beyond the amount of deposit required, until maturity date although provision is made for any estimated unrealized losses.

DEPRECIATION AND DEVELOPMENT CHARGES

Depreciation of property, buildings and equipment and amortization of development expenditures are based on the estimated service lives of the assets calculated using the method appropriate in the circumstances, for the most part straight-line for fixed assets and unit of production for development. Assets held under capital leases are generally amortized over the terms of the respective leases and the amortization amounts are included in depreciation.

EXPLORATION

Mineral and petroleum exploration expenditures are charged against current earnings, unless they relate to properties from which a productive result is reasonably certain or on which work is in process. Gains on sale or recoveries of costs previously written off are normally credited against exploration expense.

INCOME TAXES

Under the income tax laws, some costs and revenues are included in taxable income in years which are earlier or later than those in which they are included in income reported in the

financial statements. As a result of these timing differences, income taxes currently payable normally differ from the provisions for taxes charged to earnings. The differences are shown in the consolidated balance sheet as "Taxes provided not currently payable".

Potential tax savings arising from losses incurred and investment tax credits are not reflected in earnings in the year they arise unless there is virtual certainty that they will be realized.

INTEREST

Generally interest expense is accrued and charged against income except interest that can be identified with a major capital expenditure program. Such interest is capitalized during the construction period.

START-UP COSTS

Start-up costs on major projects are deferred until the facility achieves commercial production volumes. These deferred costs are written off over a reasonable period on either a straight-line or a unit of production basis.

CAPITAL LEASES

The Company and its subsidiaries lease certain property, buildings and equipment under long-term capital leases which are recorded in the financial statements as fixed assets and long-term debt.

PENSION COSTS

The Company and its subsidiaries have various contributory pension plans which cover substantially all of the employees. Current service pension costs are charged to earnings and funded as they accrue. Past service costs are charged to earnings and funded at rates which, based on annual independent actuarial estimates, will fully provide for the obligations over periods not longer than those permitted by various regulatory bodies.

Consolidated Balance Sheet

December 31
NORANDA MINES LIMITED
(Incorporated under the laws of Ontario)

ASSETS	1980	1979
	(in thousands)	
Current assets		
Cash and short-term notes	$ 64,147	$ 10,033
Marketable investments, at cost less amounts written off (quoted market value $222,205,000; 1979 — $20,027,990)	161,280	15,370
Accounts, advances and tolls receivable	578,063	702,902
Inventories	805,992	760,488
	1,609,482	1,488,793
Investment in and advances to associated and other companies (note 2)	529,364	406,089
Fixed assets		
Property, buildings and equipment, at cost	2,622,634	2,158,502
Accumulated depreciation	(1,085,754)	(922,472)
	1,536,880	1,236,030
Other assets (note 4)	262,495	189,298
	$3,938,221	$3,320,210

Auditors' Report

To the Shareholders of
Noranda Mines Limited

We have examined the consolidated balance sheet of Noranda Mines Limited as at December 31, 1980 and the consolidated statements of earnings, retained earnings and changes in financial position for the year then ended. Our examination of the financial statements of Noranda Mines Limited and those subsidiaries and associated companies of which we are the auditors was made in accordance with generally accepted auditing standards, and accordingly included such tests and other procedures as we considered necessary in the circumstances. We have relied on the reports of the auditors who examined the financial

LIABILITIES	1980	1979
	(in thousands)	
Current liabilities		
Bank advances (note 5(c))	$ 182,197	$ 170,334
Accounts payable	476,283	459,741
Taxes payable	115,051	126,118
Debt due within one year (note 5)	14,430	45,237
	787,961	801,430
Deferred liabilities and revenues	26,929	29,897
Taxes provided not currently payable	342,834	229,189
Long-term debt (note 5)	580,477	602,483
Minority interest in subsidiaries	199,038	193,961
Shareholders' equity		
Capital stock (note 7)	772,656	512,301
Retained earnings	1,394,969	1,113,510
	2,167,625	1,625,811
Less the company's pro rata interest in its shares held by subsidiary and associated companies	(166,643)	(162,561)
	2,000,982	1,463,250
	$3,938,221	$3,320,210

(See accompanying notes)

On behalf of the Board

A. POWIS, Director

W. P. WILDER, Director

statements of certain other subsidiaries and associated companies.

In our opinion, these consolidated financial statements present fairly the financial position of the company as at December 31, 1980 and the results of its operations and the changes in its financial position for the year then ended in accordance with generally accepted accounting principles applied on a basis consistent with that of the preceding year.

Clarkson Gordon
Chartered Accountants

Toronto, Canada,
February 19, 1981.

Consolidated Statements of Earnings and Retained Earnings

For the years ended December 31

EARNINGS	1980	1979
	(in thousands)	
Revenue	$2,889,295	$2,484,690
Expense		
Cost of production	1,942,612	1,520,455
Administration, selling and general expenses	161,835	126,037
Depreciation ($113,866,000; 1979 — $89,073,000) and development charges	129,959	96,699
Exploration written off	57,261	67,612
Interest — net (including long-term debt interest of $39,373,000; 1979 — $60,758,000)	48,421	65,259
	2,340,088	1,876,062
	549,207	608,626
Income and production taxes	242,242	227,045
Minority interest in profits of subsidiaries	28,894	57,163
	271,136	284,208
Earnings before the following	278,071	324,420
Share of earnings in associated companies (note 2)	83,096	85,775
Unusual items (note 11)	47,188	(15,686)
Earnings	$ 408,355	$ 394,509
Earnings per share	$ 4.06	$ 4.70

RETAINED EARNINGS	1980	1979
	(in thousands)	
Balance, beginning of year	$1,113,510	$ 789,840
Earnings	408,355	394,509
	1,521,865	1,184,349
Dividends paid (note 7(c))	126,896	70,839
Balance, end of year	$1,394,969	$1,113,510

(See accompanying notes)

Consolidated Statement
of Changes
in Financial Position

for the years ended December 31

	1980	1979
	(in thousands)	
Working capital, beginning of year	$ 687,363	$ 281,572
Source of Funds		
Operations —		
Earnings	408,355	394,509
Depreciation and development charges	129,959	96,699
Taxes provided not currently payable	108,665	112,348
Minority interest in earnings of subsidiaries	28,894	57,163
Share of earnings less dividends of associated companies	(58,681)	(54,834)
	617,192	605,885
Working capital acquired through acquisition of Maclaren (note 3(a))	105,077	—
Working capital acquired through Mattagami merger	—	69,721
Issue of shares	12,737	139,011
Long-term financing	64,050	72,327
Fixed asset disposals	17,081	12,124
	816,137	899,068
Use of Funds		
Fixed assets	292,966	284,887
Deferred development, exploration and other expenditures	87,768	34,597
Investments and advances	45,121	(2,099)
Dividends paid to — shareholders	126,896	70,839
— minority shareholders of subsidiaries	23,736	29,203
Current maturities of long-term debt	95,729	71,710
Other	9,763	4,140
	681,979	493,277
Net increase in working capital	134,158	405,791
Working capital, end of year	$ 821,521	$ 687,363

(See accompanying notes)

Notes to Consolidated Financial Statements

December 31, 1980

1. Accounting Policies

The principal accounting policies followed by Noranda Mines Limited and its subsidiaries are summarized under the caption "Accounting Policies".

2. Investments

(a) Investments in and advances to associated and other companies consist of:

	Noranda's Direct Interest	Carrying Value December 1980	1979
		(in thousands)	
Investments carried on an equity basis —			
British Columbia Forest Products Limited	28%	$101,388	$ 91,167
Craigmont Mines, Limited	20%	3,312	3,984
Kerr Addison Mines Limited	41%	6,129	141
Northwood Forest Industries Limited	50%	77,449	66,231
Pamour Porcupine Mines, Limited	49%	8,745	6,685
Placer Development Limited	33%	75,083	53,286
Tara Exploration and Development Company Limited	46%	53,248	51,553
Frialco/Friguia Guinean Consortium	20%	17,005	18,248
Frenswick Holdings Limited investment in Zinor Holdings Limited		84,772	34,400
Associated manufacturing companies		54,213	47,802
Other companies		30,111	15,726
		511,455	389,223
Other investments and advances —			
Shares, at cost less amounts written off		13,019	13,290
Advances & other indebtedness		4,890	3,576
		$529,364	$406,089

(b) Included above are shares carried at a book value of $260,612,000 which had a quoted market value of $688,968,000 at December 31, 1980 ($213,517,000 and $471,707,000, respectively, at December 31, 1979). The latter amount does not necessarily represent the value of these holdings which may be more or less than that indicated by market quotations.

3. Significant Acquisitions

(a) Maclaren Power & Paper Company

On January 14, 1980 the company made an offer to the shareholders of Maclaren Power & Paper Company to purchase all the issued Class A and Class B shares.

The basis of the offer was 11 common shares of Noranda for each 6 Class A or Class B shares of Maclaren or, at the option of the Maclaren shareholder, $40 cash for each Maclaren share.

As a result of this offer Noranda acquired all the Class A and Class B shares of Maclaren in exchange for 10,674,794 shares of Noranda and $1,017,000 cash.

The transaction is summarized as follows:

(in thousands)

Net assets acquired:	
Non-current assets	
Fixed — including increase to fair value of $97,427	$137,539
Other	4,942
	142,481
Long-term liabilities	14,653
	127,828
Working capital — including increases to fair value of $14,726	105,077
Total consideration	$232,905

The accompanying consolidated statement of earnings includes the results of Maclaren from date of acquisition.

(b) Fraser Inc.

On February 19, 1980 the company acquired a further 666,000 shares of Fraser Inc., bringing its interest to 64%, in exchange for 527,810 shares of the company, for a total consideration of $14,713,000.

4. Other Assets

	1980	1979
	(in thousands)	
Deferred development costs	$133,053	$134,802
Deferred preproduction costs	76,000	15,600
Deferred exploration expenditures	36,502	20,982
Other deferred assets	12,250	12,650
Debenture and revenue bond discount and financing expenses, at cost less amortization	4,690	5,264
	$262,495	$189,298

The majority of the deferred preproduction costs in the current year were incurred on new mining projects.

5. Debt

(a) Long-term debt *(in thousands)*:

	Dec. 31 1980	Dec. 31 1979
(i) Bonds, debentures, notes		
Noranda Mines Limited		
9¾% notes due July 15, 1982	$ 25,000	$ 25,000
9¾% notes due November 1, 1980	—	25,398
9¾% sinking fund debentures May 1, 1994	39,860	42,300
7½% sinking fund debentures October 1, 1988	19,978	21,751
9¼% sinking fund debentures October 15, 1990	32,227	33,548
Norandex Inc.		
5½%-9¼% mortgage notes payable in monthly instalments to 1990 — ($5.275 U.S.; 1979 — $5,894 U.S.)	5,683	6,274
Noranda Aluminum Inc.		
10½% secured notes due October 1, 1995 ($71,200 U.S.; 1979 — $75,600 U.S.)	73,192	76,885
9.75% note due January 10, 1987 ($30,000 U.S.; 1979 — $30,000 U.S.)	35,229	35,229
9.75% note due 1985 ($20,000 U.S.; 1979 — $20,000 U.S.)	23,400	23,400
8% pollution control revenue bonds due April 1, 2001 — ($10,500 U.S.; 1979 — $10,500 U.S.)	10,315	10,315
Notes payable ($25,000 U.S.)	29,250	—
Brunswick Mining and Smelting Corporation Limited		
5.85% first mortgage sinking fund bonds series "A" maturing April 1, 1986	4,579	7,254
7.25% general mortgage sinking fund bonds, series "A" maturing August 15, 1987	5,207	6,040
11% general mortgage sinking fund bonds, series "B" maturing December 1, 1996	17,349	17,434
Fraser Inc.		
6⅛% sinking fund debentures due April 1, 1987 — ($5,250 U.S.; 1979 — $6,000 U.S.)	5,755	6,545
10¾% sinking fund debentures due June 1, 1992 — ($35,000 U.S.; 1979 — $35,000 U.S.)	36,023	35,612
Notes payable	56,000	42,600
Maclaren Power & Paper Company		
5¾% sinking fund debentures due 1987	9,388	—
Sundry indebtedness	21,930	9,993
	450,365	425,578

	Dec. 31 1980	Dec. 31 1979
(ii) Obligations under capital leases		
Noranda Aluminum Inc.		
5.90% Sinking fund industrial revenue bonds, maturing November 1, 1993 ($57,360 U.S.; 1979 — $64,800 U.S.)	61,518	69,824
Other leases	6,249	7,100
	67,767	76,924
(iii) Other Debt:		
Notes payable (note 5(b))	76,775	145,218
	594,907	647,720
Debt due within one year	14,430	45,237
Long-term debt	$580,477	$602,483

Maturities of long-term debt are as follows: 1982 — $52,502,000; 1983 — $43,221,000; 1984 — $67,176,000; 1985 — $42,804,000 and subsequent $374,774,000.

(b) $76,775,000 of notes payable, representing promissory notes with maturities in 1981 have been classified as long-term debt to the extent of the unconditional commitment the Company has received from its bankers for contractual term credits expiring December 31, 1984 and October 31, 1986.

(c) Shares of Frenswick Holdings Limited held by certain subsidiaries have been pledged as collateral for bank demand loans of $102,435,000 to those companies.

6. Commitments and Contingent Liabilities

(a) Approved capital projects outstanding total approximately $950,000,000 at December 31, 1980, extending over three years.

(b) The Company and its subsidiaries had guaranteed or were contingently liable for repayment of loans of associated companies to the extent of approximately $34,400,000 at December 31, 1980.

(c) As at December 31, 1980 some of Noranda's pension plans are overfunded and some are underfunded.

The total unfunded obligation is estimated at $28,000,000 and will be funded and absorbed against income through annual instalments not exceeding $2,800,000 within the time limits imposed by government regulations pertaining to pension plans. The overfunding in the other plans exceeds the unfunded amount.

(d) The Company is one of 29 original defendants described as uranium producers and located in various countries to a private antitrust action instituted in 1976 by Westinghouse Electric Corporation in the United States District Court alleging the existence of a conspiracy among such producers to restrain interstate and foreign commerce in uranium. Some of the original defendants have entered into settlement agreements with Westinghouse Electric Corporation and the action has been dismissed as against them. A second action alleging the existence of the same conspiracy was brought against the Company and seven other defendants in 1977 by the Tennessee Valley Authority.

The damages claimed by the plaintiffs are substantial. The Company is defending these actions and is taking appropriate steps to minimize any ultimate liability.

The Company and three associated companies are among fourteen defendants in an action instituted in the Superior Court of the Province of Quebec by various groups of and individual Cree Indians for damages of $8,034,000 and injunctive relief in respect of alleged environmental contamination and other interference with alleged territorial rights of the Cree Indians in Northern Quebec. The Company is defending this action and believes it has a good defence on the merits.

7. Shareholders' equity

(a) Authorized Capital:

At a meeting of shareholders held April 25, 1980 the authorized capital was increased from 120,000,000 to 150,000,000 common shares of no par value and 5,000,000 preferred shares with a par value of $100 each were created.

(b) The following table summarizes the share account:

	December 31 1980	December 31 1979
	(shares)	(shares)
Total common shares issued — beginning of year	101,536,449	75,517,632
Issued under stock option plan	125,200	216,740
Issued as stock dividends (note 7(a))	309,694	148,898
Issued under share purchase plan	99,900	—
Issued for Maclaren acquisition (note 3(a))	10,674,794	—
Issued for increased ownership of Fraser (note 3(b))	527,810	—
Issued on merger with Mattagami	—	11,653,179
Issued to Zinor	—	14,000,000
Total common shares issued — end of year	113,273,847	101,536,449
Company's pro rata interest in its shares held by subsidiary and associated companies	11,484,371	11,247,062
Net shares	101,789,476	90,289,387

The earnings per share calculations have been based on the weighted average number of shares outstanding, 100,574,355 in 1980 and 83,865,396 in 1979.

(c) During the year the following dividends were declared:

Common — $1.25/share (1979 — $.68/share)	$141,132,000	$60,790,000
Class A — (1979 $.17/share)	$ —	$11,725,000
Class B — (1979 $.17/share)		871,000
Total	141,132,000	73,386,000
Less the Company's pro rata share of dividends paid to subsidiary and associated companies	14,236,000	2,547,000
Net charge to retained earnings	$126,896,000	$70,839,000

(d) (i) During the year ended December 31, 1980, 125,200 shares were issued under the Company's stock option plan for $1,419,760 and 99,900 shares were issued under the Company's share purchase plan for $2,897,100.

   (ii) Options on 255,200 shares were granted under the provisions of the stock option plan during the year ended December 31, 1980. Options on 1,550 shares were cancelled.

   At December 31, 1980 options on 395,310 shares were outstanding exercisable at prices varying from $8.34 to $22.91 for periods up to 1986.

(e) Under the Company's share purchase plan, shares are sold to a trustee for resale to employees financed by an interest-free loan from the Company. At December 31, 1980, the amount of the loan included in accounts receivable was $5,062,000.

(f) Shareholders have the right to receive either cash dividends or the equivalent in common stock. Under an exemption order of the Ontario Securities Commission the Company may purchase for cancellation on an annual basis through the facilities of the Toronto Stock Exchange a number of common shares approximately corresponding in number to the common shares issued by it as stock dividends, subject to certain conditions. During 1980 309,694 shares were issued as stock dividends and no shares were purchased for cancellation.

8. Oil and Gas

The Company conducts oil and gas programs in which certain other parties have earned an interest. At December 31, 1980 the Company's interest was 64.58% in the Elmworth/Wapiti properties and 60.42% in other properties. Net expenditures to date by the Company on these programs are reflected on the balance sheet in the amount of $230,174,000.

9. Related Party Transactions

The following summarizes the related party transactions during the year between Noranda and associated companies.

(a) Sale of goods and services in the normal course of business amounted to $39,065,000 and gave rise to accounts receivable at December 31, 1980 of $3,306,000.

(b) Purchase of goods and services in the normal course of business amounted to $28,820,000 and gave rise to accounts payable at December 31, 1980 of $6,402,000.

(c) Certain corporate costs which were shared with associated companies amounted to $1,289,000.

(d) The Company and its subsidiary and associated companies participate in a short term investment pool. Interest charges and credits are calculated at market rates.

10. Business Segment Information

Operations and identifiable assets by industry segment are set out on page 40 in the table of Industry Segment Information.

Components of each industry segment are described in their respective sections of the annual report on pages 12 to 28.

Operations and identifiable assets by geographic segment, as well as export sales of domestic operations, are as follows:

	1980	1979
	(in thousands)	
Revenue		
Canada — domestic	$ 988,968	$ 955,818
— export	1,100,828	853,915
	2,089,796	1,809,733
U.S.A.	799,499	674,957
Total revenue	2,889,295	2,484,690
Segment operating profit		
Canada	593,827	654,574
U.S.A.	108,250	86,925
Total	702,077	741,499
Identifiable assets		
Canada	3,059,136	2,768,912
U.S.A.	653,658	525,895
	$3,712,794	$3,294,807
Cash and marketable investments	225,427	25,403
Total	$3,938,221	$3,320,210

1‼. Unusual Items

(a) Sale of Koongarra —
   During the year the company disposed of its interest in the Koongarra uranium project in Australia. The proceeds were $57,300,000 resulting in a gain on sale of $47,188,000. The sale agreement provides for a further payment of about $75,000,000 U.S., contingent upon the decision to place the property in production.

(b) The unusual items in 1979 consisted of Noranda's share of the write down by Kerr Addison Mines Limited of its investment in the Agnew Lake uranium mine, $24,528,000, and Noranda's share of the gains realized by Kerr Addison resulting from the sale of certain assets, $8,842,000, net of tax.

Industry Segment Information

	1980	1979
	(in thousands)	
Revenue (1)		
Copper operations	$ 599,524	$ 512,938
Other mining & metallurgical operations	747,296	726,300
Mining & metallurgical operations	1,346,820	1,239,238
Manufacturing operations	1,111,342	948,486
Forest products operations	619,607	457,417
	3,077,769	2,645,141
Less: inter-segment sales	(200,000)	(170,000)
Plus: investment income	11,526	9,549
Total	$2,889,295	$2,484,690

	1980	1979
Segment operating profit		
Copper operations	$ 196,550	$ 243,386
Other mining & metallurgical operations	295,521	347,620
Mining & metallurgical operations	492,071	591,006
Manufacturing operations	112,227	86,587
Forest products operations	97,779	63,906
Total Segment Operating Profit	702,077	741,499
Exploration written-off	(57,261)	(67,612)
Income and production taxes	(242,242)	(227,045)
Minority interest	(28,894)	(57,163)
Share of earnings in associated companies	83,096	70,089
Interest expense	(48,421)	(65,259)
Net earnings	$ 408,355	$ 394,509

	1980	1979
Earnings after taxes		
Copper operations	$ 121,423	$ 178,152
Other mining & metallurgical operations	178,348(3)	148,522(2)
Gross mining & metallurgical operations	299,771	326,674
Less: exploration written-off	30,023	28,707
Net mining & metallurgical operations	269,748	297,967
Manufacturing operations	84,211	67,519
Forest products operations	74,217	63,699
Earnings before borrowing cost	428,176	429,185
Less: cost of borrowing* (net of tax)	19,821	34,676
Net earnings	408,355	394,509

*net of investment income

	1980	1979
	(in thousands)	
Total assets employed		
Copper operations	$ 647,386	$ 830,830
Other mining & metallurgical operations	1,568,482	1,262,308
Total mining & metallurgical operations	2,215,868	2,093,138
Manufacturing operations	829,490	800,100
Forest products operations	767,436	506,569
Less: inter-segment receivables/payables	(100,000)	(105,000)
	3,712,794	3,294,807
Cash and marketable investments	225,427	25,403
Total	$3,938,221	$3,320,210

	1980	1979
Capital expenditures		
Copper operations	$ 38,534	$ 23,786
Other mining & metallurgical operations	183,520	186,918
Total mining & metallurgical operations	222,054	210,704
Manufacturing operations	37,959	15,693
Forest products operations	32,953	58,490
Total	292,966	284,887

	1980	1979
Depreciation and amortization		
Copper operations	$ 27,780	$ 17,821
Other mining & metallurgical operations	54,233	40,971
Total mining & metallurgical operations	82,013	58,792
Manufacturing operations	26,353	25,346
Forest product operations	21,593	12,561
Total	$ 129,959	$ 96,699

	1980	1979
Return on net assets (4)		
Mining & metallurgical operations	16.7%	20.4%
Manufacturing operations	12.4%	10.2%
Forest product operations	11.7%	16.3%
Consolidated	14.7%	17.1%

(1) Excludes Noranda's share of revenues of associated companies accounted for on an equity basis, as follows: mining operations $294,383,000, manufacturing $259,000,000, forest products $374,992,000 ($241,310,000, $207,125,000 and $343,123,000 respectively in 1979).

(2) Includes $15,686,000 net loss on unusual items.

(3) Includes $47,188,000 gain on sale of Koongarra.

(4) Earnings before borrowing cost expressed as a percentage of net assets employed (operating working capital, fixed assets at cost less accumulated depreciation, investments and other assets at book value).

FALCONBRIDGE NICKEL MINES LIMITED

FINANCIAL REPORT

ACCOUNTING RESPONSIBILITIES, PROCEDURES AND POLICIES

The Board of Directors which, among other things, is responsible for the consolidated financial statements of the Company, delegates to management the responsibility for the preparation of the statements. Responsibility for their detailed review is delegated by the Board to the Company's audit committee, which reports its findings to the Board. Each year the shareholders appoint independent auditors to examine and report directly to them on the financial statements.

In preparing the financial statements great care is taken to use the appropriate generally accepted accounting principles and estimates considered necessary by management to present fairly and consistently the consolidated financial position and the results of operations. The significant accounting policies followed by Falconbridge are summarized on pages 22 and 23.

The accounting systems employed by Falconbridge include appropriate controls, checks and balances to provide reasonable assurance that Falconbridge's assets are safeguarded from loss or unauthorized use as well as facilitating the preparation of comprehensive, timely and accurate financial information. The internal auditors, who are employed by the Company as part of management, play an integral part in the effective operation of the system. There are limits inherent in all systems of internal accounting control based on the recognition that the cost of such systems should not exceed the benefits to be derived. Falconbridge believes its systems provide the appropriate balance in this respect.

The Company's audit committee is appointed by the Board of Directors annually and is comprised of four non-management directors. The committee meets with management and with the independent auditors (who have free access to the audit committee) to satisfy itself that each group is properly discharging its responsibilities and to review the financial statements and the independent auditors' report. The audit committee reports its findings to the Board of Directors for its consideration in approving the financial statements for issuance to the shareholders.

D. E. Lewis, Q.C.
Chairman of the
Audit Committee

H. T. Berry
President and Chief
Executive Officer

J. D. Krane
Vice-President
Corporate Affairs
and Secretary

Clarkson Gordon

Chartered Accountants

P.O. Box 251
Toronto-Dominion Centre
Toronto Canada M5K 1J7
(416) 864-1234

AUDITORS' REPORT

To the Shareholders of
 Falconbridge Nickel Mines Limited:

We have examined the following financial statements of Falconbridge

Nickel Mines Limited:

> Consolidated financial position as at December 31,
> 1980 and 1979;
> Consolidated earnings, consolidated retained earnings
> and changes in consolidated financial position for
> the three years ended December 31, 1980;
> Segmented information as at December 31, 1980, 1979
> and 1978 and for the three years ended December 31,
> 1980; and
> Investment in associated and other companies as at
> December 31, 1980, 1979 and 1978 and for the three
> years ended December 31, 1980.

Our examination was made in accordance with generally accepted auditing standards,

and accordingly included such tests and other procedures as we considered necessary

in the circumstances.

In our opinion, the above-mentioned financial statements present

fairly the financial position of the company, the results of its operations and

the changes in its financial position at the dates and for the periods indicated

in accordance with accounting principles generally accepted in Canada, consistently

applied.

Toronto, Canada,
January 30, 1981.

Clarkson Gordon

Chartered Accountants

FALCONBRIDGE NICKEL MINES LIMITED

ACCOUNTING POLICIES

The consolidated financial statements of Falconbridge Nickel Mines Limited have been prepared in accordance with accounting principles generally accepted in Canada, consistently applied. In these statements, references to the Company mean only Falconbridge Nickel Mines Limited, the parent company, and references to Falconbridge include the Company, its consolidated subsidiaries and significantly influenced companies. The principal accounting policies followed by Falconbridge are summarized hereunder to facilitate review of the consolidated financial statements.

A. Basis of consolidation and accounting standards

Investments in subsidiary companies (owned more than 50%) and significantly influenced companies are accounted for as follows:

(i) Falconbridge generally consolidates the financial statements of subsidiary companies and accounts on an equity basis for those companies over which it exercises significant influence. Those companies incorporated in foreign countries in which there are significant restrictions on the transfer of funds are accounted for on a cost basis;

(ii) The differences between the interest in the book value of the net assets of consolidated subsidiaries and the carrying value of the investments are allocated to the subsidiary's asset accounts based on their fair values at the date of acquisition. For consolidated operating subsidiaries, the differences are depreciated, depleted or amortized in accordance with the Company's accounting policy for the related asset; and

(iii) For consolidation purposes foreign subsidiaries' foreign currency financial statements are restated to accord with the Company's accounting policies.

B. Translation of foreign currencies

Foreign currency transactions and account balances have been translated into Canadian dollars as follows:

(i) Current assets and current liabilities are translated into Canadian dollars at approximate quoted rates of exchange at year end;

(ii) Items included in property, plant and equipment, other assets, and non-current liabilities are translated into Canadian dollars at rates of exchange prevailing when they were acquired or incurred;

(iii) Revenues and expenses are translated into Canadian dollars at the approximate average monthly quoted rates of exchange, except that provisions for depreciation, depletion and amortization are translated at the rates used to translate the related assets;

(iv) Realized foreign exchange gains and losses are included in earnings; and

(v) On translation of foreign subsidiaries' financial statements for consolidation purposes, net unrealized gains are deferred and losses are reflected in earnings.

C. Revenue recognition

Revenues from the sale of refined metals, ferronickel, industrial minerals and metal castings are recorded in the accounts when legal title passes to the buyer.

Where metals contained in concentrate are sold under contracts, estimated revenues are recorded in the accounts during the month when the concentrates are produced. The estimated revenues may be subject to adjustment on or before final settlement, usually three or four months after the date of production, to reflect changes in metal market prices and weights and assays.

D. Valuation of inventories

Inventories are valued as follows:

(i) Metals inventories are valued at the lower of cost and net realizable value. Cost includes direct labour and material costs as well as administrative expenses at the operating properties but excludes development and preproduction expenditures and depreciation.

The cost of inventories derived from the Company's ore is determined monthly on a "last-in, first-out" basis, the cost of inventories derived from the subsidiaries' ore and other sources is determined monthly on a "first-in, first-out" basis; and

(ii) Supplies inventories are valued at the lower of average cost of acquisition and replacement cost.

E. Property, plant and equipment

Property, plant and equipment and related expenditures are accounted for as follows:

(i) All property, plant and equipment and related deferred development and preproduction expenditures are generally recorded at cost and include, where appropriate, the fair value adjustments referred to in policy A (ii) above. Investment tax credits related to plant and equipment expenditures are recorded as a reduction of the cost of the related asset;

(ii) The Company depreciates plant and equipment on a straight-line basis over the lesser of their useful lives or the lives of the producing mines to which they relate, limited to a maximum of twenty-five years. Generally the subsidiary companies calculate depreciation on a straight-line basis at rates varying from 5% to 25%. Depreciation is provided on the unit of production basis by the Company's Wesfrob Mining Division and by Corporation Falconbridge Copper for certain of its properties;

(iii) Idle plant and equipment resulting from temporary curtailments of operations continue to be depreciated. Care and maintenance costs during standby periods are expensed as incurred;

(iv) Idle plant and equipment resulting from the termination of operations are carried at estimated salvage value. Upon sale or abandonment, the cost of the fixed assets and the related accumulated depreciation are removed from the accounts and any gains or losses thereon are taken into earnings;

(v) Depletion of properties is provided over a period equal to the lesser of the estimated life of the resources recoverable from the properties, or twenty-five years;

(vi) Development and preproduction expenditures are capitalized until the commencement of commercial production. These, together with certain subsequent development expenditures which are also capitalized are amortized over periods not longer than the lives of the producing mines or properties, limited to a maximum of twenty-five years; and

(vii) Repairs and maintenance expenditures are charged to operations or development and preproduction; major betterments and replacements are capitalized.

F. Exploration

Exploration costs incurred to the date of establishing that a property has reserves which have the potential of being economically recoverable are charged against earnings; further costs are generally capitalized and then amortized as appropriate under policy E above.

G. Research and process development

Research and process development costs are charged against earnings as incurred.

H. Retirement plans

The costs of retirement plans are charged against earnings in the year required fundings are payable and include amounts for current service and amortization of past service costs. Past service costs are generally being amortized and funded over periods of up to fifteen years.

I. Income and mining taxes

All companies follow the deferral method of applying the tax allocation basis of accounting for income and mining taxes. Under this method timing differences between the period when income or expenses are reported for tax purposes and the period when they are recorded in the accounts result in deferred taxes.

Where appropriate, income taxes and withholding taxes are provided on the portion of any interest in consolidated foreign subsidiaries' undistributed net income since acquisition which it is reasonable to assume will be transferred in a taxable distribution.

J. Stock option plan

The cost to the Company of shares optioned under the plan is allocated over a period of four years from the date options are granted, according to the terms of the plan, and is measured as the amount by which the quoted market value of the Company's shares covered by the grant exceeds the option price specified under the plan throughout the period that options remain outstanding.

Stock option plan costs expensed are included in the accounts payable and accrued charges classification of the statement of financial position until the options are exercised (see note 9 C (ii), page 33).

K. Interest costs

Interest costs incurred prior to the commencement of commercial production for projects which are specifically financed by debt are capitalized. Interest costs incurred after the commencement of commercial production are expensed.

L. Earnings per common share

Earnings per common share are computed using the weighted average number of shares outstanding during the year (excluding shares held by subsidiary companies).

The preference shareholder's prior claim is deducted from earnings for purposes of this calculation.

FALCONBRIDGE NICKEL MINES LIMITED
(Incorporated under the laws of Ontario)

CONSOLIDATED FINANCIAL POSITION

ASSETS

	December 31.	
	1980	1979
	(000's)	(000's)
CURRENT:		
Cash and temporary investments, at cost which approximates market value	**$ 243,080**	$ 259,353
Accounts and metals settlements receivable (note 11, page 33)	**108,938**	155,980
Inventories of metals (note 6, page 29)	**145,384**	80,664
Inventories of supplies	**50,923**	40,369
	548,325	536,366
PROPERTY, PLANT AND EQUIPMENT (note 7, page 30):		
Producing assets —		
Plant and equipment, at cost	**663,122**	626,579
Land and properties, at cost	**24,613**	24,248
	687,735	650,827
Less accumulated depreciation and depletion	**401,547**	373,940
	286,188	276,887
Development and preproduction expenditures, at cost less amounts written off . . .	**104,323**	87,749
	390,511	364,636
Non-producing assets —		
Properties and projects, at cost less amounts written off	**115,620**	105,743
	506,131	470,379
OTHER:		
Investment in associated and other companies (Statement 5, page 42)	**100,442**	57,337
Deposits, long-term accounts receivable and other assets, at cost	**2,169**	2,533
Debt discount and issue expenses, at cost less amounts written off	**2,027**	2,756
	104,638	62,626
	$ 1,159,094	$ 1,069,371

(See notes to consolidated financial statements)

LIABILITIES AND SHAREHOLDERS' EQUITY

	December 31,	
	1980	1979
	(000's)	(000's)
CURRENT:		
Bank indebtedness	$ **5,075**	$ 4,185
Accounts payable and accrued charges (note 3, page 28)	**96,197**	72,770
Salaries and wages payable	**23,169**	17,976
Income and other taxes payable	**43,347**	46,130
Long-term debt maturing within one year	**18,418**	14,422
	186,206	155,483
LONG-TERM DEBT (notes 3 and 8, pages 28 and 31):		
Falconbridge Nickel Mines Limited	**167,678**	171,994
Falconbridge Dominicana, C. por A.	**103,850**	108,394
Other companies	**14,273**	6,782
	285,801	287,170
DEFERRED INCOME AND MINING TAXES (note 5, page 28)	**85,284**	41,973
MINORITY INTEREST (Statement 4, page 36)	**95,662**	88,824
COMMITMENTS AND CONTINGENCIES (note 11, page 33)		
PREFERENCE SHARES (note 9, page 32):		
Authorized:		
7,000,000 Preference shares of the value of $25 each (3,000,000 shares in 1979)		
Issued:		
None at December 31, 1980 (3,000,000 shares in 1979)		75,000
COMMON SHAREHOLDERS' EQUITY:		
Capital (note 9, page 32) —		
Authorized:		
25,000,000 Common shares without par value		
Issued:		
5,024,755 Common shares	**89,368**	89,368
Retained earnings (notes 8 and 10, pages 31 and 33)	**419,952**	334,732
	509,320	424,100
Less 45,483 Common shares held by subsidiary companies, at cost	**(3,179)**	(3,179)
	506,141	420,921

On behalf of the Board:

Director

Director

	$ 1,159,094	$ 1,069,371

Falconbridge Nickel Mines Ltd.   **203**

CONSOLIDATED EARNINGS AND RETAINED EARNINGS

CONSOLIDATED EARNINGS
(See additional details — Statement 4, page 36)

	Year ended December 31,		
	1980	1979	1978
	(000's)	(000's)	(000's)
Revenues	**$ 757,815**	$ 789,418	$ 508,211
Operating expenses:			
Costs of metal and other product sales	**455,793**	469,083	379,995
Selling, general and administrative	**40,114**	34,136	29,932
Development and preproduction	**23,820**	11,019	11,731
Depreciation and depletion	**30,311**	31,613	29,182
Other charges (note 14, page 34)	**15,306**		
	565,344	545,851	450,840
Operating profit	**192,471**	243,567	57,371
Interest and other income	**37,466**	21,815	8,183
	229,937	265,382	65,554
Interest and debt expenses	**39,112**	36,089	33,690
Exploration (note 12, page 33)	**28,284**	14,297	7,662
Research and process development	**6,636**	3,960	3,086
	74,032	54,346	44,438
	155,905	211,036	21,116
Income from investment in associated and other companies (Statement 5, page 42).	**9,588**	17,589	4,751
Earnings before taxes and other items	**165,493**	228,625	25,867
Income and mining taxes (note 5, page 28):			
Current	**48,227**	54,100	19,087
Deferred	**31,873**	36,898	(6,466)
	80,100	90,998	12,621
Earnings before minority interest and extraordinary item	**85,393**	137,627	13,246
Minority shareholders' interest in earnings of subsidiary			
companies (Statement 4, page 36)	**13,971**	27,066	7,428
Earnings for the year before extraordinary item	**71,422**	110,561	5,818
Extraordinary item (note 2, page 28)	**37,700**	20,000	
Earnings for the year	**109,122**	130,561	5,818
Dividend requirement on preference shares	**6,475**	5,911	4,732
Earnings applicable to common shares	**$ 102,647**	$ 124,650	$ 1,086
Earnings per common share:			
Before extraordinary item	**$13.04**	$21.01	22¢
Extraordinary item	**7.57**	4.02	
For the year	**$20.61**	$25.03	22¢

CONSOLIDATED RETAINED EARNINGS

Retained earnings, beginning of year	**$ 334,732**	$ 225,020	$ 223,934
Earnings for the year	**109,122**	130,561	5,818
	443,854	355,581	229,752
Dividends:			
Common shares (per share: 1980 — $3.50; 1979 — $3.00; 1978 — Nil)	**(17,427)**	(14,938)	
Preference shares (per share: 1980 — $2.158; 1979 — $1.970;			
1978 — $1.577)	**(6,475)**	(5,911)	(4,732)
Retained earnings, end of year	**$ 419,952**	$ 334,732	$ 225,020

(See notes to consolidated financial statements)

CHANGES IN CONSOLIDATED FINANCIAL POSITION

	Year ended December 31,		
	1980	1979	1978
	(000's)	(000's)	(000's)
Sources of working capital (funds):			
Operations —			
Earnings for the year before extraordinary item	$ 71,422	$ 110,561	$ 5,818
Charges (credits) not requiring outlay of funds:			
Depreciation and depletion	30,311	31,613	29,182
Development and preproduction	23,820	11,019	11,731
Amortization of debt expenses	175	223	269
Income and mining taxes deferred	30,729	38,286	(6,466)
Minority shareholders' interest in earnings of subsidiary companies	13,971	27,066	7,428
Gains on disposal of fixed assets, net	(449)	(107)	(1,198)
Gains on disposals and write-off of investments, net	(631)	(1,666)	(245)
Interest in earnings of companies accounted for on an equity basis in excess of dividends received	(1,357)	(8,669)	(1,191)
Total from operations	167,991	208,326	45,328
Cash proceeds from disposal of investments (note 2, page 28)	9,165	6,890	381
Proceeds from disposal of fixed assets	1,561	1,962	1,859
Issue of common shares, stock options exercised (note 9, page 32)		8	360
Decrease (increase) in other non-current assets	364	189	(204)
Reclassification of long-term debt maturing within one year			7,828
	179,081	217,375	55,552
Applications of working capital:			
Redemption of preference shares	75,000		
Property, plant and equipment expenditures	50,116	34,072	29,197
Development and preproduction expenditures	40,879	24,280	13,767
Dividends paid by consolidated subsidiary companies and purchase of minority interest of $3,033,000 in 1978	7,133	4,425	4,756
Decrease in long-term debt, net	815	7,650	3,908
Dividend payments on the preference shares	6,475	5,911	4,732
Dividend payments on the common shares	17,427	14,938	
	197,845	91,276	56,360
Increase (decrease) in working capital during the year	$ (18,764)	$ 126,099	$ (808)
Changes in components of working capital:			
Increase (decrease) in current assets —			
Cash and temporary investments	$ (16,273)	$ 155,827	$ (17,761)
Accounts and metals settlements receivable	(47,042)	25,301	44,717
Inventories	75,274	3,003	(50,281)
	11,959	184,131	(23,325)
Increase (decrease) in current liabilities —			
Bank indebtedness	890	105	(6,621)
Long-term debt maturing within one year	3,996	8,584	(7,414)
Other current liabilities	25,837	49,343	(8,482)
	30,723	58,032	(22,517)
Increase (decrease) in working capital during the year	(18,764)	126,099	(808)
Working capital, beginning of year	380,883	254,784	255,592
Working capital, end of year	$ 362,119	$ 380,883	$ 254,784

(See notes to consolidated financial statements)

FALCONBRIDGE NICKEL MINES LIMITED

NOTES TO CONSOLIDATED FINANCIAL STATEMENTS

1. **Accounting policies**
   The principal accounting policies followed by Falconbridge are summarized on pages 22 and 23.

2. **Extraordinary item**
   As a result of the public offer made by The Superior Oil Company, Houston, Texas (Superior), to purchase all of the capital stock of Canadian Superior Oil Ltd. (Canadian Superior), at a price of 1.145 common shares of Superior and U.S. $25.00 cash for each share of Canadian Superior the Company received, on January 29, 1980, 336,793 shares of Superior (with a quoted market value of $59,214,000) and Cdn. $8,534,000 for its 294,143 Canadian Superior shares, which were carried in the Company's accounts at $17,465,000. The transaction resulted in a gain of $37,700,000 (net of a $12,583,000 provision for income taxes).

   The extraordinary item for 1979 of $20,000,000 reflects the reduction of deferred income taxes resulting from the carry-forward of prior years' losses.

3. **Translation of foreign currencies**
   (a) If translated into Canadian dollars at the year end rates of exchange, long-term debt as at December 31, 1980 would increase by $29,235,000 to $315,036,000 (at December 31, 1979 it would increase by $27,925,000 to $315,095,000). This change is not necessarily indicative of the amount repayable when the obligations are retired.

   (b) Net realized exchange losses on foreign currency transactions amounting to $407,000 in 1980 (1979 − gains, $1,151,000; 1978 − gains, $28,000) have been charged to earnings; net unrealized gains on translation of foreign subsidiaries' financial statements for consolidation purposes, before minority interest, amounting to $12,144,000 at December 31, 1980 (1979 − $10,582,000; 1978 − $12,729,000), have been deferred and included in accounts payable and accrued charges.

   (c) The average and year end rates of exchange for foreign currencies in which Falconbridge conducts a significant portion of its business were as follows:

	U.S. $1 = Cdn. $			Norwegian Kroner 1 = Cdn. $		
	1980	1979	1978	1980	1979	1978
Average for the year	$ 1.17	$ 1.17	$ 1.15	$ 0.24	$ 0.23	$ 0.22
At year end	1.19	1.17	1.19	0.23	0.24	0.23

4. **Retirement plans**
   The Company and certain of its subsidiaries maintain retirement plans providing retirement, death and termination benefits for substantially all salaried and hourly rated employees.

   Total pension expense for the year was $12,850,000 (1979 − $8,798,000; 1978 − $9,741,000) including past service costs of $6,317,000 (1979 − $3,238,000; 1978 − $4,584,000). Based on the most recent actuarial evaluation, the unfunded past service costs for all pension plans in effect at December 31, 1980 are estimated to amount to approximately $47,000,000 (1979 − $52,500,000; 1978 − $32,500,000) including $24,000,000 (1979 − $36,500,000; 1978 − $18,000,000) which is computed to have vested. The companies' present intention is to provide for the unfunded past service costs over periods of up to fifteen years.

5. **Income and mining taxes**
   (a) Consolidated income and mining tax expense consists of the following:

	1980 (000's)	1979 (000's)	1978 (000's)
Canadian taxes −			
Current	$ 45,844	$ 51,482	$ 18,026
Deferred	35,296	32,985	(179)
	81,140	84,467	17,847
Foreign taxes −			
Current	2,383	2,618	1,061
Deferred	(3,423)	3,913	(6,287)
	(1,040)	6,531	(5,226)
	$ 80,100	$ 90,998	$ 12,621

   (b) The provision for consolidated deferred tax expense results from timing differences between the period when income or expenses are reported for tax purposes and the period when they are recorded in the accounts. The sources and tax effect of these differences are as follows:

	1980 (000's)	1979 (000's)	1978 (000's)
Depreciation claimed for tax purposes over (under) depreciation expensed in the accounts, net	$ 9,069	$ 3,543	$ (3,072)
Exploration, preproduction and mine development costs claimed for tax purposes over (under) amounts expensed in the accounts, net	7,970	12,282	3,702
Inventories recorded in accounts on LIFO basis and on tax returns on FIFO basis	(9,229)	4,262	(4,500)
Non-capital loss	29,756	15,606	
Expenses (losses) carried forward	(2,060)	2,754	(3,618)
Other	(3,633)	(1,549)	1,022
	$ 31,873	$ 36,898	$ (6,466)

At December 31, 1980 deferred taxes on the statement of financial position amount to $85,284,000. This amount will be reflected as a component of current tax expense in subsequent years as timing differences are reversed.

(c) The difference between the amount of the reported consolidated provision for income and mining taxes and the amount computed by multiplying the earnings before taxes by the Company's statutory tax rates is as follows:

	1980				1979				1978			
	Federal and provincial income taxes (000's)	Provincial mining taxes (000's)	Foreign taxes (000's)	Total (000's)	Federal and provincial income taxes (000's)	Provincial mining taxes (000's)	Foreign taxes (000's)	Total (000's)	Federal and provincial income taxes (000's)	Provincial mining taxes (000's)	Foreign taxes (000's)	Total (000's)
Earnings before taxes	$ 162,414	$ 162,414	$ 3,079	$ 165,493	$ 198,682	$ 198,682	$ 29,943	$ 228,625	$ 38,340	$ 38,340	$ (12,473)	$ 25,867
Statutory tax rates	51%	28%*	51%		49%	29%*	49%		49%	18%*	49%	
Earnings before taxes multiplied by the statutory tax rates	$ 82,831	$ 45,476	$ 1,570		$ 97,354	$ 57,618	$ 14,672		$ 18,787	$ 6,901	$ (6,112)	
Taxes reported in accounts .	52,179	28,961	(1,040)	$ 80,100	55,756	28,711	6,531	$ 90,998	10,590	7,257	(5,226)	$ 12,621
Difference to be reconciled .	$ (30,652)	$ (16,515)	$ (2,610)		$ (41,598)	$ (28,907)	$ (8,141)		$ (8,197)	$ 356	$ 886	
Reconciliation, tax effect of —												
(1) Non-claimable expenses .	$ 2,125	$ 12,106	$ 4,778		$ 2,498	$ 14,339	$ 1,075		$ 660	$ 3,695	$ 163	
(2) Resource, depletion, processing and inventory allowances	(30,723)	(11,352)	(844)		(37,066)	(22,438)	(393)		(8,966)	(2,823)		
(3) Adjustments because of differences in companies' statutory tax rates	207	(3,241)	2,057		(739)	(5,353)	(1,395)		(765)	1,126	2,498	
(4) Increase in unrecorded deferred tax debit									2,384			
(5) Non-taxable income	(2,261)	(14,028)	(8,601)		(6,291)	(15,455)	(7,428)		(1,510)	(1,642)	(1,775)	
	$ (30,652)	$ (16,515)	$ (2,610)		$ (41,598)	$ (28,907)	$ (8,141)		$ (8,197)	$ 356	$ 886	

*Average determined from the graduated scale which ranged from 0% to 40% from January 1, 1978 to April 10, 1979 and 0% to 30% from April 11, 1979 to December 31, 1980.

(d) No taxes have been provided by the Company in respect of the earnings of its wholly-owned subsidiary, Falconbridge International Limited (Bermuda), as a result of the present intention not to transfer, to Canada, its earnings of U.S.$35,592,000 accumulated to December 31, 1980 (U.S.$20,459,000 to December 31, 1979).

(e) Falconbridge Dominicana, C. por A. (Falcondo), a subsidiary company, has received income tax assessments from the Dominican Government for the 1972 and 1973 fiscal years approximating Cdn. $5,800,000. Falcondo is presently appealing these assessments, the outcome of which management cannot reasonably predict. As a result no provision has been made by the company or in the consolidated accounts.

6. **Inventories of metals**

Consolidated metals inventories consist of the following:

	1980		1979	
	Metals in process (000's)	Finished metals (000's)	Metals in process (000's)	Finished metals (000's)
Derived from:				
Company's ore	$ 20,267	$ 50,234	$ 14,460	$ 18,168
Subsidiaries	6,990	50,532	5,593	37,922
Other sources	10,693	6,668	3,535	986
	$ 37,950	$ 107,434	$ 23,588	$ 57,076
Total inventories of metals	$ 145,384		$ 80,664	

For information on the effect of general inflation on inventories and the current cost of inventories, see page 46, ''Impact of inflation — financial reporting and changing prices.''

FALCONBRIDGE NICKEL MINES LIMITED

7. Property, plant and equipment

(a) The following table details the consolidated property, plant and equipment on a functional basis (see note 3 (b) of the notes to statement of segmented information, page 38):

	1980			1979		
	Cost (000's)	Accumulated depreciation and depletion (000's)	Net book value (000's)	Cost (000's)	Accumulated depreciation and depletion (000's)	Net book value (000's)
Property, plant and equipment:						
Producing assets —						
Plant and equipment:						
Mines, mining plants and ancillary mining assets	$ 400,409	$ 255,220	$ 145,189	$ 378,050	$ 241,144	$ 136,906
Smelter	107,963	30,644	77,319	104,633	27,383	77,250
Refinery	97,876	62,233	35,643	89,999	56,457	33,542
Townsites and other company housing	16,972	11,394	5,578	16,844	10,276	6,568
Transportation assets and facilities	10,314	9,918	396	10,150	9,771	379
Other	29,588	14,730	14,858	26,903	13,039	13,864
	663,122	384,139	278,983	626,579	358,070	268,509
Properties	22,887	17,408	5,479	22,489	15,870	6,619
Land	1,726		1,726	1,759		1,759
	24,613	17,408	7,205	24,248	15,870	8,378
	$ 687,735	$ 401,547	286,188	$ 650,827	$ 373,940	276,887
Non-producing assets			40,273			30,881
			326,461			307,768
Development and preproduction expenditures:						
Producing assets			104,323			87,749
Non-producing assets			75,347			74,862
			179,670			162,611
			$ 506,131			$ 470,379

For information on the effect of general inflation on property, plant and equipment and the current cost of property, plant and equipment, see page 46, "Impact of inflation — financial reporting and changing prices."

(b) The following assets are included under the caption "Non-producing assets":

Company and project	1980 (000's)	1979 (000's)
Falconbridge Nickel Mines Limited —		
Fraser mine (i)	$ 50,835	$ 32,171
Other projects (ii)	5,677	5,577
Corporation Falconbridge Copper —		
Corbet mine (i)		24,229
Other (ii)	231	127
Falconbridge Nikkelverk Aktieselskap —		
Process revision program (i)	9,017	672
Kiena Gold Mines Limited (i)	8,916	2,763
New Quebec Raglan Mines Limited —		
Subsidiary's Cape Smith-Wakeham Bay properties (iii)	35,185	34,031
Other subsidiary companies' projects (ii)	5,759	6,173
	$ 115,620	$ 105,743

(i) In the preproduction or construction stage; Corbet mine commenced commercial production in January, 1980.

(ii) Includes the costs related to certain projects upon which further work has been suspended pending more favourable economics. Falconbridge believes these costs will be recovered.

(iii) Exploration, development and other expenditures relating to New Quebec Raglan Mines Limited (a 68.4% owned subsidiary) and its wholly-owned subsidiary company, Raglan Quebec Mines Limited, incurred in the development of the latter company's Cape Smith-Wakeham Bay properties.

These costs have been capitalized with the intention that they will be amortized by charges against income from future mining operations. Since 1971, when underground work on the properties was suspended, studies have continued on the feasibility of alternate methods of bringing the properties into production. Profits commensurate with the risks of operating in such a remote northern location must be indicated before development to production. The exploration permits and development licences pertaining to these properties expire in 1982 and the Company believes that new permits will be issued.

8. Long-term debt

A. Details of long-term debt are as follows:

	1980 (000's)	1979 (000's)
(i) Falconbridge Nickel Mines Limited		
7.75% Sinking fund debentures maturing February, 1991 (a)	$ 43,750	$ 45,000
8.85% Sinking fund debentures maturing May, 1996 (U.S. $47,000,000) (b)	48,028	51,094
Bank loan due December 31, 1986 (18.5% at December 31, 1980) (c)	75,900	75,900
Total (1980 net of $793,000 maturing within one year)	$ 167,678	$ 171,994

(a) The Company is required to make sinking fund payments sufficient to retire $1,250,000 principal amount of the 7.75% debentures in each of the years 1981 to 1990.

(b) The Company is required to make sinking fund payments sufficient to retire U.S.$3,000,000 principal amount of the 8.85% debentures in each of the years 1982 to 1995.

(c) The bank loan is part of a line of credit of $180,000,000 extended by a Canadian bank until December 31, 1986. Interest is payable monthly at the rate of $\frac{1}{4}$ of 1% over the bank's minimum commercial lending rate.

(ii) Falconbridge Dominicana, C. por A. (Falcondo) (RD$1 equals U.S.$1)		
(a) Due to Loma Corporation (Loma)* (Payable in U.S. currency) —		
8.73% Series C demand mortgage notes	RD$ 60,950	RD$ 68,570
8.5% Series D demand subordinated notes	34,000	34,000
	94,950	102,570

* Payment will only be demanded under certain specified circumstances, the most significant being to meet payments due on notes of Loma (a U.S. financing company) issued in the same principal amounts and at the same interest rates as the above demand notes, as follows:

8.73% Series C secured sinking fund notes, due in semi-annual payments of U.S.$5,080,000 1981 to 1986 inclusive (this schedule of repayments reflects the 1978 deferment of principal repayments aggregating U.S.$15,240,000); and
8.5% Series D guaranteed sinking fund notes, due in semi-annual payments of U.S.$3,400,000 1987 to 1991 inclusive.

(b) Due to International Bank for Reconstruction and Development (IBRD) —		
7% Loans, due semi-annually to 1984, payable in various currencies	14,620	17,139
	109,570	119,709
(c) Housing —		
9.5% Mortgages on houses repayable monthly to 1993 in Dominican Republic currency	1,873	1,969
(d) Contingent monthly payment subordinated notes (Payable in U.S. currency) —		
Advances from the Company and the other sponsor under the terms of the agreement which requires the Company and the other sponsor to provide, respectively, 60% and 40% of the funds required by Falcondo to meet its cash requirements — interest rates vary from 12% to 15.5%, due not later than December 31, 1991	14,223	
(e) Other—		
Unsecured borrowings payable in U.S. funds, bearing interest at 10.5%, due in semi-annual installments to 1985	1,714	
	127,380	121,678
Less long-term debt maturing within one year	14,264	11,144
Total — As reported by Falcondo in Dominican Republic currency, translated at year-end rates of exchange	RD$ 113,116	RD$ 110,534
Total — Expressed in Canadian currency and reflecting consolidation adjustments and Falconbridge's translation policy (1980 net of $17,028,000 maturing within one year)	$ 103,850	$ 108,394
(iii) Other companies		
Various maturity dates and interest rates.		
Total (1980 net of $597,000 maturing within one year)	$ 14,273	$ 6,782

FALCONBRIDGE NICKEL MINES LIMITED

(iv) **Maturity and sinking fund requirements**

Maturity and sinking fund requirements (stated at 1980 year-end rates of exchange) for the next five years are as follows:

1981 — $18,418,000	1984 — $23,411,000
1982 — $22,782,000	1985 — $18,398,000
1983 — $23,396,000	

B. Guarantees, covenants and restrictions:

(i) Falconbridge Nickel Mines Limited (the Company) has guaranteed portions of the long-term debt and other obligations of Falconbridge Dominicana, C. por A. (Falcondo), the details of which are as follows:

(a) Loans to Falcondo amounting to RD$109,570,000 are secured by a first mortgage on the assets of the project, which have a net aggregate carrying value of RD$170,705,000 at December 31, 1980. The Company has agreed to buy all ferronickel of commercial value produced by Falcondo and is also obligated to provide 60% of the funds required by Falcondo to enable it to meet its operating costs and debt service obligations in the event receipts from the sale of ferronickel produced by Falcondo and other receipts are insufficient for that purpose. (The Company has been required since July, 1980, in accordance with the terms of the financing agreements to provide funds totalling U.S.$8,534,000, representing 60% of the total amount required by Falcondo to meet its cash requirements. The funds so provided to Falcondo are evidenced by notes, which are subordinated to all other debt instruments and can only be repaid under certain circumstances, and bear interest at rates related to the U.S. prime rate which is in effect on the date the notes are issued). The loans from Loma Corporation are covered by a specific risk insurance issued by the Overseas Private Investment Corporation.

(b) The Company has pledged all of its shareholdings in Falcondo against repayment of the Loma Series C demand mortgage notes and the IBRD loans. In addition, the Company has made a direct guarantee for repayment of 60% of the Loma Series D demand subordinated notes.

(c) In accordance with the terms of the loan agreements, funds of $1,980,000 (1979 — $3,224,000) (included with cash and temporary investments) are on deposit with the Trustee for use in paying current debt service and operating expenses of Falcondo.

(ii) During the period that the Falcondo loans are outstanding, there are certain restrictions placed on the amount and nature of borrowing that the Company may undertake. Covenants given by the Company in this respect are substantially the same (other than the restriction on the payment of dividends) as those given by the Company under its 8.85% debentures which include limitations as to:

(a) The amount of dividends which may be paid by the Company (see note 8 B (iii) below);
(b) The assumption of additional debt; and
(c) Guarantees which it may give on certain indebtedness of its subsidiary and other companies.

(iii) At December 31, 1980, the portion of retained earnings restricted under the 8.85% debenture covenants and not available for dividend payment and share repurchase was $170,905,000 (1979 — $95,905,000).

9. Capital

A. On April 15, 1980 at the Annual and a General Meeting, shareholders authorized several amendments to the Articles of the Company including:

(i) Reclassifying the authorized Class A and Class B convertible shares without par value, whether issued or unissued, as common shares without par value.

(ii) Increasing the authorized capital of the Company by the creation of —
(a) An additional 17,998,000 common shares without par value; and
(b) An additional 7,000,000 shares, designated as Preference Shares, with a par value of $25.00 each, issuable in series.

(iii) Providing that the Company may purchase any of its issued common shares.

B. Preference shares

(i) The creation of an additional 7,000,000 shares (see note 9 A above) increased the authorized preference shares from 3,000,000 to 10,000,000 at April 15, 1980.

(ii) The 3,000,000 Variable Rate Cumulative Redeemable Preference Shares, Series "A", which were issued in 1977 to a Canadian bank, were redeemed at their par value, and cancelled on December 30, 1980. The shares had a cumulative variable dividend rate calculated on a quarterly basis, equal to one-half of the bank's minimum lending rate plus 1.5%; and the dividend rate averaged 8.63% during 1980 (1979 — 7.88%; 1978 — 6.31%).

C. Common shares

(i) The common share capital as at December 31, 1979 was as follows:

Authorized:
7,001,000 Convertible shares without par value
1,000 Common shares without par value

Issued:
5,024,755* Convertible shares $89,368,000

*Includes 45,483 shares held by subsidiary companies.

(ii) In 1979, the Company reserved 200,000 unissued common shares without par value for the purpose of granting options to purchase shares of the Company to certain full time employees of the Company or a subsidiary or associated company. The price for which the shares may be optioned shall be the closing bid price for the common shares on the business day immediately preceding the granting of the option less a discount of 10%. Options are exercisable, over a period of four years, at the rate of 25% of the shares optioned times the number of periods of twelve months each which have elapsed since the date the option was granted less the aggregate number of options already exercised or surrendered. The optionee may also be given the right, at the time of exercise, to surrender the right to purchase shares under the options in return for receipt of cash equal to the excess of the fair market value of the shares over the option price thereof. No options have been granted to date.

(iii) No common shares were issued during 1980. Under the previous stock option plan, 300 common shares were issued for $7,500 in 1979; and 14,400 common shares were issued for $360,000 in 1978.

10. **Interest in investees' undistributed earnings**
Consolidated retained earnings includes the Company's share of the undistributed earnings of its (i) consolidated subsidiaries; and (ii) equity accounted for companies, which, respectively, amounted to $89,627,000 and $15,565,000 (1979 — $82,900,000 and $14,208,000 respectively; 1978 — $44,186,000 and $5,439,000 respectively).

11. **Commitments and contingencies**
(a) There are commitments outstanding at December 31, 1980 aggregating approximately $6,200,000 (December 31, 1979 — $6,700,000) in connection with capital expenditure programs.

(b) The following are under continuing study and discussion with Government officials:

(i) The construction in Canada of facilities for refining ores mined in Ontario. The Company has received, however, an exemption by the Ontario Government, until December 31, 1989, from a requirement to refine in Canada ores mined from certain properties of the Company in Ontario, such exemption being limited to the quantity of nickel-copper matte capable of producing not more than 100,000,000 pounds of refined nickel per year;

(ii) The requirement that, by December 31, 1983, the Company take such steps as are necessary to reduce emissions of sulphur dioxide from its Sudbury smelter complex so that in the aggregate they comply with the standards prescribed by the Ontario Government; and

(iii) The mounting concern of Environment Canada (an agency of the Federal Government) regarding acid rain and long range transport of pollutants.

It is presently not practicable to estimate the potential costs to Falconbridge which may arise from these items.

(c) During 1980, 1979 and 1978 a portion of accounts receivable was either sold without recourse or discounted with recourse. The cost, which was charged against earnings, amounted to $3,603,000 in 1980 (1979 — $2,062,000; 1978 — $1,705,000). At December 31, 1980 the Company has a contingent liability of U.S.$18,180,000 (1979 — U.S.$41,001,000) in respect of discounted bills of exchange drawn on its accounts receivable.

(d) The Company is committed to subscribe, proportionately with the other shareholders, to an issue of shares by Western Platinum Limited (the proceeds of which will be used to finance capital expenditures). The Company will acquire 25% of the shares issued at a cost of approximately $7,500,000.

(e) No material provision for doubtful accounts has been made and none is considered necessary.

(f) See notes 4, 5 (e) and 8 B (i), pages 28, 29 and 32, respectively, which detail other commitments and contingencies.

12. **Transactions with related companies**
Falconbridge is a member of a group of related companies. The Company's holdings in this group are described in Statement 5, page 42. Other significant holdings within the group include The Superior Oil Company's (Superior) 24% interest in Western Platinum Limited (Western Platinum) and its 100% interest in Canadian Superior Oil Ltd. (Canadian Superior). McIntyre Mines Limited (McIntyre), which holds a 36.8% interest in Falconbridge, is owned 26.7% by Superior and 26.4% by Canadian Superior.

The following significant transactions of an ongoing nature occurred between Falconbridge and other members of the group:
(a) Matte produced from Western Platinum ore is refined on a fee basis and the refined metals are marketed on an agency basis by Falconbridge. Fees and commissions totalled $7,061,000 in 1980 (1979 — $6,648,000; 1978 — $4,537,000).

(b) The Company engages in a number of mineral exploration programs with Superior and other members of the related group. The Company's participating interest in these projects ranges up to 51%, and the Company's cost is equal to its share of the overall cost.

The most significant of these ventures include:

(i) Exploration and development of the Quebrada Blanca mining claims in northern Chile pursuant to July, 1977 agreements between the Company, Superior, Canadian Superior, McIntyre and the government of Chile. The Company's 20% participation to date has been $4,670,000 of which $2,162,000 was expended in 1980 (1979 — $1,431,000; 1978 — $1,077,000);

(ii) Exploration for minerals in various African countries pursuant to an agreement between the Company and Superior. The Company's participating interest is 50% and to date $7,545,000 has been expended on these projects, of which $4,799,000 was expended in 1980 (1979 — $2,118,000; 1978 — $628,000); and

(iii) The exploration for diamonds in North America. Participation, with Superior, ranges up to 51% and to date $2,195,000 has been expended of which $1,762,000 was expended in 1980 (1979 — $433,000).

See also notes 2 and 8 B (i) (a), pages 28 and 32, for other transactions which occurred between the Company and related members of the group.

FALCONBRIDGE NICKEL MINES LIMITED

13. Earnings per common share

Earnings per common share are based on the weighted average number of common shares outstanding during each year (excluding shares held by subsidiary companies) as follows:

1980 — 4,979,272; 1979 — 4,979,184; and 1978 — 4,965,618

The preference shareholder's prior claim is deducted from earnings for purposes of this calculation.

Common shares issuable under employee stock option plans are excluded from the aforementioned weighted average number of common shares because their dilutive effect is not material in any period reported. The exercisable options outstanding at the end of each period are as follows:

1980 and 1979 — Nil; 1978 — 300

14. Other charges

Other charges, in 1980, represent the ongoing costs during the five-month shut down of Falconbridge Dominicana, C. por A.'s ferronickel production operations.

15. Compensating balances and borrowing arrangements

No company within the Falconbridge group of companies is required to maintain a compensating balance under any borrowing arrangement. Falconbridge Dominicana, C. por A. is required, under loan agreements, to keep funds on deposit with the Trustee for use in paying current debt service and other expenses (see note 8 B (i) (c), page 32).

The various borrowing arrangements, which have been established over a period of years, are as follows:

FALCONBRIDGE NICKEL MINES LIMITED

The Company has an unsecured $75,900,000 term loan from a Canadian bank (the Bank) pursuant to a line of credit of $180,000,000 extended by it to the Company. Use of this line of credit is restricted under guarantees and covenants (see note 8 B, page 32). Interest is payable at a rate of 1/4 of 1% above the Bank's minimum commercial lending rate. A fee of 1/4 of 1% will apply to any undrawn portion of the credit, payable monthly. Interest was payable at the rate of 18.5% at December 31, 1980 and averaged 14.69% during the year. The Company has an additional $40,000,000 operating line of credit with the same bank. The interest rate for this line is 1/4 of 1% above the Bank's prime lending rate. This line of credit may also be used to discount U.S. trade paper at rates prevailing at the time of discounting. There is no commitment fee on this line which may be withdrawn at the Bank's discretion.

The Company also has two $25,000,000 lines of credit with a second Canadian bank. One line of credit can be converted to U.S. dollar loans at the bank's option (exchange risk for the account of the Company). The interest rate for Canadian dollar drawings under this line is the bank's prime lending rate. For U.S. dollar borrowings the rate is the bank's U.S. base rate. The second $25,000,000 line of credit is available to discount U.S. trade paper at rates prevailing at the time of discounting. There are no commitment fees and both lines may be withdrawn at the bank's discretion.

INDUSMIN LIMITED

At December 31, 1980 Indusmin Limited (Indusmin) has an unsecured demand loan totalling $3,842,000 outstanding to a Canadian bank (the Bank) pursuant to a line of credit of $9,000,000 extended by the Bank. No commitment fee is payable for this line of credit which can be withdrawn at the Bank's discretion. Interest is payable at the Bank's prime lending rate. During the year, the largest amount of indebtedness outstanding at any one time was $4,919,000 and the average was $3,343,000. Interest was payable at 18.25% at December 31, 1980 and averaged 15.04% during the year. The aforementioned $9,000,000 line of credit may also be utilized by way of banker's acceptances. Indusmin pays 3/8 of 1% to the Bank for their acceptance. At December 31, 1980 $2,000,000 banker's acceptances were outstanding at an average 14.84%.

Fahramet Limited (Fahramet), a wholly-owned subsidiary of Indusmin, has arranged with a Canadian bank a $7,000,000 revolving credit and term loan facility, secured by hypothecation of shares of Fahramet owned by Indusmin. This loan is repayable in quarterly installments over a five year period commencing December 15, 1982. The loan gives Fahramet various currency and interest rate options. No commitment fee is payable for this loan facility. $4,000,000 of the $7,000,000 line of credit utilized in 1980 was by way of banker's acceptances. The largest amount of indebtedness outstanding at any one time in 1980 was $4,000,000 and the average for the year was $4,000,000. Fahramet pays 3/8 of 1% to the bank for their acceptance. Interest was payable at 14.84% as at December 31, 1980 and averaged 13.41% during the year.

At December 31, 1980, American Nepheline Corporation (ANC), a wholly-owned subsidiary of Indusmin, has a term loan totalling U.S.$2,300,000, from a U.S. bank, secured by hypothecation of shares of Lawson-United Feldspar and Mineral Company (a wholly-owned subsidiary of ANC). The loan is repayable in quarterly installments over a five year period and bears interest at 1% above the U.S. dollar London Inter-bank rate for Eurodollars for selected maturities. The largest amount of indebtedness outstanding at any one time in 1980 was U.S.$2,700,000 and the average for the year was U.S.$2,500,000. Interest was payable at 12.94% at December 31, 1980 and averaged 12.70% during the year.

KIENA GOLD MINES LIMITED

Kiena Gold Mines Limited (Kiena) has arranged a $25,000,000 revolving term loan, due December 31, 1986, with a Canadian bank. The loan is secured by a fixed and floating charge upon Kiena's assets. Interest on this loan is payable at 1/2 of 1% above the bank's prime lending rate. Kiena also has an option to utilize this term loan facility by way of banker's acceptances. Kiena pays 3/8 of 1% to the bank for their acceptance. The largest amount of indebtedness outstanding at any one time in 1980 was $8,100,000, the average for the term of the loan was $5,700,000 and $8,100,000 was outstanding at December 31. Interest was payable at 15.74% at December 31, 1980 and averaged 12.75% during the term of the loan. No commitment fee is payable for this term loan.

16. Reconciliation of earnings (loss) prepared in accordance with generally accepted accounting principles (GAAP) in Canada to accord with accounting principles which are generally accepted in the United States (U.S.):

	Year ended December 31,		
	1980	1979	1978
	(000's)	(000's)	(000's)
Earnings for the year, as reported	$ 109,122	$ 130,561	$ 5,818
Deduct extraordinary item, as reported (iv)	(37,700)	(20,000)	
Adjustments to accord with U.S. GAAP:			
1. Record long-term debt at exchange rate current at the end of each year (i)	(1,151)	4,050	(13,635)
2. Record gains which were deferred on translation of foreign subsidiaries' accounts for consolidation purposes (i)	1,582	(1,459)	4,947
3. Adjust income tax reassessments (ii)		3,296	(115)
4. Record capitalization of interest cost (iii)	3,324		
Earnings (loss) from continuing operations in accordance with U.S. GAAP	75,177	116,448	(2,985)
Disposal of Canadian Superior shares (iv)	37,700		
Extraordinary item under U.S. GAAP (iv)		20,000	
Earnings (loss) for the year in accordance with U.S. GAAP	$ 112,877	$ 136,448	$ (2,985)
Earnings (loss) per common share in accordance with U.S. GAAP:			
From continuing operations	$13.80	$22.20	$(1.55)
Disposal of Canadian Superior shares	7.57		
From extraordinary item		4.02	
For the year	$21.37	$26.22	$(1.55)

(i) Under Canadian GAAP Falconbridge translates long-term debt into Canadian dollars at rates of exchange prevailing when the debts were incurred and defers net unrealized gains on translation of foreign subsidiaries' financial statements for consolidation purposes. U.S. GAAP require recognition of all gains or losses resulting from translation of foreign currencies at year-end exchange rates.

(ii) Under Canadian GAAP Falconbridge gives retroactive accounting treatment to reassessments of prior years' tax. For fiscal years beginning 1978, the U.S. professional pronouncements require that the cumulative effect of the tax reassessments be given recognition in current income.

(iii) Consistent with the Canadian mining industry's policy of capitalizing all costs incurred during the preproduction stage of a project, Falconbridge capitalizes interest costs incurred prior to the commencement of commercial production for projects which are specifically financed by debt capital. Interest costs incurred after the commencement of commercial production are expensed.

    For fiscal years beginning in 1980 U.S. GAAP require the capitalization of interest costs as part of the historical cost of acquiring certain assets whether or not the assets are specifically financed by debt.

(iv) See note 2, page 28.

FALCONBRIDGE NICKEL MINES LIMITED

SEGMENTED INFORMATION *(Thousands of dollars)*

	Integrated Nickel Operations	Unallocated corporate	Wesfrob Mining Division	Corporation Falconbridge Copper	Falconbridge Dominicana, C. por A.	Indusmin Limited	Oamites Mining Company (Proprietary) Limited	Other	Consolidation adjustments	Consolidated total	Integrated Nickel Operations	Unallocated corporate	Wesfrob Mining Division
% ownership	(100%) (note 2)	(100%) (note 2)	(100%) (note 8)	(50.2%) (note 9)	(65.7%) (note 3)	(69.0%)	(74.9%)		(note 3)		(100%) (note 2)	(100%) (note 2)	(100%) (note 8)
EARNINGS (note 3):													
Revenues	$ 350,496	$ 5,443	$ 18,473	$171,428	$137,614	$ 63,945	$ 20,003	3,913	$ (13,500)	**$757,815**	$ 348,973	$ 5,937	$ 21,069
Operating expenses —													
Costs of metal and other product sales	192,906		15,673	93,897	104,214	46,536	14,121	1,560	(13,114)	**455,793**	208,589		12,829
Selling, general and administrative	19,604	6,095	2	1,767	10,332	6,830	2,387	1,284	(8,187)	**40,114**	17,919	4,130	168
Development and preproduction .	12,430		226	10,011	1,498	31	127		(503)	**23,820**	5,613		315
Depreciation and depletion	14,729	166	455	3,062	7,141	3,016	1,194	404	144	**30,311**	13,893	306	556
Other charges					15,306					**15,306**			
	239,669	6,261	16,356	108,737	138,491	56,413	17,829	3,248	(21,660)	**565,344**	246,014	4,436	13,868
Operating profit (loss)	110,827	(818)	2,117	62,691	(877)	7,532	2,174	665	8,160	**192,471**	102,959	1,501	7,201
Interest (net) and debt expenses . . .	(5,150)	(2,575)		(9,955)	13,651	1,332	(133)	(37)	4,513	**1,646**	1,571	786	
Exploration	5,127	13,560		7,569	214	75		1,739		**28,284**	2,390	6,848	586
Research and process development	6,289					347				**6,636**	3,640		
	6,266	10,985		(2,386)	13,865	1,754	(133)	1,702	4,513	**36,566**	7,601	7,634	586
Earnings (loss) before investment income and taxes	104,561	(11,803)	2,117	65,077	(14,742)	5,778	2,307	(1,037)	3,647	**155,905**	95,358	(6,133)	6,615
Investment income		9,489		101		157		23	(182)	**9,588**		17,589	
Earnings (loss) before taxes	104,561	(2,314)	2,117	65,178	(14,742)	5,935	2,307	(1,014)	3,465	**165,493**	95,358	11,456	6,615
Income and mining taxes	47,189	(2,001)	614	34,845	(5,193)	2,248	920	69	1,409	**80,100**	33,145	294	1,941
Earnings (loss) for the year before other items	$ 57,372	$ (313)	$ 1,503	$ 30,333	$ (9,549)	$ 3,687	$ 1,387	$ (1,083)	$ 2,056	**$ 85,393**	$ 62,213	$ 11,162	$ 4,674
Minority shareholders' interest in earnings (loss)				$ 15,109	$ (2,621)	$ 1,135	$ 348			**$ 13,971**			
Falconbridge's interest in above earnings (loss) after consolidation adjustments (note 3)	$ 57,372	$ (313)	$ 1,503	$ 15,152	$ (4,516)	$ 2,398	$ 909	$ (1,083)		**$ 71,422**	$ 62,213	$ 11,162	$ 4,597
FINANCIAL POSITION (note 2) —													
Working Capital (note 5):													
Current assets	$ 324,825	$ 9,548	$142,138	$ 80,835	$ 26,972	$ 8,295	$ 2,369	$ (46,657)		**$548,325**	$ 334,899	$ 12,753	
Current liabilities	136,411	3,027	35,155	28,691	13,843	4,378	3,844	(39,143)		**186,206**	106,718	2,566	
	$ 188,414	$ 6,521	$106,983	$ 52,144	$ 13,129	$ 3,917	$ (1,475)	$ (7,514)		**$362,119**	$ 228,181	$ 10,187	
Property, Plant and Equipment (notes 3 and 6):													
Producing assets, at net book value —													
Plant and equipment	$ 161,548	$ 2,922	$ 10,225	$ 78,290	$ 20,443	$ 3,655	$ 1,418	$ 482		**$278,983**	$ 153,413	$ 2,927	
Land and properties	3,546			1,839	1,273	65	886	(404)		**7,205**	3,789	42	
Development and preproduction expenditures	55,141	880	17,036	35,345	372	1,297		(5,748)		**104,323**	52,705	1,700	
	$ 220,235	$ 3,802	$ 27,261	$115,474	$ 22,088	$ 5,017	$ 2,304	$ (5,670)		**$390,511**	$ 209,907	$ 4,669	
Non-producing assets, at cost less amounts written off	$ 67,165		$ 266		$ 639		$ 54,605	$ (7,055)		**$115,620**	$ 40,059		
Long-term debt	$ 167,678			$113,763	$ 5,995		$ 8,278	$ (9,913)		**$285,801**	$ 171,994		
Minority shareholders' interest in equity				$ 63,185	$ 14,984	$ 8,639	$ 1,548	$ 7,306		**$ 95,662**			
DIVIDEND PAYMENTS TO													
— Company				$ 6,510		$ 725	$ 801	$ 17		**$ 8,053**			
— Others	$ 23,902			$ 6,461		$ 326	$ 268			**$ 30,957**	$ 20,849		
CAPITAL EXPENDITURES	$ 64,946	$ 484	$ 9,306	$ 3,234	$ 3,331	$ 1,706	$ 7,988			**$ 90,995**	$ 37,008		$ 99
MARKET VALUE OF FALCON-BRIDGE'S SHAREHOLDINGS (note 7)			$ 78,116		$ 12,090		$102,856			**$193,062**			
PRINCIPAL LOCATION OF ASSETS . . .	Ontario and Norway	British Columbia	Quebec and Ontario	Dominican Republic	Ontario, Quebec and U.S.A.	Namibia					Ontario and Norway		British Columbia
PRINCIPAL PRODUCTS	Nickel, copper and cobalt	Iron and copper	Copper, zinc and precious metals	Ferronickel	Industrial minerals and metal castings	Copper					Nickel, copper and cobalt		Iron and copper
MAJOR MARKETS FOR PRINCIPAL PRODUCTS	Europe, U.S.A. and Japan	U.S.A. and Japan	Canada and Europe	Europe, U.S.A. and Japan	Canada and U.S.A.	Europe					Europe, U.S.A. and Japan		U.S.A. and Japan

(See notes to statement of segmented information)

December 31, 1979

	Corporation Falconbridge Copper (50.2%) (note 9)	Falconbridge Dominicana, C. por A. (65.7%) (note 3)	Indusmin Limited (69.0%)	Oamites Mining Company (Proprietary) Limited (74.9%)	Other	Consolidation adjustments (note 3)	Consolidated total
	$204,818	$160,648	$56,038	$18,495	3,807	$(30,367)	$789,418
	100,665	116,344	38,859	12,222	1,279	(21,704)	469,083
	1,554	7,253	5,887	1,821	600	(5,196)	34,136
	3,973	1,486	30	105		(503)	11,019
	5,271	7,050	2,851	1,090	450	146	31,613
	111,463	132,133	47,627	15,238	2,329	(27,257)	545,851
	93,355	28,515	8,411	3,257	1,478	(3,110)	243,567
	(4,201)	13,155	1,011	(12)	(71)	2,035	14,274
	3,593	153	92		635		14,297
			354			(34)	3,960
	(608)	13,308	1,457	(12)	564	2,001	32,531
	93,963	15,207	6,954	3,269	914	(5,111)	211,036
	86		50		22	(158)	17,589
	94,049	15,207	7,004	3,269	936	(5,269)	228,625
	47,500	5,324	2,871	1,179	215	(1,471)	90,998
	$46,549	$9,883	$4,133	$2,090	721	$(3,798)	$137,627
	$23,186	$2,091	$1,274	525	$(10)		$27,066
	$23,277	$4,508	$2,714	$1,360	$730		$110,561
	$128,127	$83,027	$23,717	$8,301	1,838	$(56,296)	$536,366
	42,933	26,997	12,650	4,841	393	(41,615)	155,483
	$85,194	$56,030	$11,067	$3,460	1,445	$(14,681)	$380,883
	$3,280	$82,400	$20,112	$4,122	$1,276	979	$268,509
	862	1,891	1,303	86	851	(446)	8,378
	2,520	36,843	403	424		(6,846)	87,749
	$6,662	$121,134	$21,818	$4,632	$2,127	$(6,313)	$364,636
	$25,059		$632		$46,457	$(6,464)	$105,743
		$108,394	$6,557		$225		$287,170
	$54,537	$17,606	$7,829	$1,468	$7,384		$88,824
	$3,906		$725	$793	$186		$5,610
	$3,876		$326	$269			$25,320
	$10,489	$1,022	$7,124	$772	$1,838		$58,352
	$65,097		$12,896		$58,740		$136,733
	Quebec and Ontario	Dominican Republic	Ontario, Quebec and U.S.A.	Namibia			
	Copper, zinc and precious metals	Ferronickel	Industrial minerals and metal castings	Copper			
	Canada and Europe	Europe, U.S.A. and Japan	Canada and U.S.A.	Europe			

December 31, 1978

	Integrated Nickel Operations (100%) (note 2)	Unallocated corporate (100%) (note 2)	Wesfrob Mining Division (100%) (note 8)	Corporation Falconbridge Copper (50.2%) (note 9)	Falconbridge Dominicana, C. por A. (65.7%) (note 3)	Indusmin Limited (69.0%)	Oamites Mining Company (Proprietary) Limited (74.9%)	Other	Consolidation adjustments (note 3)	Consolidated total
	$209,915	$2,021	$13,222	$132,429	$89,469	$46,686	$13,380	2,095	$(1,006)	$508,211
	162,737		10,851	87,443	76,092	32,665	10,079	883	(755)	379,995
	14,231	3,354	63	1,050	6,776	5,235	1,313	597	(2,687)	29,932
	4,282		520	4,459	2,844	30	99		(503)	11,731
	12,006	540	898	3,816	7,621	2,901	883	297	220	29,182
	193,256	3,894	12,332	96,768	93,333	40,831	12,374	1,777	(3,725)	450,840
	16,659	(1,873)	890	35,661	(3,864)	5,855	1,006	318	2,719	57,371
	7,061	3,588		(1,366)	13,825	815	51	(30)	1,563	25,507
	1,215	3,515	347	2,163	82	7			333	7,662
	3,006					132			(52)	3,086
	11,282	7,103	347	797	13,907	954	51	303	1,511	36,255
	5,377	(8,976)	543	34,864	(17,771)	4,901	955	15	1,208	21,116
		3,966						785		4,751
	5,377	(5,010)	543	34,864	(17,771)	4,901	955	800	1,208	25,867
	(1,181)	279	5	17,267	(6,042)	1,836	336	163	(42)	12,621
	$6,558	$(5,289)	538	$17,597	$(11,729)	$3,065	619	637	1,250	$13,246
		$10,040	$(3,706)	942	156	$(4)				$7,428
	$6,558	$(5,289)	551	$7,498	$(6,596)	$2,027	405	664		$5,818
	$236,211		$6,188	$65,807	$56,155	$17,566	$4,479	1,887	$(36,058)	$352,235
	77,386		2,360	20,282	11,577	9,299	2,410	645	(26,508)	97,451
	$158,825		$3,828	$45,525	$44,578	$8,267	$2,069	1,242	$(9,550)	$254,784
	$146,543		$3,430	$5,125	$89,204	$15,831	$4,438	541	$1,151	$266,263
	3,753		50	2,796	1,943	1,333	108	417	(454)	9,946
	52,124		2,015	5,351	38,309	434	509		(7,350)	91,392
	$202,420		$5,495	$13,272	$129,456	$17,598	$5,055	958	$(6,653)	$367,601
	$31,298			$16,822		$632		$46,510	$(6,349)	$88,913
	$173,244				$118,554	$3,018		$187		$295,003
				$35,227	$15,516	$6,882	$1,212	$7,346		$66,183
				$1,302		$725	$383			$2,410
	$4,732			$1,292		$326	$132			$6,482
	$30,429		$241	$8,543	$834	$2,024	$278	$615		$42,964
				$43,940		$11,284		$15,786		$71,010
	Ontario and Norway	British Columbia	Quebec and Ontario	Dominican Republic	Ontario, Quebec and U.S.A.	Namibia				
	Nickel, copper and cobalt	Iron and copper	Copper, zinc and precious metals	Ferronickel	Industrial minerals and metal castings	Copper				
	Europe, U.S.A. and Japan	U.S.A. and Japan	Canada and Europe	Europe, U.S.A. and Japan	Canada and U.S.A.	Europe				

FALCONBRIDGE NICKEL MINES LIMITED

NOTES TO STATEMENT OF SEGMENTED INFORMATION

1. **Translation of foreign currencies**
   Foreign currency items have been translated into Canadian dollars as explained in accounting policy B on page 22.

2. **Integrated Nickel Operations and Unallocated corporate**
   Included under the caption "Integrated Nickel Operations" are the accounts of the Company and all its wholly-owned subsidiaries engaged in the integrated operations of mining, milling, smelting, refining and marketing of nickel mainly derived from Canadian ore. The Integrated Nickel's production operations are interdependent and are carried on in Canada (mainly mining and reducing ore to matte at Sudbury) and in Norway (matte refining). The Marketing Division is structured to serve worldwide markets and contracts the processing of material containing cobalt, nickel and other metals, on a fee basis (refined metals produced from these sources are either marketed on an agency basis or returned to the owner of the material). That portion of the Company's net corporate expenditures relating to the overall direction and management of other activities of the Falconbridge group of companies and income from investment in associated and other companies have been segregated under the caption "Unallocated corporate". It is not practicable to segregate the Integrated Nickel Operations and the Company's corporate financial position items.

   The Integrated Nickel Operations and Company's corporate financial position at December 31, 1980 includes identifiable assets of $49,914,000 in Norway (1979 — $38,536,000; and 1978 — $34,917,000).

   The 1979 Integrated Nickel Operations and Unallocated corporate earnings have been restated to reflect the reclassification of $2,829,000 commissions earned on certain agency sales.

3. **Consolidation adjustments**
   Adjustments have been made on consolidation as follows:
   (a) Falconbridge Dominicana, C. por A. (Falcondo)
   The ferronickel produced by Falcondo is purchased and marketed by the Company. The earnings of Falcondo include profits on all ferronickel sold to the Company whereas consolidated earnings exclude the profits relating to inventories of ferronickel held by the Company at December 31, for subsequent resale to customers.

   (b) Fair value adjustments
   The difference between the interest in the book value of the net assets of certain consolidated subsidiaries and the carrying value of the investments are accounted for as explained in accounting policy A (ii) on page 22. The investment in consolidated subsidiaries is $10,245,000 less than the equity in net assets of these subsidiaries at December 31, 1980 ($11,682,000 at December 31, 1979) and this difference is included in the consolidated balance sheet as follows:

	1980	1979
	(000's)	(000's)
Increase (decrease)		
Property, plant and equipment —		
Producing assets		
Plant and equipment	$ 5,656	$ 6,007
Accumulated depreciation	5,173	5,029
Land and properties	6,100	6,100
Accumulated depletion	6,505	5,847
Development and preproduction expenditures	(10,069)	(10,664)
Accumulated amortization	(4,321)	(3,818)
Non-producing assets	(4,999)	(6,471)
Investment in associated and other companies	50	50
Other	374	354
Excess of interest in net assets of subsidiaries over carrying value of investments	$ (10,245)	$ (11,682)

   The depreciation, depletion and amortization of the fair value adjustments included in the consolidated statement of earnings increased the 1980 depreciation and depletion expenses by a net $144,000 (1979 — $1,514,000; 1978 — $34,000) and decreased the amortization of development and preproduction expenditures by $503,000 in each of the years 1980, 1979 and 1978.
   (c) Other inter-company transactions have been adjusted to prevent duplication.

4. **Interest in consolidated subsidiary companies' undistributed earnings**
   See note 10, page 33, of the notes to consolidated financial statements.

5. **Working capital**
   (i) Working capital includes the estimated realizable value of metal settlements receivable and concentrates in transit of $40,128,000, or 37% of consolidated accounts and metal settlements receivable, in respect of certain consolidated subsidiaries (1979 — $74,020,000, or 47%).
   (ii) See note 8 B (i) (c), page 32, of the notes to consolidated financial statements for particulars of funds held in trust in respect of Falconbridge Dominicana, C. por A.

6. **Property, plant and equipment**
   See note 7, page 30, of the notes to consolidated financial statements.

7. **Market value of Falconbridge's shareholdings**
   The market values shown are based on Canadian stock exchanges' closing bid prices at year end. Because of the number of shares held by Falconbridge (representing control of the companies concerned), the amounts that could be realized if these securities were to be sold may be more or less than their indicated quoted market value.
8. **Wesfrob Mining Division**
   On January 2, 1980, the dissolution of Wesfrob Mines Limited, a wholly-owned subsidiary was approved. The operation of the mine is continuing as the Wesfrob Mining Division of the Company.
9. **Corporation Falconbridge Copper**
   The company's name was changed from Falconbridge Copper Limited on April 29, 1980.
10. **Segmented data**
    Although the Company and its subsidiary and significantly influenced companies basically constitute a one industry segment (mining industry) the data contained on Statement 4, page 36, and these notes thereto, present a more detailed review of the various group operations.
    (i) The following table shows the revenues of the consolidated companies in the Falconbridge group on a segmented and product basis by amount and approximate percentage:

	Year ended December 31,					
	1980		1979		1978	
	Amount	%	Amount	%	Amount	%
	(000's)		(000's)		(000's)	
Integrated Nickel and corporate operations:						
Nickel	$206,719	27	$226,794	29	$158,640	31
Copper	62,385	8	44,352	6	20,722	4
Cobalt	40,158	5	44,197	6	17,619	4
Gold	3,568	1	2,309		662	
Silver	2,396		953		459	
Platinum	8,025	1	8,163	1	2,780	1
Palladium	3,366	1	2,741		682	
Other revenues	29,322	4	25,401	3	10,372	2
	355,939	47	354,910	45	211,936	42
Other operations:						
Ferronickel	128,340	17	134,110	17	90,741	18
Copper	98,742	13	115,003	15	81,452	16
Zinc	24,073	3	41,445	5	32,892	6
Gold	31,563	4	22,568	3	15,284	3
Silver	41,487	5	51,351	6	18,379	3
Industrial minerals						
Nepheline syenite	11,961	2	10,936	1	9,711	2
Silica	16,798	2	14,900	2	13,500	3
Aggregates	7,056	1	5,227	1	5,112	1
Steel castings	23,481	3	20,439	3	14,867	3
Other metals and products	18,375	3	18,529	2	14,337	3
	401,876	53	434,508	55	296,275	58
	$757,815	100	$789,418	100	$508,211	100

(ii) Sales revenues, by product source, of the companies in the Falconbridge group which are accounted for on an equity basis were as follows:

	Year ended December 31,					
	1980		1979		1978	
	Amount	%	Amount	%	Amount	%
	(000's)		(000's)		(000's)	
Gold	$27,968	47	$30,914	37	$22,206	51
Lead	1,443	2	3,729	4	3,119	7
Silver	29,997	51	49,417	59	18,412	42
	$59,408	100	$84,060	100	$43,737	100

(iii) Consolidated sales revenues by geographical area were as follows:

	Year ended December 31,					
	1980		1979		1978	
	Amount	%	Amount	%	Amount	%
	(000's)		(000's)		(000's)	
Europe	$197,639	26	$222,712	28	$194,633	38
U.S.A.	282,266	37	249,076	32	166,345	33
Others	51,462	7	67,350	8	54,096	11
*Total foreign	531,367	70	539,138	68	415,074	82
Canada	226,448	30	250,280	32	93,137	18
*World total	$757,815	100	$789,418	100	$508,211	100
*Includes sales by domestic operations to foreign customers of	$335,877		$339,936		$287,841	

FALCONBRIDGE NICKEL MINES LIMITED

(iv) Sale of principal metals and products by the consolidated companies in the Falconbridge group were as follows:

			Year ended December 31,			
	1980		1979		1978	
	Consolidated total	Company share*	Consolidated total	Company share*	Consolidated total	Company share*
	(000's)	(000's)	(000's)	(000's)	(000's)	(000's)
Integrated Nickel Operations:						
Nickel (pounds)	54,159	54,159	84,454	84,454	71,341	71,341
Copper (pounds)	53,686	53,686	42,460	42,460	30,027	30,027
Cobalt (pounds)	1,386	1,386	1,294	1,294	1,255	1,255
Gold (ounces)	5	5	6	6	3	3
Silver (ounces)	108	108	79	79	75	75
Platinum (ounces)	10	10	16	16	9	9
Palladium (ounces)	14	14	20	20	10	10
Other operations:						
Copper (pounds)	86,971	49,287	104,459	59,405	108,571	61,142
Ferronickel (pounds of nickel)	34,567	22,710	47,628	31,292	43,477	28,564
Iron concentrate (tons)	677	677	638	638	560	560
Steel castings (tons, not 000's)	5,685	3,924	6,131	4,230	4,869	3,360
Zinc (pounds)	50,984	25,594	91,710	46,038	85,337	42,839
Gold (ounces)	44	22	48	24	63	32
Silver (ounces)	2,011	1,067	2,575	1,349	2,774	1,462
Industrial minerals (tons) —						
Nepheline syenite	429	296	430	297	422	291
Silica	977	674	920	635	963	664
Aggregates	2,950	2,035	2,452	1,692	2,405	1,659
Sales on an agency basis:						
Nickel (pounds)	5,612		5,195		3,543	
Copper (pounds)	3,666		2,273		2,049	
Cobalt (pounds)	391		208			

*Includes the subsidiary companies' sales prorated on the basis of the Company's percentage ownership.

(v) Sales of metals and products of the companies in the Falconbridge group which are accounted for on an equity basis were as follows:

			Year ended December 31,			
	1980		1979		1978	
	Total	Company share*	Total	Company share*	Total	Company share*
	(000's)	(000's)	(000's)	(000's)	(000's)	(000's)
Silver (ounces)	1,672	807	2,496	1,204	2,763	1,331
Lead (pounds)	3,296	1,596	5,620	2,721	7,521	3,642
Gold (ounces)	38	7	75	14	95	18

*Significantly influenced companies' sales are prorated on the basis of the Company's percentage ownership.

(vi) The following table sets forth certain information respecting metal prices during the periods indicated. The pricing bases used therein are the most representative prices that the Falconbridge group received for its metal products and metals in concentrates:

Metal	Pricing unit	Prices at December 31, 1980	Falconbridge (6) average prices during		
			1980	1979	1978
			(U.S. Dollars)		
Refined nickel	pound	$ 3.24(1)	$ 3.25	$ 2.31	$ 1.94
Ferronickel	pound	3.21(1)	3.18	2.41	1.82
Copper	pound	0.86(2)	0.94	0.93	0.64
Gold	ounce	589.50(3)	611.03	367.61	205.55
Silver	ounce	15.65(4)	16.00	16.64	5.77
Platinum	ounce	578.00(5)	678.55	421.47	254.41
Cobalt	pound	25.00(1)	24.36	29.12	12.25

(1) Producer prices.
(2) London Metal Exchange cash wirebar prices.
(3) London Metal Exchange final prices.

(4) Prices quoted by Hardy and Harman. New York.
(5) New York Dealer prices.
(6) Includes sales on an agency basis.

(vii) The following table shows the approximate percentage of revenues, earnings, working capital and property, plant and equipment of the consolidated companies in the Falconbridge group on a segmented basis (see Statement 4, page 36, for corresponding dollar amounts).

	Revenues (a) Year ended December 31,			Earnings (b) Year ended December 31,			Working capital Year ended December 31,			Property, plant and equipment (producing assets) Year ended December 31,		
	1980 %	1979 %	1978 %	1980 %	1979 %	1978 %	1980 %	1979 %	1978 %	1980 %	1979 %	1978 %
Integrated Nickel Operations	46	44	41	80	56	113	52	60	62	56	58	55
Unallocated corporate	1	1			10	(91)						
Corporation Falconbridge Copper	23	26	26	21	21	129	29	22	18	7	2	4
Falconbridge Dominicana, C. por A.	18	20	18	(6)	4	(113)	14	15	17	30	33	35
Indusmin Limited	8	7	9	3	3	35	4	3	3	6	6	5
Oamites Mining Company (Proprietary) Limited	3	2	3	1	1	7	1	1	1	1	1	1
Wesfrob Mining Division	2	3	3	2	4	9	2	3	2	1	1	2
Other consolidated subsidiaries	1	1		(1)	1	11			1			1
Consolidation adjustments	(2)	(4)					(2)	(4)	(4)	(1)	(2)	(2)
Consolidated total	100	100	100	100	100	100	100	100	100	100	100	100

(a) The 1980 revenues include $144,984,000, 19% of the consolidated total (1979 — $191,748,000, 24%; 1978 — $118,721,000, 23%) from sales by Corporation Falconbridge Copper to a single customer.

(b) Earnings (loss) contributions are after consolidation adjustments, before extraordinary items.

(viii) Segmented earnings (loss) contributions, working capital, capital expenditures and metal sales for the years 1971 through 1980 are presented in the ten-year review on page 43.

Section V:

Multiple-Subject Situations

ADAMS CORPORATION

Adams Corporation (AC) is privately owned and incorporated under a provincial Corporations Act. It has been in existence for 15 years. The financial statements have never been audited in these 15 years, and most of the accounting principles were selected bearing in mind that minimizing income tax payments was an important objective of accounting during that time.

In September 19x3 senior management began to press the owners of AC for an incentive plan so that important managers would be rewarded for successful activity and high productivity. After two months of debate the owners and managers decided to adopt a "phantom stock option plan" (PSOP) commencing January 1, 19x4. At this date an audit would be performed and consistent principles of accounting would be adopted for subsequent years for the PSOP.

The PSOP operates as follows. Key managers or employees would be granted a "percentage ownership" in the company each January 1. The employees would not actually own a share of the company; instead, they would receive a percentage of increases in owners' equity from January 1 to the following January 1. The PSOP differs from a plan in which an employee receives a bonus based on net income because under the PSOP dividends are deducted first for common and preferred shareholders. The PSOP agreement sets out at some length how dividends may be calculated, and the maximum that can be paid out in any year.

You have been hired to conduct the audit of AC for 19x4 and to do a "balance sheet only" audit as of December 31, 19x3. You also have been asked to recommend appropriate accounting principles for AC for the years commencing January 1, 19x4. During your review of AC's accounts as of January 1, 19x4 you learn of the following:

1. AC carries out mechanical and electrical installations in new buildings and factories, as well as those in need of repair and overhaul. As a result, it has to bid on contracts, and these contracts may extend over more than one year. Sometimes AC has to incur significant costs in developing techniques for overhauling complex factories or assembly lines.

2. AC leases some of its heavier equipment on both short-term and long-term bases. For example, it uses an overhead crane that has been leased for 10 years. But, automobiles are leased for only two or three years.

3. AC is obligated to pay for "warranty" repairs on its installations for up to one year from the date of completion of its work.

4. AC claims maximum capital cost allowance every year on the machinery and equipment that it owns. In some years AC may encounter a loss, but over a period of years it has been quite profitable.

5. AC subcontracts some portions of the contracts that it obtains from successful bidding. It withholds 20 percent of the subcontractor's fee for 90 days after the subcontractor's work has been completed.

6. AC has negotiated a new bond issue payable to an industrial finance company, to replace a bond coming due in March 19x4. The bond is secured by several assets of AC, and personal guarantees of the owners of AC. A $200,000 placement fee will be payable in March 19x4. The new bond will expire in March 19x9.

7. AC currently has one contract that will be completed in mid 19x4. The overall loss on the contract is projected at $600,000. As of December 31, 19x3 the contract is one-third complete.

Required:
A. Assume the role of auditor and adviser to AC. What financial and

management accounting principles do you recommend for the above transactions and activities of AC? Why?

B. Identify important audit and income tax problems, and explain how you would satisfactorily resolve each.

AN ACQUISITION

Your client, A Ltd., incorporated under the Canada Business Corporations Act and listed on major Canadian stock exchanges, has just acquired a portion of the shares of B Ltd., which until March 1, 19x3 had always been a privately-owned company. The terms of purchase are:

A. A Ltd. acquired 40 percent (400,000) of the common shares of B Ltd. on March 1, 19x3 by issuing A Ltd.'s common shares. At this date the closing bid price of A Ltd.'s common shares was $24.50 per share; 224,000 shares of A Ltd. were issued. The purchase-sale agreement was finalized on February 15, 19x3, when A Ltd.'s common shares had a bid price of $25 per share.

B. Another 35 percent (350,000) of B Ltd.'s common shares must be acquired on or before March 1, 19x7 for $14 per common share plus or minus any change in book value per common share between March 1, 19x3 and the date of exercise of the agreement (requiring purchase of the additional 35 percent of the shares.) The agreement states that accounting principles are to be determined "in accordance with generally accepted accounting principles."

C. A Ltd. acquired 100 percent (15,000) of B Ltd.'s convertible preferred shares for $140 cash per share effective March 1, 19x3. One convertible preferred share is convertible into 10 common shares any time after January 1, 19x2.

You have been A Ltd.'s auditor for many years and have also handled income tax and special assignments for them. They rely on you to keep them advised of implications of their business dealings.

B Ltd.'s financial statements in the years to December 31, 19x2 have been audited, but not by a CA. You have been appointed auditor of B Ltd. for the year ended December 31, 19x3. During your year end audit you discover the following:

1. In early 19x1 B Ltd. had its main building appraised. At the time, the net book value was $1.6 million and undepreciated capital cost was $1.4 million. The appraiser would give the building a value of $2.4 million if it were sold to a third party who could thereby have an undepreciated capital cost of $2.4 million. B Ltd. recorded the $2.4 million valuation in its books, and credited the $800,000 increase over book value to "Allowance for repairs." Depreciation for 19x1, 19x2 and 19x3 have been based on the $2.4 million figure. The following charges were made to the "Allowance for repairs" account for repairs and maintenance to all of the company's assets: 19x1, $62,500; 19x2, $75,200; 19x3, $181,900.

2. As of December 31, 19x2 the previous auditor had not requested adjustments to the financial statements for the following:

   a. Overstatement of supplies at December 31, 19x2 by $120,000 because spare parts for manufacturing machinery were incorrectly counted as inventory.

   b. Understatement of accounts payable by $101,800 as a result of computer programming deficiencies that caused discounts to be deducted from invoices when interest should have been added for delayed payment.

   c. Understatement of accounts receivable of about $125,000 for inventory that was shipped but not invoiced. (The uninvoiced purchasers were not known for certain at the date that the financial statements were finalized.)

   This information was received over the telephone from the previous auditor of B Ltd.

3. B Ltd. has always based its pension expense on whatever it was required to fund per requests from the consulting actuary for the pension plan. On April 1, 19x3 the actuary informed officials of B Ltd. that, as requested, he had changed actuarial funding methods from the "accrued benefit" to the "projected benefit" method. As a result the company was short $778,000 in funding as of April 1, 19x3 to meet the requirements of the new method. The actuary proposed that the deficiency plus interest be funded over three years.

   As of March 1, 19x3 unfunded past service liability amounted to $2,110,000, and was being funded over 15 years. The pension fund assets were valued at March 1, 19x3 and were $492,000 short of that required to meet requirements under the accrued benefit method. Management of B Ltd. decided to fund the deficiency over three years, but to expense the amount funded over 10 years.

4. B Ltd. has used direct costing for income tax purposes since the company was incorporated. The financial statements prepared by the controller of B Ltd. incorporate the following standard cost figures:

	As of December 31	
	19x3	19x2
Standard cost:		
Inventory of finished goods and work in process, at direct cost-beginning of year	$ 3,883,700	$ 3,644,200
Add:		
Direct material and labor and variable manufacturing cost incurred during the year	11,422,665	10,982,370
	15,306,365	14,626,570
Less:		
Goods sold (FIFO basis) and inventory spoilage during year	11,112,310	10,735,640
	4,184,055	3,890,930
Add:		
Fixed manufacturing overhead incurred during the year	2,240,600	2,050,000
	6,424,655	5,940,930
Less:		
Taxes on fixed overhead		
46% x 2,240,600	1,030,676	
46% x 2,050,000		943,000
Closing inventory at standard cost	$ 5,383,979*	$ 4,997,930*

* These figures were used on the balance sheets and for income determination.

For 19x2 and 19x3 the following differentials existed between actual cost and standard cost:

	Variances for year ended December 31	
	19x3	19x2
	(Bracketed figures indicate where standard cost exceeded actual cost)	
Direct material	$ 52,300	$(346,500)
Direct labor	127,740	(32,300)
Variable manufacturing overhead	17,890	(8,290)
Fixed manufacturing overhead	22,660	10,500
	$220,590	$(376,590)

(Standard costs were used in preparing financial statements.)

5. As of December 31, 19x2 B Ltd. was aware that one of its customers was experiencing financial difficulty. The customer owed $675,000 at December 31, 19x2, and as of the date that the financial statements were finalized (February 1, 19x3) no payments had been received. An allowance for bad debts of $500,000 was recorded in 19x2 for this customer. On March 1, 19x3 $225,000 of cash was received from the customer; but, on April 1, 19x3 the customer was placed in receivership. As of December 31, 19x3 the receiver was offering 30¢ on the dollar for principal balances outstanding to unsecured creditors, such as B Ltd. B Ltd.'s accounts receivable at December 31, 19x3 showed $450,000 principal plus $92,600 accrued interest owing from the customer. The bad debt provision of $500,000 for this customer still existed at December 31, 19x3.

6. Effective October 1, 19x3 B Ltd. exchanged warehouses with another company. B Ltd.'s warehouse had a net book value of $720,000, and an undepreciated capital cost of $500,000 when the exchange occurred. On October 1, 19x3 the replacement cost, in used condition, of the warehouse was $1,050,000 and the mortgage payable was $450,000 at 16 percent interest per annum. The warehouse that B Ltd. received in the arm's length exchange had these financial characteristics:

Replacement cost in used condition	$1 million
Net book value, per "seller's books"	900,000
Undepreciated capital cost, per "seller's books"	700,000
Mortgage payable on warehouse, at 15 percent	650,000

B Ltd. received a cheque for $150,000 from the other company when legal title to the warehouses had been exchanged, and each had assumed the mortgage that was previously the responsibility of the other party. B Ltd.'s accountant credited the $150,000 to accumulated depreciation.

Required:

In your role as auditor and financial adviser to A Ltd., and auditor of B Ltd., provide supported recommendations concerning all important problems facing the two companies.

ANTIQUES LIMITED

Antiques Limited (AL) was incorporated under federal corporate legislation on April 1, 19x3 after being operated as a sole proprietorship for many years. On incorportion, because ownership was not changing, the assets were transferred to AL at estimated cost or book value to the proprietorship. The books of the proprietorship were not always accurate; as a result, in many cases cost of the inventory of antiques had to be estimated. On incorporation inventories represented 75 percent of the assets of AL.

It is now April 20, 19x4 and the company has completed its first year ending March 31, 19x4. AL's banker has requested financial statements, audited or otherwise, but prepared in accordance with generally accepted accounting principles (GAAP). The proprietorship did not have GAAP statements.

AL maintains perpetual inventory cards for items that cost it over $100. Charges to cost of goods sold are based on the price shown on the inventory card. Items costing less than $100 are accounted for under a retail basis of inventory control. Approximately two-thirds of sales revenue is from items costing AL less than $100.

Inventory turns over about one time per year, on average. Items below $100 in cost turn over about six times per year.

AL plans to expand its operations and open up a new store. The present store is located in a small shopping centre. The 10-year lease was signed on February 1, 19x1. AL fortunately received an excellent monthly rental price on the store, $500 per month, primarily because the owner was having difficulty finding tenants. Now, the shopping centre is fully rented. If a lease were signed today monthly rental would be $900 to $1,000.

In order to open a new store large sums would have to be borrowed from a bank. The bank has asked the owner of AL to provide a schedule indicating how and when the loan would be repaid, and what security could be provided. The owner is thinking of selling more common shares in AL if someone can be found who will allow his personal assets to be pledged to the bank.

Besides the inventory, the other main tangible assets of AL are receivables, leasehold improvements, office and display equipment and a little cash. The only intangible asset is goodwill of $5,000 which was transferred from the proprietorship, which had paid this sum to buy out a competitor.

Required:
Advise the owner of AL about accounting and related matters.

BELL ENTERPRISES LIMITED

Bell Enterprises Limited (BEL) was incorporated under federal legislation many years ago by the Bell family. BEL, still privately owned by several members of the family, is a holding company with large investments in several companies.

During the year just ended, December 31, 19x4, BEL acquired common shares in three companies, A Ltd., B Ltd. and C Ltd. As BEL's accounting adviser you have been consulted about suitable accounting for the three companies, each of which is in effect controlled by BEL. In particular you have been asked how to account for and report the following in the financial statements of the individual companies, and of BEL consolidated:

1. A Ltd. is a trust company 40 percent owned by BEL. Trust officers of A Ltd. administer the pension plans of B Ltd. and two other companies owned by BEL and included in the consolidated financial statements of BEL. The trust officers also administer pension plans of some of the directors of BEL, and of companies controlled by BEL. Three senior management persons of B Ltd. and C Ltd. have mortgages on their residences, that are payable to A Ltd.

2. When B Ltd. was acquired, BEL signed an agreement entitling it to acquire any rights or warrants to purchase common shares in B Ltd. if the holder of the rights did not exercise them. That is, B Ltd. previously had issued bonds with warrants to purchase common shares of B Ltd. in 19x4, 19x5 and 19x6. If a bondholder did not exercise the warrant, BEL could buy the equivalent number of common shares from B Ltd. for fair market value. During 19x4 a few warrants were not exercised by the expiry date. However, in 19x5 many are not expected to be issued because the exercise price is not attractive. BEL hopes that, over the years, its 35 percent ownership of B Ltd. will increase to over 50 percent.

3. Sixty percent of C Ltd. was acquired for $3 million cash in July 19x4, shortly before its year end of July 31, 19x4. The purchase price was less than the book and fair value of C Ltd.'s assets and liabilities. BEL has a "put-call" option with the holders of the remaining 40 percent of C Ltd.'s shares. Under the option the 40 percent owners may "put", or require, BEL each year to purchase one-quarter of the remaining 40 percent of the shares of C Ltd. (or 10 percent of the issued shares) for $600,000 or six times current net income of C Ltd., whichever is higher. The "call" part of the option allows BEL to exercise its right to acquire one-quarter of the 40 percent each year for the next four years for the same consideration.

Required:

A. Advise the managements of each of the companies (BEL, A, B and C) as to appropriate accounting and reporting for the above transactions.

B. Identify important auditing and income tax aspects of the above transactions and explain how you would resolve each.

MANN OIL LIMITED

Mann Oil Limited (MOL) is incorporated under federal corporate legislation and listed on a major stock exchange. The company is primarily an exploration and refining enterprise in the oil industry. Its products are sold to independent distributors.

MOL's refinery was judged to be inadequate in 19x1 (two years ago) and management decided to modernize the process. The cost was estimated at $15 million ($12 million plus $3 million for "start up" costs needed to ensure a smooth running operation).

Most of the work has been completed as of December 31, 19x3 at a cost of $26 million ($18 million plus $8 million for "start up"). Approximately $22 million was incurred in the financial year ended December 31, 19x3. The selling price of oil products has increased in two years. However, refinery capacity is far more than is needed in the region where MOL is located.

A refinery such as MOL's produces about six main products. Main product costing has been affected by the modernizations because not all products were affected by the new equipment that was installed. The cost accountant for MOL had a formula for allocating costs—such as depreciation, and of various joint product costs—before modernization, and is now uncertain about his former procedure.

The auditors of MOL knew that the company was having difficulty with the modernization program, but have only recently (January 19x4) learned about specific cost problems.

Required:

Assume the role of auditor of MOL.

A. What accounting and reporting of the above would you recommend to the company? Why?

B. What advice can you provide to the company's cost accountant?

MODERN METALWORKS LIMITED

Modern Metalworks Limited (MML) has recently been incorporated under federal corporate legislation. All of the outstanding shares are owned by one businessman and his son. MML will manufacture a wide variety of metal products, such as childrens' swing and slide sets, grating devices for use around basement windows of houses and gas furnace parts whenever it is able to receive orders from distributors and manufacturers. One distribution chain has already expressed an interest in buying some of MML's leisure equipment.

Most of MML's manufacturing assets were recently acquired at bankruptcy sales. They still have to be transported to a building, that MML is renting under a 20-year agreement, and installed and readied for use. The major items which were acquired (shears, brakes, etc.) cost $445,000 and a further $100,000 is expected to be incurred in installation. $40,000 is estimated as installation costs and $60,000 is for "debugging" after the manufacturing operations commence.

Sales are expected to be made on two bases:

1. Direct sales to distributors and manufacturers on terms of net 90 days. Defective merchandise will be returnable to MML for 100 percent credit. Any goods damaged by distributors will be returnable for refurbishing by MML; only out-of-pocket costs of repairs will be chargeable to the distributor when such goods are returned.
2. Delivery to department stores on a consignment basis.

Each product will be produced in batches for a few weeks, and stored. Production is expected to be seasonal for a few years until a more balanced line of winter sale products is developed. Working capital needs are to be financed by a bank loan. The bank requires monthly repayments but is willing to negotiate higher loans if the need can be proven.

MML is located in an area that is eligible for government grants. The company receives a subsidy each year for five years for creating jobs. It also has been provided with a loan to buy manufacturing equipment; the loan is forgivable at one-fifth per year over five years.

Management wishes to set up accounting principles and a system suitable for the company.

Required:

A. Assume the role of financial adviser to the management of MML and recommend suitable accounting principles and a management accounting system. Explain your recommendations, including the detailed disclosure you would adopt for external financial statements.

B. Provide income tax advice and any other comments that are within the expertise of a public accountant.

MOUNT ROYAL MANUFACTURING LIMITED

Mount Royal Manufacturing Limited (MRML) was incorporated under federal legislation many years ago. It has been privately owned since incorporation but was sold this year, 19x4, to another syndicate of business persons. The new owners intend to modernize the manufacturing plant, close out unsuccessful product lines, and expand sales of successful products.

You have been hired to assist the new owners in selecting accounting and reporting policies that would be appropriate for the new business. Its financial year ends on February 28. On reviewing the company's accounting records and financial reports and after interviewing officials you learn that:

1. Financial statements have been prepared for many years but they have not been audited. No management accounting reports have been prepared; estimates are used in quoting prices to customers.

2. Approximately $200,000 of fully depreciated fixed assets are shown on the balance sheet. Management ignores depreciation in costing products for quoting purposes.

3. The company has always employed income tax methods and rates in depreciating its fixed assets for accounting purposes, with one exception. The exception occurred two years ago when the company wrote off $175,000 of fixed assets being used to produce an unprofitable product. These assets are still in use but may be scrapped next year. The product being manufactured is now considered to be profitable.

4. The company has always accrued repair and maintenance costs on its depreciable assets. Such information is used for quoting selling prices of finished products. Whenever an asset is acquired its lifetime repair and

maintenance costs are estimated. From this sum a subtraction is made for estimated equipment salvage value, after taking into account the effects of rising replacement costs on salvage estimates. The net sum is then charged evenly over the life of the asset by crediting "Allowance for repairs." As repairs are made the "Allowance" account is credited. Every five years, accruals are revised.

5. For income tax purposes, manufacturing costs such as licenses, insurance, property taxes, supervisory salaries and heat and light are expensed in the year that they are incurred.

6. Intense competition exists for most of MRML's products. As a result it incurs substantial selling costs that are expensed when incurred. Quantity purchase discounts are paid to customers each August 31 for purchases in the previous 12 months ended June 30. The rates of discount vary in order to keep regular customers from purchasing from competitors.

7. Out-of-pocket manufacturing costs are largely material and labor. Shipping can also be expensive.

8. New products have to be designed in order to be competitive. MRML expenses design costs as they are incurred. The company also has standard lines that it produces on a year-round basis.

Required:

Assume the role of an adviser to the company.

A. Recommend appropriate financial accounting and reporting policies for MRML.

B. Recommend an effective management accounting and control system to officials of MRML, and explain its use.

C. Provide any other advice that you think would help management.

URBAN MAGAZINE LIMITED

Urban Magazine Limited (UML) was incorporated under federal legislation many years ago. It is privately owned by five businesspersons and their families. However, funds will be needed from the public in the near future to permit expansion. The company's year end is December 31.

UML publishes six magazines, four on a monthly and two on a bi-monthly basis. Two of the four monthlies were added this year, 19x3.

All four monthlies are sold for prices between 40¢ to $1.00. The bi-monthlies are distributed free of charge in parts of larger Canadian cities.

The addition of the two new monthlies should more than triple 19x3 revenue of UML after an initial start up period of up to two years. Magazine #5 was started by UML in April 19x3. Magazine #6 was acquired in October 19x3. These additional magazines and the need to borrow from the public have caused management of UML to have to reexamine the company's financial and managerial accounting and reporting systems. Several expenditures arose in 19x3 as a result of the additions.

Expenditures on Magazine #5:

Advertising its existence	$ 126,500
Investigation of its market potential	96,200
Salaries paid prior to first magazine being produced on June 10, 19x3	73,150
Fixed assets acquired especially for this magazine, mainly equipment	196,215
Special paper stock—one year's consumption	720,000°
New stationery	20,000
Miscellaneous	26,175
	$1,261,240

Expenditures incurred and expected on Magazine #6:

Cost of acquisition–payment to owner	$1,200,000
–due annually, $1 million November 19x4 to 19x7	4,000,000
Salaries paid prior to first magazine being published on November 15, 19x3	126,800
Special paper stock acquired for cash— about three month's consumption	590,000
Equipment acquired especially for this magazine	96,200
Assumption of lease on premises used by former owner of magazine	100,000°°
Miscellanenous	121,190
	$6,234,190

° Being financed at 14 percent interest per annum; 12 equal payments due August 1, 19x3 to July 1, 19x4.

°° UML paid this to the former owners of Magazine #6 because there is a five-year lease that requires monthly rental payments well below current rates. Even with the $100,000 payment the monthly rental cost is very favorable to UML.

Magazine #6 is sold in stores, at newstands, and has a regular group of subscribers who pay one year in advance. Much of the $5.2 million purchase price was for the magazine's reputation and subscribers' list. The magazine's cash receipts from advertising and subscriptions are well in excess of the cash operating expenditures each month. Most advertising is placed through agencies. UML receives a net price from the agencies, who deduct their fee from amounts paid by their clients. Advertising rates are based on the number of subscribers. Hence, UML spends a considerable amount of effort in attracting new subscribers.

Magazine #5 is not expected to make a profit for the first two years. A quality magazine must be produced in order to attract subscribers who in turn attract advertisers. In its first year of operations, cash operating expenses (excluding the outlays listed previously) are expected to exceed cash revenue by $600,000. The second year excess of expenses is budgeted at $200,000. A small excess of revenue over expenses is expected for the third year.

In order to attract subscribers for magazine #5, bargain rates are being offered on one-, two- or three-year bases. These are roughly 60 percent of planned rates to be charged after July 1, 19x4.

Prior to the acquisition of magazines #5 and #6 officials of UML were able to operate without a management control system. Now, because staff has more than doubled, and different physical locations are necessary for editorial, advertising and subscriber relations staff, some cost controls may be worth considering.

All typesetting and printing is contracted to other companies. UML handles its own distribution network, which involves having small offices in several cities. One advertising representative would use the same office facility in each city. All editorial staff are located in Toronto.

Required:

Assume the role of an accounting adviser to UML.

A. Explain how the company should report the start up of magazines #5 and #6 and the related receipts and expenditures in its financial statements for the year ended December 31, 19x3.
B. Select appropriate financial accounting principles for the magazine, especially for #5 and #6.
C. Design a suitable management control system for UML and explain how management can use it effectively.

XAVIER SOFTDRINKS LIMITED

Xavier Softdrinks Limited (XSL) is incorporated under federal legislation. The company's common shares are privately held by a group of business people. Virtually all of its borrowings to finance expansion have been from private sources such as insurance companies and indirectly from foreign government agencies that finance exports of machinery to countries like Canada. Usually, for the latter, payments are made directly to an agent of the manufacturer of the machinery.

Two years ago, in 19x2, XSL had eight bottling and concentrate plants across Canada. Sales had been expanding steadily. Eighteen months ago two larger competitors of XSL stepped up their competition by lowering prices and engaging in extensive advertising. In the past 15 months XSL's sales have been suffering, and are down 30 percent in 19x4 from those for comparable months in 19x2.

In October of this year, 19x4, XSL began "mothballing" bottling plants. To XSL's year end of December 31, 19x4 three plants had been closed and the following costs were incurred:

Severance pay and pension payments	$762,000
Preparing machinery for closing down	105,000
Production variances in excess of standard cost; inefficiencies incurred during closing down period	92,500
Lease payments on idle machinery (two months)	30,000
Interest on debt incurred to finance closed down plants (two months)	110,000
Other costs of close down	20,500
	$1,120,000

During 19x2 the plants that were closed down accounted for 28 percent of XSL's sales. By 19x3 the percentage had dropped to 25.

Management of XSL does not know when the plants may be reopened. It is hoped that the price war between the top two companies in the industry will cease in two to three years. If the plants had to be closed permanently, the machinery would have to be sold as scrap at a loss of $2 million or more. The buildings may have to be leased at a price below a combination of (1) operating expenses plus (2) an imputed interest charge at 12 percent after income tax on the investment in buildings and land. In order to keep the three plants "in mothballs" annual costs of $250,000 to $300,000 will be necessary to pay for insurance, property taxes, watchmen and so on.

In early 19x5, before the financial statements for 19x4 were finalized, XSL announced the closing of the fourth bottling and concentrate plant. As a result of this fourth closing, transportation costs of merchandise to serve its independent retailers are expected to increase 50 percent. Another $400,000 in costs are anticipated as a result of the fourth closing, and annual "mothball" costs for this fourth plant will be around $100,000. In 19x3 this fourth plant closed accounted for 16 percent of sales.

Excluding any costs of "mothballing" income before income tax of XSL for the year ended December 31, 19x4 was $20,500. Payments have been made on time to the various debtholders. Two of the owners of XSL invested an additional $500,000 on January 10, 19x5 in "special redeemable preferred shares" that are redeemable at the option of the holders. The special shares carry a cumulative dividend rate of 18 percent.

Required:

A. Assume the role of financial vice-president of XSL. Explain what would constitute appropriate disclosure of the foregoing transactions in the financial statements for 19x4. Give detailed illustrations of your suggestions and recommendations.

B. If you were the auditor of XSL what disclosure would you insist on for 19x4 and what "additional" (or beyond normal) audit procedures would you undertake? Why?

YARMOUTH STEEL CORPORATION LIMITED

Yarmouth Steel Corporation Limited (YSCL) is incorporated under federal legislation. Its common shares are traded over-the-counter in several Canadian cities. The company also has $70 million of debentures and $30 million of 12 percent preferred shares in the hands of the public. YSCL issues quarterly reports to shareholders and debenture holders.

YSCL has two divisions: steel making and steel fabricating and construction. Each division is separately incorporated. Last year, 19x1, each division contributed about 50 percent to the net income. Your employer has been the auditor and income tax and financial adviser to YSCL for many years. You are in charge of the YSCL audit for 19x2 on behalf of your firm.

About 20 percent of YSCL's common shares are owned by a company listed on several Canadian stock exchanges. This other company is audited by another firm of public accountants.

The year ended December 31, 19x2 has just been completed and you are currently (February 19x3) conducting the audit of YSCL. The unaudited income statements (condensed) of the steel-making company division show:

	Year ended December 31	
	19x2	19x1
	(in thousands of dollars)	
	UNAUDITED	
Revenue	$107,070	$85,412
Cost of sales	84,345	61,202
Gross profit	22,725	24,210
Selling, distribution and administrative expense	4,510	4,000
Interest expense	8,120	7,900
Depreciation and amortization	9,995	10,210
	22,625	22,110
Operating income before income tax	100	2,100
Income tax	45	975
Net income	$ 55	$ 1,125

Your audit staff has discovered the following:

1. Revenue has traditionally been recognized in the steel-making division on three different bases:
   a. For steel produced for special order, on which a 25 percent or more down payment has been received, revenue is recognized when the steel has been manufactured.
   b. For steel purchased from the warehouse revenue is recognized on shipment from YSCL's warehouse.
   c. For steel sold to YSCL's fabricating company revenue is recognized monthly for any steel that has been sold to customers of the fabricating company.

Throughout 19x2, as a result of heavy demand for Canadian steel, nearly all of the steel division's customers made the 25 percent down payment so that they would be assured of supply. In 19x1 less than 20 percent (in sales dollars) of the customers made the 25 percent down payment.

2. The main reason that the steel company's cost of sales has been increasing is that all of its older furnaces use petroleum as fuel. Petroleum prices steadily rose throughout 19x2 to 30 percent over December 31, 19x1, so that, on average, fuel cost became 18 percent of cost of sales in 19x2. These older furnaces account for 80 percent of the company's production capacity. In total, manufacturing costs per ton of steel rose 14 percent in 19x2 compared to 19x1.

3. In the six weeks to February 15, 19x3 petroleum prices have risen another 20 percent.

4. YSCL's steel-making competitors use furnaces fueled by natural gas, coal and other energy sources that rose in price by 9 percent in 19x2 and 3 percent in the first six weeks of 19x3.

5. At December 31, 19x1 the steel company's inventory was shown on the balance sheet at a cost of $11,422,000. It was sold for approximately $15 million.

6. In the first two weeks of February 19x3 sales in the steel-making division have slowed appreciably in response to an economic slowdown. Selling prices per ton of steel have remained constant and are not expected to increase in 19x3. Fortunately, YSCL did not have any finished goods inventory at December 31, 19x2 and had only $500,000 of work in process inventory.

7. YSCL's plant and equipment, per the unaudited balance sheet, show the following at December 31, 19x2:

(In thousands of dollars)

	Cost	Accumulated depreciation	Net
Furnaces, petroleum-fired	$72,500	$30,100	$42,400
Furnaces, natural gas-fired	31,750	3,205	28,545
Equipment	52,665	20,430	32,235
Land	1,800	—	1,800

8. Repair, maintenance and relining costs in 19x2 amounted to $6,250,000 for the petroleum-fired furnaces. These costs are being amortized over 36 months.

9. At December 31, 19x2 the fabricating company held $10,520,000 of steel that it bought in 19x2 from the steel-making company, which

stands to gain a gross profit of $2 million when the steel is sold to outsiders.

10. Current liabilities at December 31, 19x2 included the following debenture payments:

(In thousands of dollars)

	Outstanding Principal	Current Portion Due in 19x3
Debenture, 12%, due 19x9	$20,000	$1,000
Debenture, 10%, due 19x7	20,000	1,000
Debenture, 9%, due 19x4	30,000	1,500

11. In prior years your audit firm has used an overall 8 percent materiality factor in establishing maximum tolerable deviation for determining extent of audit testing. It has sought a 95 percent confidence level. As a result of discussion with management and this testing, prior years' revenue and cost of sales have been adjusted at the year end as follows:

Year ended December 31	Revenue	Cost of Sales
19x1	Nil	2,000,000°
19x0	Nil	Nil

The audit work completed to date shows that due to December 31, 19x2 cutoff problems cost of goods sold could be understated by as much as $2.2 million at 95 percent confidence limits. Revenue could be understated by as much as $500,000 and other expenses understated by as much as $600,000.

12. Your audit staff has made the following notes after reading various minutes and contracts pertaining to the steel-making company:

a. Board of Directors, October 17, 19x2: "Our bankers desire an interest rate of about 21 percent on $3 million needed to pay for repairs to the steel-making plant...the board approves that...(YSCL)...guarantee any bank loan made to...(the steel-making division)."

b. Board of Directors, December 30, 19x2: "...the income tax reassessment of $1,350,000 for 19x0 and 19x1...that was received on December 28, 19x2...not be accrued in the balance sheet for 19x2 because our controller believes that it can be successfully fought.... It represents an assessment for capital cost allowance claimed on the portion of a government grant that we did not credit to "equipment" but instead credited to "contributed surplus.""

° Audit adjustment increase in cost of sales.

c. Board of Directors, December 30, 19x2: "...and thereby the board approves of a feasibility study to consider replacing the present petroleum-fired furnaces with more modern furnaces, by 19x8.... The study should be available for the next board meeting."

Required:

Identify the important problems that you should bring to the attention of your audit partner, and explain in detail the recommendations that you have for resolving the problems.

YARROW CORPORATION

Yarrow Corporation (YC) is incorporated under federal legislation and its common shares are privately owned. The company has two debenture issues outstanding that were acquired by the general public. One issue comes due in two years, the other in eight years.

YC manufactures and distributes a line of automotive supplies and outdoor equipment. It has two manufacturing plants, one in the West and one in the East. The company has nine of its own retail stores, plus it sells manufactured goods to over 100 other retail stores across Canada.

Inflation has been causing YC a variety of difficulties. The board of directors, with the agreement of the president, have come to you for advice. After some preliminary investigations you learn the following:

1. The board of directors of YC are deeply concerned that managers are receiving unwarranted incentive bonuses based on gross profit in their store or their plant, and in their division (i.e., East or West), as well as on net income for the entire company. Cost of goods sold is computed in FIFO cost flows, and all other costs are based on original dollar expenditures.

   Although senior management has remained responsive to the Board's concerns, most of the middle management have adopted the following operating methods:

   a. Adding significantly to their inventories, whenever price increases are expected.

   b. Maximizing volume, even if this means receiving a small contribution margin on some sales.

c. Selling on longer credit terms, or with negligible down payments, or with subsidized interest rates.

2. Larger sums are having to be borrowed from short-term credit sources such as banks, in order to finance current assets. The banks are hinting that YC is reaching its credit limit.

3. Unfortunately variances between budget and actual have been increasing in the past 18 months.

4. Net income as a percentage of owners' equity has increased slightly in the past two years.

5. Senior management is complaining that income taxes are excessive.

6. The owners are complaining that the dividend has not increased to keep pace with inflation.

7. The manufacturing division is separately incorporated and has a 10 percent owner who does not own any of the remainder of YC. According to a binding agreement, the 10 percent owner is assured that goods transferred from the manufacturing to the retail operation are at fair market value.

8. The owners and some of the debenture holders were unhappy with the "minimal" disclosures in the most recent annual report.

Required:

Provide concrete advice to the board of directors concerning how to solve the important problems that face the company. Explain your recommendations in terms that the board would understand. (All important assumptions should be stated.)

ZEBALLOS FISHING COMPANY LIMITED

Zeballos Fishing Company Limited (ZFCL) is incorporated under federal legislation and is privately owned. Last year, 19x2, its sales were over $30 million, a rise of 20 percent over average sales of the previous two years ending December 31.

The current year, 19x3, has been a busy and sometimes difficult one for the company. In particular:

1. A 100 percent owned subsidiary company, Canso Limited (CL), that operated one fish cannery, was sold in March 19x3 for $2 million to be paid in March 19x5. CL was carried on ZFCL's books at $2,650,000, which represented a figure arrived at by using equity basis accounting for the first three years that ZFCL owned CL, and cost plus three years' equity income for the subsequent eight years. The buyer of CL, a local Indian band, is currently (February 19x4) experiencing some financial difficulties, but is hoping to make the $2 million payment in March 19x5.

2. ZFCL suffered through a two-month strike, which has these "costs and benefits":

Legal and negotiation cost	$ 80,000
Security guards	26,500
Unrecorded depreciation on plant and equipment	(60,000)
Interest on unsold inventory	79,000
Miscellaneous savings—salaries of supervisors who would not cross picket line	(29,000)
Charged to strike expense	$96,500

3. ZFCL acquired 100 percent of the common shares of a small logging company in July 19x3 for $8.5 million. The fair value of the net assets acquired was:

Equipment	$ 3,200,000
Forest lands — discounted value	12,000,000
Working capital	800,000
Long term debts payable, face value, 10 percent interest rate, due 19x8	(10,000,000)

4. ZFCL temporarily had to borrow the $8.5 million from a bank at 20 percent interest because the owners were not able to negotiate a debenture issue to a private lender until September 19x3. The interest on the bank loan amounted to $285,000 and has been added to the $8.5 million cost of the investment in the logging company.

5. At year end, December 31, 19x3, the logging company had $2 million of inventory, at cost, of one grade of log that it had been holding for 12 months waiting for an increase in selling price. At year end and in February 19x4 the net realizable value of these logs was $800,000.

6. Most of ZFCL's inventory at December 31, 19x3 consisted of canned fish that was stored in warehouses awaiting sale to markets throughout the world. Selling prices of fish tend to be set in the world market place

and not locally. The inventory is carried at "the lower of net realizable value or cost."

"Cost" includes the following:

Fish bought, at cost of acquisition
Fish caught by company crews, at cost of labor plus
  cash operating costs of boats
Cannery labor
Cannery cash operating costs
Interest on investment in inventory in storage

Net realizable value exceeded cost of canned fish at December 31, 19x3.

7. Several of ZFCL's fishing boats were built under subsidization programs provided by various levels of government. During 19x3, ZFCL received $4 million from governments to build new boats. The $4 million is forgivable over 10 years as long as the company employs the boats in fishing operations using labor from specified regions.

The logging company's operations consist of cutting trees, hauling the logs by truck to water for storage, and shipping the logs by water to whoever pays the highest price. The operation is highly mechanized but logging costs per unit vary considerably because of the terrain and proximity of the trees to water.

The fishing operations consist of buying fish from independent boat operators, or sending out the company's fleet, canning the fish, and storing the canned goods until sale. Fishing operations are seasonal. Labor cost is much more significant in fishing than in logging. Lately fish prices have been rising steadily.

Required:

A. Identify the accounting problems that affect ZFCL's 19x3 financial statements and give supported recommendations for resolving each.
B. Identify income tax problems arising in 19x3 and explain how you would resolve each.
C. How should the management accounting and control systems differ between the logging and the fishing company? Be specific. Make necessary assumptions and outline a suitable management accounting system for each company. Explain how your system would aid management.